ETERNAL
SALVATION

Russell A. Young

ETERNAL SALVATION

This book is written to provide information and motivation to readers. Its purpose is not to render any type of psychological, legal, or professional advice of any kind. The content is the sole opinion and expression of the author, and not necessarily that of the publisher.

Copyright © 2019 by Russell A. Young

All rights reserved. No part of this book may be reproduced, transmitted, or distributed in any form by any means, including, but not limited to, recording, photocopying, or taking screenshots of parts of the book, without prior written permission from the author or the publisher. Brief quotations for noncommercial purposes, such as book reviews, permitted by Fair Use of the U.S. Copyright Law, are allowed without written permissions, as long as such quotations do not cause damage to the book's commercial value. For permissions, write to the publisher, whose address is stated below.

All Scripture quotations, unless otherwise indicated, are taken from the HOLY BIBLE, NEW INTERNATIONAL VERSION, Copyright 1973, 1978, 1984 International Bible Society, Used by Permission of Zondervan Bible Publishers

Printed in the United States of America.

ISBN   978-1-64552-017-7   (Paperback)
ISBN   978-1-64552-018-4   (Digital)

Lettra Press books may be ordered through booksellers or by contacting:

Lettra Press LLC
18229 E 52nd Ave.
Denver City, CO 80249
1 303 586 1431 | info@lettrapress.com
www.lettrapress.com

PREFACE

The proclamation that "I'm Okay! You're Okay!" when it comes to a person's eternal state deserves real reflection and confirmation. It is easy, and perhaps common, to accept teachings from those whom we respect as learned in theology as being truth and of letting those nagging questions that bring doubt to be put to rest without further consideration. Disquiet in my soul concerning Romans 5:9-10 which presented the thought that "justification" through the blood of Jesus was not enough to avoid the wrath of God prompted me to examine Biblical teachings much more thoroughly and *to let them lead* me rather than to allow myself the comfort of the teachings of others.

In the course of my studies I have come to realize that much of current protestant theology rests on the two pillars of God's "grace" and on pre-creation "election." Ever since the inception of these "doctrines" teachings have evolved based on them, and a departure from the truths of God's Word has been significantly replaced by the imaginations of men. It is time to carefully re-examine Biblical revelation in order to satisfy the heart that a person is truly "okay" when it comes to his or her eternal salvation.

In order to avoid having the formulation of my understanding being tainted by the teachings of man, I have fearfully endeavoured to let the Spirit and the Word lead in the revelation of the truths presented in this writing. It is fair and accurate to say that I did not know where the journey would take me when I began my studies and was somewhat excited, surprised, and even disturbed as unfamiliar truths were exposed and confirmed in various passages throughout the Word.

The writings in this document include only a portion of the many issues examined. At its inception I had already spent many years and thousands of hours in committedly researching the topic of 'salvation' and in writing through various issues relevant to it. Issues such as grace, works, faith, belief, freedom, justification, obedience, and redemption and many others had to be considered more fully and brought into context, not just in the context of specific passages and of the books and chapters in which they were addressed but into the context of the whole body of the Word of God.

This project was instigated by a pastor who wistfully presented that it was too bad that there was not a book *Salvation for Dummies*. Although such a book even though helpful would be truly condescending, the reality of the need for a book on the topic that was clear, unambiguous, and accurate would be beneficial. Having spent many years is research, I took up the challenge.

This writing had the objective of presenting as clearly as possible teachings on eternal salvation as revealed in the Word of God. A strenuous effort has been made to avoid the dangers of falling into the biases of any particular spiritual or denominational perspective; after all, my quest for truth was firstly to satisfy my own heart with the knowledge of truth. To gain truth, I have allowed the Scriptures to lead me rather than to let my understanding interpret God's Word. The many Biblical references have been included in order to anchor the writing in truth. I am, and was, very much aware of the condemnation by God of those who bring in false teachings. References have been made available so that the reader might compare the presentations with Scripture. The references also provide anchor for the points being made so that they would not be accepted as conjecture which would have the potential of rendering the writing as being one person's opinion. Although the many references allow for the examination of truths, they also tend to make the document quite academic in style.

Although some of the truths that I present challenge current teachings, I have tried to avoid discussion of the discrepancies in order not to complicate understanding. Diversions to explain, compare, and to justify differences would have led to many long and complicated digressions from a simple presentation of the theme. Instead, I have chosen to rely upon references to the Word of God in order to validate the concepts in this writing.

During the writing process, the understandings that I have learned to accept have been frequently challenged by teachings that I was hearing from pulpits and through other media sources; consequently, I have had to thoroughly and frequently re-examine and to validate my thoughts. In the end, I have full confidence that the "truths" of eternal salvation have been accurately presented.

I found it difficult to set aside the comfort of my own long-standing beliefs and denominational perspective. However, through much study, prayer, and meditation I have found an understanding that is consistent with the Scriptures and which allows comfort in the knowledge on which my own eternal hope is based. In the end, each believer needs to find peace in his own mind since he or she is not just dealing with a life and death issue, but with *his* or *her* life and death issue.

Russell A. Young

"Eternal" Salvation "I'm Okay! You're Okay!" Really?

CONTENTS

Chapter 1: God and Humankind 1
  1.1 Understanding the Issue 1
  1.2 About Humankind 3
  1.3 God: Sovereign, Just, and Holy 7
  1.4 God Declared His Creation to be "Very Good!" So,
      What Happened? 9
  1.5 Sin and Humankind 12
  1.6 Becoming an Offering Acceptable to God 17

Chapter 2: The Gospel 23
  2.1 The Gospel of Christ 23
  2.2 A Synopsis of Eternal Salvation 29
  2.3 Putting "Salvation," "Saved," and "Eternal Salvation"
      into Perspective 31
  2.4 The Sacrifice of Christ on the Cross 37
  2.5 The New Covenant 40

Chapter 3: Necessary Understandings 43
  3.1 Being "in" Christ 43
  3.2 The Path to Eternal Salvation 45
  3.3 More About Gaining the Spirit 54

Chapter 4: The Life of Faith 58
  4.1 Understanding "Faith" 58
  4.2 Death to Self 64
  4.3 Slavery and the Believer 68
  4.4 Eternal Salvation through Relationship 69
  4.5 The Practice of Being Led by the Spirit 74
  4.6 The Leading of the Spirit for Righteousness 81
  4.7 The Leading of the Spirit for Service 83

4.8 Facing Trials 85
4.9 The Fight for Victory 88
4.10 Gaining Victory 90

Chapter 5: Putting Issues into Perspective 96
5.1 Repentance and Salvation.. 96
5.2 The Issue of "Works" and "Grace" 97
5.3 The Law and Salvation... 102
5.4 Conditions Applied to Eternal Salvation 105
5.5 How Can You Know that You Enjoy the Hope of
    Eternal Salvation? 108

Chapter 6: Judgment 111
6.1 The Basis of Judgment 114
6.2 Destruction of the World 118
6.3 Abuse of God's Grace 118
6.4 Judgment for Service 121
6.5 Christ, the Judge 121
6.6 Reward Following Judgment... 122
6.7 The Millennium and Judgment 123

Chapter 7: Challenging Thoughts 126
7.1 Where is the Heavenly Kingdom?................................... 126
7.2 A Place for the Disobedient 127
7.3 Life in the Spirit and Religion 129
7.4 Common Misrepresentations/Confusions Concerning
    Salvation 131

Chapter 8: Conclusion... 147

Chapter 9: Questions Answered 150

Chapter 10: Study Guide.. 166

Chapter 11: Sharing Your Faith...185

INTRODUCTION

The title of this book might challenge the sensibilities of some, but the question needs to be asked: Am I okay? Are you okay? Eternity is a long time to be *not* "okay." A very positive attitude, and even certainty of a person's eternal hope, pervades much teaching that is commonly presented even though Paul, the author of many of the epistles from which the hope for humanity is derived, revealed that *his* hope had not yet been secured. He told the Philippians that he had to persist and suffer like Christ so that *"somehow"* (Phil 3:11) he might attain the resurrection. In spite of Paul's testimony, most feel confident that the requirements of God have been satisfied and that their eternal state has been secured. If Paul was not confident of his own state, on what is your confidence based?

There are many teachings in the Scriptures that deserve a second look and more complete consideration. Issues such as 'obedience,' 'freedom,' 'judgment,' and even 'grace,' 'works,' 'faith,' and 'belief' need careful examination since they are the bases on which so much interpretation is constructed.

The doctrine of 'eternal salvation' is the doctrine of God's plan to draw humankind once more into an eternal *relationship* with himself. It is the deliverance of a people from their disobedience and depravity into a relationship of love, obedience, and holiness, and *into his eternal kingdom*. In a sense the creation story has yet to be completed. God is building a kingdom suitable for his pleasure. It is easy to look at God's salvation plan and to accept that it is all about people when, in fact, it is *all* about God. The plan needs to be understood as it relates to God accomplishing *his* good pleasure. This reality should never be confused. In Timothy we read, *"And God so loved the world…"* That is, God loved all that he had created and one day his creation will be restored to the state that he declared to be "very good." People are being restored to the state to which they had been created in order to fulfill God's purposes. People are being to the state that will bring God the pleasure for which humankind had been created.

God had told the Israelites, "And now, Israel, what does the Lord require of you? He requires only that you fear[1] the LORD your God, and live in a way that pleases him, and to love[2] him and serve him with all your heart and soul." (Deut 10:12)[3] Jesus repeated this requirement during His ministry, "You must love the Lord your God with all your heart, all your soul, and all your mind. This is the first and greatest commandment." (Mt 22:37-38, NLT) This teaching of commitment through love will *never* be set aside for the person that will dwell with God. Eternal salvation is based on a person's *love relationship* with his Creator-God.

The question needs to be asked: How committed is your love for the Lord? Is it with all of your heart, mind, soul, body and strength? Caution needs to be given to your response. Each person has his own understanding of what love means but the Lord has revealed his characterization.

There is more than one element to the plan of "eternal" salvation, and this has resulted in confusion and the spawning of numerous understandings. The evil one has been able to utilize half-truths and bewilderment to lead many astray. For instance, some would say that Christ has saved everyone from destruction regardless of his or her choices and actions in life. Some would permit that after a person quotes the "Sinner's Prayer," his place in the Father's heavenly kingdom is assured. Others suggest that continuous striving is necessary for "salvation", while still others rest their confidence in the symbolic washing of water through baptism. And, of course, there are many who view the concept of salvation as being mythical and lacking in any reality.

Of those who accept its need, for many "salvation" has the understanding of being accomplished through redemption[4] from sin with the promise of

---

[1] "fear" is translated from the Hebrew word *'yare'* which means "to fear; morally, to revere; caus. to frighten: —affright, be (make) afraid, dread(-ful), (put in) fear (-ful, -fully, -ing), (be had in) reverence(-end), X see, terrible (act, -ness, thing)."- Strong's Hebrew Dictionary #3372

[2] "love" is translated from the Hebrew word *'ahab'* which means "to have affection for (sexually or otherwise): (be-)love (-d, -ly, -r), like, friend." – Strong's Hebrew Dictionary #157

[3] Also, Deut 11:13; 13:3; Josh 22:5; 1 Sam 7:3, 12:20, 12:24; Joel 2:12

[4] Redemption: the purchase back of something that had been lost, by the payment of a ransom. The Greek word so rendered is *apolutrosis*, a word occurring nine times in Scripture, and always with the idea of a ransom or price paid. -Easton's Bible Dictionary

heaven to follow. No seeker would suggest that God's "heavenly Kingdom" and "eternal life" are not his true hope. It is less well understood that redemption from sin, although necessary, is only the *beginning* of God's salvation plan. The limited insight that has been endorsed as the full gospel may satisfy humankind, however, from God's point of view such a narrow perception will not achieve the goals for which humans had been created. The means of "eternal salvation" is bound with the life of Christ in a person following that redemption and is gained through, and for an *intimate relationship* between that person and his Creator and this must be developed and maintained.

> People must be careful not to allow assumptions and presumptions to invade his thinking.

People must be careful not to allow assumptions, presumptions, and the intrusion of philosophical thought to invade their thinking. (This has happened, and some issues have been addressed at the end of this book.) No matter what is taught, God is the author of salvation and it is his determination as to who will dwell with him. His Word has revealed the truths that would allow a person into his eternal presence and *it must be properly examined and understood*. God will not alter his plan according to errant ideas and presentations concerning it. Gaining eternal salvation is the primary task of a person's earthly life since his or her choices during their natural life will determine the reality of their eternal existence.

The Greek word, 'soteria,' from which 'salvation' is derived means "rescue or safety (physically or morally): --deliver, health, salvation, save and saving." [5] It has also been stated as meaning: "to *effect successfully the delivery of someone or something from impending danger.*"[6] Thinking of salvation as meaning 'deliverance' from impending danger might help expand a person's thinking and dispel the connotations that limit understanding. That is, "delivering" someone from danger does not necessarily mean that one has been eternally saved; his or her salvation might have been more limited as from a particular threat. With this in mind, it must be appreciated that each believer needs to be *delivered* from, or saved from, a number of dangers and entanglements if he or she is to satisfy their holy Creator. A right relationship with God must be established,

---

[5] Strong's Greek Definition # 4991
[6] Willmington, Dr. H. L., Willmington's Guide to the Bible, Tyndale House Publishers, Inc., Wheaton, Illinois, 1984, page 727

the penalty of his or her sin must be dealt with, *the practice of their sinning must be addressed*, that sinner must be *transformed into the image of Christ*, and their love for the one who has redeemed them must be reflected through submission to the one they call "Lord!"

Confusion results when salvation is thought of *only* as deliverance from the penalty of sin, whereby the forgiven person is said to gain assurance of access into the kingdom of heaven. Being rescued from the consequences of sin does not by itself satisfy the need and the plan of God. A person's sanctification is an essential requirement. The biblical understanding of 'faith' and 'works' must be made clear, and the means of salvation must be understood if a person is to achieve his or her eternal hope. Since there are many resting their hope on a state that they do not have, a picture of true and eternal salvation needs to be made clear. Because salvation is by the *grace of God and* understanding the place of grace in salvation is not often made complete, commitment has been replaced by the cheap treatment of the blessed and horrible work of Christ on the cross while neglecting *his ministry that follows*. The believer's hope rests in Christ in him or her and cannot be achieved solely by Christ's sacrificial offering.

> There are many resting their hopes on a state that they do not have.

Chapter 1
God and Humankind

1.1 Understanding the Issue

It is easy to get misled concerning the means of "eternal salvation" unless the issue of its need is clearly understood. That is, *why* does a person have to be "saved" in the first place? *What* is God trying to accomplish? What is the strategy that God has set in place to achieve his purpose?

The salvation plan of God is not arbitrary. It is not something that has been put in place merely for the collection of a group of people. His people will be a "peculiar people" (Titus 2:14; 1 Pet 2:9, KJV); they will be a people who suit his eternal plan. In a sense, the creation story has not been completed, and it will not be completed until God has set up the *eternal* kingdom that he had envisioned.

The nature of God's kingdom is not difficult to grasp since it existed *before* the rebellion of Adam and Eve in the Garden of Eden. The Lord had looked at what he had created and had declared it to be "very good." (Gen 1:31) Shortly after, however, it is revealed that he was "grieved that he had made man on the earth, and his heart was filled with pain." (Gen 6:6) It is the heart need of God and the inclination to evil in people that eternal salvation must address. The heart of humankind was, and is, the issue that God must make suitable for his presence in order to accomplish a person's eternal salvation and for his plan to be satisfied. The believer must be restored and transformed into the image in which humankind had been created. "Neither circumcision nor uncircumcision means anything; what counts is a new creation." (Gal 6:15) It is the transformation process that reveals God's salvation plan and that results in a person's *eternal* salvation. Paul said, "God gave me the priestly duty of proclaiming the gospel of God, so that the Gentiles might become an offering acceptable to God, sanctified by the Holy Spirit." (Rom 15:16) A person's cleansing and transformation into the likeness of the Son of God making them an acceptable offering is needed to bring about their eternal salvation.

The issue of salvation cannot be considered from a human's perspective, but it must be examined according to God's goal for eternity. Salvation is *all* about God the Creator and the fulfillment of his plans. The plan of creation is God's, and he has created for the accomplishment of his pleasure. (Rev 4:11) He had a purpose in mind for his handiwork and it is for this objective that his plan is being completed even in the eternal salvation of a person. God's desired state for humankind was revealed in the very first book of the Bible, and it is to this created state that people must be returned: "Let us make man in our own image; in the image of God he created him." (Gen 1:26) Humans were created pure and regular of heart and mind—holy in state. Although they did not maintain this image for long, it is still the condition that God requires in order to fulfil his plan. Those who will be privileged to dwell with him must be in his likeness. Paul has recorded that those who God foreknew "he also predestined to be conformed to the likeness of his Son." (Rom 8:29) Whatever a person understands to be the route to eternal salvation, it must ensure the transformation of the believer back to the image in which humans had been created in the first place- the image of God's Son. The state of the human heart has brought "pain" (Gen 6:6) to the heart of God, and it should not be accepted that God will allow those who bring pain to his heart to dwell with him eternally.

> Salvation is *all* about God the Creator and the fulfillment of his plans.

The issue in all human history has been the rebellion of created people against God's person and authority, and the hearts that have allowed it. Nevertheless, God loved his creation and still does. "For God so loved the world that he gave his one and only Son." (Jn 3:16) An elaborate and costly plan was put in place in order to rescue his creation which would require the development of a new heart for those who would dwell with him, thus allowing his purpose to be accomplished.

The issue of humankind is very complicated. Humans are a special creation with the ability to gain knowledge and to exercise reason. Along with that, God permitted people the right to practice their own free-will. Undoubtedly, he wants humans to freely choose righteousness through knowledge of him and through the exercise of reason. Allowing humankind to enjoy free-will and yet to be conformed to the image of Christ is the complex issue that eternal salvation addresses.

Some have taken offense that not all people will be included in the Lord's enduring creation. The first great truth to be accepted is that *creation is God's plan and it is to accomplish his purposes.* This being the case, only those whose moral state allows for the fulfilment of God's plan will find a presence with him; the others will be cast out and separated from the holy kingdom that he will form.

Although some teach that a person's eternal salvation comes solely through having been pardoned for sin, it must be recognized that God is setting up an *eternal* kingdom. If those in it have not made a commitment to honor and love their creator through humble obedience, the same issues of pride and self-determination will rear themselves in the kingdom to come and God's work will never be completed. Individuals who have been pardoned for their sin have merely been allowed release from its consequences; the hearts that caused the sin are not changed through a pardon. Not only are individuals to be transformed, they are to prove this transformation through their actions[7] and are to become sacrifices acceptable to the Lord.

It is difficult for the human ego to permit that humanity is not the focus of the creation story, and it is difficult to accept that people must reckon themselves to be created beings subject to the interests of one greater. Unless, and until, the truth dawns that creation and humankind belong to another who has a particular purpose for them—and until they are willing to humble themselves to the authority of that one—the truths of salvation will never be understood and a person's hope of being a part of the grand eternal story will have vanished. All who have been given breath on this earth need to understand that they are the created and have been formed by one far superior to themselves; they must understand that they must fit into *his* plan for the accomplishment of *his* purposes.

1.2 About Humankind

There is no doubt that humans are a special creation and have been given attributes and rights that are exceptional. It is the uniqueness of people that allows them to hold a special place in God's heart, although God loves

---

[7] Acts 26:20.

all of his creation. *Humans were created in God's likeness.* Failure to honor this state is the issue that caused humankind to "fall," and it is his or her renewal and restoration to it that will result in satisfying God's eternal plan and humankind's designated place in it.

Humanity's greatest blessings, and those qualities which glorify God most, have also turned out to be the greatest weaknesses in people. That is, humans were given the ability to collect knowledge and to make reasoned and informed decisions and were also granted the right to act on them. When it comes to God, people have been allowed to exercise their own will regarding whether they will attend to, and honor, their Creator God or whether they will deny him the glory that he deserves.

Unique to created beings, humans were given souls.[8] Accordingly, they have the right through their souls to affect their own course and in their own manner. Humans do not have to respond by instinct to their surroundings; they can apply memory and reason in reacting to their situation. People are a special creation, fashioned in the image or likeness of God. Being of this state, humankind can relate to God in a way that can bring him the pleasure for which they have been purposed.

Along with a soul, humans have also been given a spirit. The difference between the *soul* and the *spirit* is that while the soul is the psychological aspect or personality of the person-that which, apart from physical attributes, identifies him or her among all others-, including his or her moral consciousness and mental acuity, the spirit is *the agent of interaction of the soul with the physical and spiritual worlds.* The soul and the spirit work to lead a person into seeking and to gaining specific information that motivates his or her actions. That is, an individual might feel cold and the spirit might motivate him or her to find protection. According to the state of the soul, he or she may choose by an act of the will to either earn or even steal a covering. The spirit works with the body and the soul to determine how the individual will interpret his or her surroundings and how they will respond to the environment, including those around them.

---

[8] The soul is "the spiritual, rational, and immortal substance in people, which distinguishes him or her from brutes; that part of a person which enables them to think and reason, and which renders them a subject of moral government." It might be the aspect of a person that identifies with his personality. A soul is within everyone and individuals can be identified by the nature of their souls. Souls can be purified and that is the reason why the Holy Spirit was granted to believers. The soul is not a substance and is immortal.

All individuals have their own spirits; however, some may have other spirits as well. A person may have a spirit of lust or one of anger or he or she may have one of love or of patience. The spirits that indwell mankind may be good or they may be evil; they can build up or they can destroy. They can be sent by God[9] or by "the spiritual forces of evil in the heavenly realms." (Eph 6:12)

The Holy Spirit, once he is given, persuades the soul concerning the development of the *holiness* that affects a person's decisions and the state of his or her soul. The Holy Spirit (the Spirit of or for holiness), if obeyed leads the willing to the Father's Kingdom. He has power and the authority to bring godly information and the knowledge of righteousness to the soul through his leading and enlightenment. The Holy Spirit can transform the believer's heart and mind if permitted (willed). The Holy Spirit will not over-rule the will of a person.

Evil spirits may also affect the soul and lead the affected person into unrighteous, disobedient, and disturbing paths. A person should be careful not to allow the practice of magic arts into his or her life allowing evil spirits to contest with their spirit and with the Holy Spirit.

The soul responds according to *knowledge and knowledge is gained through the senses* (taste, touch, sight, hearing, and feeling) as an individual relates to his or her environment, through a person's past experiences, and through teachings that he or she has accepted as truths (beliefs). In order to exercise *free-will* the person must 'will' something. His or her will might be to please the flesh in some manner such as through gluttony, sexual immorality, or some other form of "comfort," or it may be to raise their status through education or wealth, or through seeking favour with others. Or, a person's will might have been persuaded to obediently follow the Lord and to forgo personal wishes. The purposes for a person's actions are based on what he or she desires at that time according to his or her understanding or knowledge of how to meet the objectives of their soul.

The Word of God frequently speaks of a person's need to be on guard concerning those things that might negatively affect his or her understanding and their desires. Because the soul is often fed by a person's environment, care should be taken to control the nature of their circumstances. For instance, a person cannot subject himself or herself to pornography without it feeding their evil nature and altering their

---

[9] Ex 28:3; 1 Sam 16:14, 1 Kings 22:23, Isa 19:14.

soul. The more a person seeks to satisfy lust, the more the power and predominance of that spirit will grow and his or her soul become altered. Neither can a person allow themselves to fixate on possessions or desire for possessions or position, without that person's soul becoming tainted with envy, greed and idolatry. A soul cannot be subjected to the violence that is presented in many videos and video games without the risk of losing regard for mercy and respect for life, nor can he or she allow themselves to pass control of their being through drugs to ill-intentioned "friends" or to their circumstances. A person's soul is shaped by the way it is fed and allowed it to be impacted. Paul wrote, "Finally, brethren, whatsoever things are true, whatsoever things are honest, whatsoever things are just, whatsoever things are pure, whatsoever things are lovely, whatsoever things are of good report; if there be any virtue, and if there be any praise, *think on these things*." (Phil 4:8, KJV) The nature of a person's environment feeds his senses and consequently his mind and his soul.

The soul and the spirit[10] leave the body at physical death; they do not die but are eternal.[11] The flesh does not survive death; it is the soul of a person that is the person and is God's greatest concern. An indestructible body[12] will *instantly* be given to the redeemed at Christ's return; however, the soul requires the duration of a person's life-long walk with the Lord to be transformed into that which pleases their creator; it is God's masterpiece (Eph 2:10, NLT) or workmanship. The transformation of the soul comes through the great ministry of the Spirit and is the purpose for Christ's presence in a person's life.

> The Spirit was given to make the soul of the redeemed "an offering acceptable to God, sanctified by the Holy Spirit."

The Spirit was given to make the soul of the redeemed "an offering acceptable to God, sanctified by him" (Rom 15:16); the soul is "God's workmanship," (Eph 2:10) the 'product' of his transforming work. A person's soul can either have been developed by his evil nature or by allowing the Holy Spirit to complete his ministry during the believer's lifetime. It is for this reason Paul taught that salvation is not by works. People cannot transform their souls from the outside and without this transformation they cannot be made acceptable for God's eternal kingdom.

---

[10] Eccl 12:7
[11] Rev 20:4-5
[12] 1 Cor 15:52

Apart from the persuasion and power of the Holy Spirit a person's evil nature will overpower his or her good intentions. Holiness of state can only be achieved through righteous practices which the Spirit must bring about. He and his ministry are essential for a person's eternal salvation.[13]

1.3 God: Sovereign, Just, and Holy

It is not possible to present a true picture of God. The Word tells us that no one can see God and live, although he has been made visible through his Son, the Lord Jesus Christ. For salvation purposes it is sufficient, however, to have a very limited understanding and that understanding in itself should be over-whelming. It might be trite to say but God is real. He is also holy and very much in control of his creation.

God is God and all creation was made by him and for him. He will not give his authority or glory to another. Neither will God allow himself to be made something that he is not in the mind of any person. He is not only *love*, he is *sovereign*, he is *just*, and he is *holy*. To see him in a different light is error. Day and night the four living creatures in heaven never stopped crying, "Holy, holy, holy is the Lord God Almighty, who was and is, and is to come." (Rev 4:8, KJV) And "the twenty-four elders fall down before him who sits on the throne and worship him. They lay their crowns before the throne and say, 'You are worthy, our Lord and God, to receive glory and honor and power, for you created all things and by your will they were created and have their being.'" (Rev 4:10-11) He is awesome and compels humility and honor by those who know him. It is he who is completing his divine plan.

The holiness of God cannot be overstated. He is pure and without moral defect. Those confessing his name are told that they are to be holy because he is holy[14] and the writer of Hebrews has stated that without holiness no one will see him.[15] God cannot dwell in the presence of sin and its darkness.

It is for the sake of developing a holy state in people that Christ came to earth. God who created the world indwells the confessor.[16] Since the

---

[13] 2 Thess 2:13; Titus 3:5-6
[14] 1 Pet 1:16
[15] Heb 12:14
[16] Col 1:27

Lord's relationship with the confessor is so intimate[17] the believer should be ever aware that nothing is hidden; all is known by God.[18] The believer can take comfort in knowing that nothing transpires in the life of the person called according to his purpose that the Lord has not ordained for that person's good.[19]

Some allow that the grace of God exempts them from being holy in heart and practice, or that he unilaterally accomplishes believer's state of holiness, but God does not change. The sin that pained his heart prior to the flood still pains his heart. The grace of God does not exempt a person from the necessity of walking in the light[20] and in obedience to him[21] but empowers him to do so.

God is just; that is his nature. He will not tolerate rebellion from one person and allow it for another. Justice will not be aborted; his nature and government demand it. His law was first revealed by command to Moses and was engraved on stone for the nation of Israel. The righteous requirements of his government were recorded for all people and for all time. Christ said that he did not come to do away with the law but to fulfil it.[22]

The Lord has made provision for the law's completion through his sacrificial offering and *through his life in the believer*.[23] Those who reject his offer of grace[24]-completion of the law through the indwelling life of Christ- must satisfy the law by themselves and are subject to its governance. God is just; those who would teach that the believer is exempt from the law are deceivers. Paul admonished his readers not to be deceived and that God would not be mocked but that "the one who sows to please the sinful nature from the sinful nature will reap destruction; the one who sows to please the Spirit from the Spirit will reap eternal life." (Gal 6:8) It is a person's sowing or living in agreement with the Holy Spirit that satisfies the

---

[17] 2 Cor 3:17-18
[18] Ps 139
[19] Rom 8:28
[20] 1 Jn 1: 5-6
[21] Heb 5:9
[22] Mt 5:17
[23] Rom 8:4
[24] Rom 8:14

righteous requirements of the law.²⁵ In the end, all will face the judgment seat of Christ and be dealt with according to the nature of their "sowing."

The love of God is immeasurable! God loved the world to the extent that he gave his Son as a sacrifice for its redemption and gave the Spirit that people might walk in the light and be transformed. It is his desire that none would be lost, and he has given his Spirit so that the person who seeks his kingdom might become an offering acceptable to Him, sanctified and holy.

God is sovereign and he is building his Eternal Kingdom. Some will be fitted for his presence while others will have rejected his grace. In the end, he will have completed his creation and it will be just as he had intended. He will dwell forever with those who have loved him with all their heart, mind, and soul.²⁶ A person's commitment cannot be "lukewarm." (Rev 3:16) His sovereignty is to be humbly respected and honored through commitment and obedience. God is creator, savior, sustainer, and sovereign and he is building his Eternal Kingdom.

1.4 God Declared His Creation to be "Very Good!" So, What Happened?

In the Garden of Eden Adam did not have to work. Food was abundant and varied. The environment provided humankind was controlled in order to allow them freedom from discomfort and from the strain of finding protection from the elements. Plants and animals were given for sustenance and enjoyment. God walked with humans and talked with them.²⁷ People only had knowledge of good, and of God.

In the middle of the garden was the tree from which Adam and Eve had been commanded not to eat -the tree of the knowledge of good and evil. The tree was a "test" for Adam and Eve. Its fruit was not a requirement for life. In fact, it was one tree among a great many. But, a command of God had been attached to that tree with the consequence of disobedience, which was death, having been made known. Would they be committed to their God or would they claim sovereignty over their lives and allow their own self-interests to prevail? They chose to defy God and to follow

---

[25] Rom 8:4
[26] Deut 6:10; 10:12; 13:3; 30:6; Mt 22:37; Mk 12:30
[27] Gen 3:8, 9

their own interests. Submitting to the temptation to appease the flesh and to disobey God caused humankind to fall; that is, a separation between God and humans occurred.[28] God is a jealous God and will not give his glory or right to rule to another. Like God, Adam and Eve had gained "knowledge" of good *and of evil*; their knowledge came from their own practice or experience. Their desire to appease the flesh and consequently to defy God introduced the knowledge of evil to people.

At creation the moral consciousness of humankind was in the likeness of their God. Their minds and their consciences had been at peace; however, Adam and Eve immediately became troubled following rejection of God's sovereignty of their lives. They became self-conscious concerning their flesh, their nakedness, and covered themselves. Peace and righteousness had deserted them.

Their disobedience, and the pleasure that disobedience brought to them, the knowledge of evil, has plagued humankind to this day. Eve had responded to her senses. "And when the woman *saw* that the tree was *good for food*, and that it was *pleasant to the eyes*, and a tree *to be desired* to make one wise, she took of the fruit thereof, and did eat, and gave also unto her husband with her; and he did eat." (Gen 3:6, KJV) Satan appealed to her through her flesh. Having "enjoyed" her defiance and the pleasure brought to her flesh Eve invited Adam into her disobedience.[29] She became knowledgeable (informed) that the body could be accommodated and rationalized her right to eat, even though doing so was rebellion against her creator. She had put her interests and her flesh above honoring her God and creator.

God had not intended to deny humankind the enjoyment of the flesh they had been given. Humans had been created to find pleasure in their bodies. It is going beyond the limitations that God had set, and in a sense allowing the body to become their god and to direct their interests that was offensive. Certainly, Adam and Eve had enjoyed many other fruits in the garden. It is the excesses and misuse of the senses with the flesh dominating the soul that is hurtful to the creator. The spirit of a person with its desire to satisfy the flesh rather than to obey God became the issue, and is still the issue, that needs to be put into proper perspective today.

---

[28] Sin separates. "But your iniquities have separated between you and your God, and your sins have hidden *his* face from you, that he will not hear." (Isa 59:2, KJV)

[29] Gen 3:6

God is to be esteemed, to be pursued, and to be honored above the flesh even today. He will not have another god before him.

As dark and as wayward as the soul can get, it can be re-trained[30] to become holy and righteous in thought and practice. The Holy Spirit was given so that humankind might defeat their flesh, and so that the obedient believer might be brought back into a state of holiness through righteous practices. Righteous living is the need of those who will dwell with their God. The obedient will enjoy a holy state once again. Those who continue to be disobedient, who continue to rebel, who prevent God's effort at renewing their souls and their hearts, will not dwell with Him. Continued defiance by the redeemed will eventually quench the Spirit of Holiness as his or her reasoning sooths their moral consciousness, preventing the "believer" from responding to his leading. Holiness will be aborted.

Adam and Eve did not commit to retaining the innocence that God had given them; instead they chose to broaden their knowledge of the forbidden with its appeal to the flesh. It is doubtful that their motivation was to rebel, however *their* interests became greater than their desire to obey. Paul spoke of this attitude to the Romans. "Since they [those who reject God's standards] did not think it worthwhile to retain the knowledge of God, he gave them over to a depraved mind, to do what ought not to be done. They have become filled with every kind of wickedness, evil, greed, and depravity.... Although they know God's righteous decree that those who do such things deserve death, they not only continue to do these very things but approve of those who practice them." (Rom 1:28, 29...32)

> Defiance of God with an interest in appeasing the flesh brought about the downfall of humankind and remains the issue for which people will be judged in the end.

Defiance of God with an interest in appeasing the flesh brought about the downfall of humankind and remains the issue for which people will be judged in the end. "For if you live according to the sinful nature, you will die; but if by the Spirit you put to death the misdeeds of the body, you will live." (Rom 8:13) The flesh remains to be conquered. Just as the forbidden fruit appealed to Eve's carnal nature, so issues of the flesh continue to entice the spirits of humankind.

Through rebellion and defiance, that which God had created and had declared to be very good has become very evil. Not only have people

---

[30] 2 Cor 4:16; Rom 8:29, 12:2

suffered through their rebellion but so has God's whole creation. "We know that the whole creation has been groaning as in the pains of childbirth right up to the present time." (Rom 8:22) The "child" that once brought pain to the heart of God and to his creation through the resistance of righteousness and a rebellious walk must mature into the product that he desires,[31] and become an "acceptable offering," (Rom 15:16) prepared to take on the life God had intended. All of creation is groaning and waiting for the product of God's handiwork to be revealed in its completion. People have a special place in fulfilling God's plan and the eternal salvation of a *particular or peculiar people is needed for the accomplishment of that plan.*

The evil that humankind has come to know must be eliminated. Rebellion must cease and the Lord must be recognized as sovereign in the heart and mind of those who will dwell with him. Being forgiven is not enough. As stated, forgiveness does nothing other than to provide judicial relief from past offences. Addressing issues of the present and the future so that they are not repeated allowing for the elimination of their practice requires a different kind of intervention. It is for this reason that God provided the presence of Christ, the Holy Spirit, the Spirit of sonship (Rom 8:15), to indwell the believer; "Christ in you, the hope of glory." (Colossians 1:27, KJV)[32] The indwelling presence of Christ is the mystery that has been kept hidden for ages and generations and has now been revealed. He is a person's hope since it is only through him that righteousness can be lived and that the believer's heart and mind can be transformed.

1.5 Sin and Humankind

The deceitfulness of a person's heart can easily allow him to dismiss sin and in his or her mind to minimize its effect on the heart of God and on their eternal hope. It was not God's plan for deceit, anger, strife, hurt, pain, disease, death, etc. to be part of his creation. Such evils were not to exist at all. People were created to live in a pure and loving relationship with each other and with their creator. The extent to which humankind has

---

[31] Eph 2:10 refers to the transformed believer as being God's "workmanship" (KJV, NIV) meaning 'product.'
[32] Note: The celebration of communion requires both the breaking *and eating* of the bread and the *drinking* of the wine. These acts of ingestion are symbolic of taking Christ into a person's body.

departed from God's plan and purpose is almost impossible for the person without the Spirit to appreciate. The "wisdom" of humans has supplanted the laws of God. Political "correctness" has encouraged abandonment of the righteousness that God demands with the acceptance of all kinds of immoral activities in order to accommodate a person's evil desires. Even nature is waiting to be liberated from bondage to decay and to be returned once more to the glorious state that existed before humankind defied God's sovereign's right to rule.[33]

Although people had originally been created in the likeness or image of God, that state and their nature, has changed to the point that God can find no pleasure in them. To appreciate God's perception of sin the effect that it has had needs to be made clear. It is recorded in Genesis: "The Lord saw how great man's wickedness on the earth had become, and that every inclination of the thoughts of his heart was only evil all the time. The Lord was grieved that he had made man on the earth and his heart was filled with pain." (Gen. 6: 5-6) The evil hearts and imaginations of humankind have brought grief and pain to the heart of God. The key to understanding eternal salvation rests in this truth. That is, *the thoughts of person's heart are only evil all the time.*" Ridding a person's heart of its constant inclination to evil is the problem that must be resolved. God will not dwell eternally with those who bring him pain; their thinking must be changed as well as the heart that motivates such thinking. Paul taught that he was given "the priestly duty of proclaiming the gospel of God, so that the Gentiles might become an offering acceptable to God, sanctified by the Holy Spirit." (Rom 15:16)

> The evil hearts and imaginations of humankind have brought grief and pain to the heart of God.

It is not enough for the sinner to be forgiven for his or her sin and rebellion, as some would teach; They must STOP it. Hope of eternal salvation should not be permitted to rest in God's willingness to forgive, or in Christ's payment for sin. Understanding eternal salvation requires appreciating the way Christ brings renewal to the deceitful and wayward heart. Access to God's provision of renewal requires the forgiveness of sin, including its just payment, but the hope of eternal life also requires the

---

[33] Rom 8:22

believer's transformation through righteous practices, to holiness of heart and mind.[34]

Sin is so prevalent in this world, and its practice so acceptable, that it is difficult to recognize its presence. The teachings and persuasions of the world permit the acceptance of acts that God condemns. The endorsing of abortions, euthanasia, adultery, and unnatural or unlawful intimacy are but a few. The flesh demands to be appeased through greed, gluttony, sexual immorality, etc. And, Satan himself would encourage a person's heart to seek its own interests and to defy God. In his or her natural state and evil nature all people would be led away from the expectations of God and the heart that he would desire. No human can change their heart by themselves;[35] such transformation requires divine intervention.[36]

Sin -rebellion and lawlessness- has separated people from their creator[37] so that the needed intervention cannot happen. However, Christ offered Himself on the cross to cleanse those who confess faith[38] in him and in

---

[34] 2 Thess 2:13; Titus 3: 5-6; Paul has taught that salvation comes through the sanctifying work of the Spirit.

[35] The impossibility of transforming a person's own heart through his own resources is what Paul meant when he taught that a person's "hope of glory" (eternal salvation) came through "Christ in you." (Col. 1:27) Christ, the Holy Spirit, must bring it about. The believer's transformation cannot be accomplished by his or her "doing" or "works," and this transformation is humankind's greatest need. The heart is so deceitful that it does not recognize sin. Each person needs to be enlightened concerning it. He must learn of sin from God's Holy Word, and from the Spirit's leading as he stirs the believer's conscience. The natural spirit would often draw a person toward the "pleasures" of sin, but the Spirit would allow him or her victory over its practice. Paul's teaching against salvation by works does not refer to the idea that by doing "good" things a person he can attempt to "earn" a place in God's heavenly kingdom; salvation by works addresses the thought of a person being able to transform his or her own mind and heart using their own resources.

[36] This Divine intervention is God's *grace*. "*We have gradually come to speak of grace as being an inherent quality in man, just as we talk of gifts; whereas it is in reality the communication of Divine goodness by the inworking of the Spirit, and through the medium of him who is "full of grace and truth.*" – Robert Girdlestone, *Synonyms of the Old Testament* (London: Longmans, Green and Co., 1871) p. 179

[37] Isa 59:2

[38] "Faith" is often taken to mean "trust;" however, different Greek words are used to represent 'trust' and 'faith.' "Faith" means "persuasion' or "having been persuaded." To have "faith" in Christ is to be persuaded that his person, ministry, and teachings are true. The persuaded person responds obediently to them

his gospel. With this cleansing they are able once more to fellowship with God. They have been made perfect, at least for the moment.

The writer of Hebrews has stated that, "by one sacrifice he has made perfect forever those who are being made holy." (Hebrews 10:14) This passage might take on greater meaning when phrased as, '*by one sacrifice those who are being made holy he has made perfect forever.*' Perfection applies only to those who *are being made* holy, *those within whom the Spirit has been allowed to work and is working.* The person who will remain perfect must be obedient.[39] Without practicing obedience a person cannot claim that he or she is in the state of perfection;[40] however, the state of those in whom the Spirit is being obeyed or who "*are being made holy*" is one of

---

because he or she accepts them as truth. The person who accepts "faith" as "trust" feels the freedom to disassociate himself or herself from any obligations regarding their own deliverance because they "trust" Christ to look after them apart from any involvement on their part.

[39] Hebrews 5:9; This is the only passage in the entire Word of God that uses the wording '*eternal salvation*" and the author records that it applies to those who "obey" Christ.

[40] Some would take issue with this teaching proclaiming that none on this earth can be perfect since all have sinned. However, this passage is not addressing those not yet redeemed and is not necessarily addressing the absence of sin. The writer may be relating perfection to complying to the requirement of obedience *to the Spirit's leadership.* God knows the heart of a person and he knows the difficulties experienced concerning its transformation. The believer's wholehearted commitment to walking in the light is as perfect as he or she can be. Walking in the light or in accordance with the Spirit's leading is perfection according to God's plan and expectations. It is those who are "being made holy" who have humbled themselves to God. There is nothing more that they can do and nothing more that is expected. Of course, "perfect" can also mean free from sin and the believer has been given "*all that is needed for life and godliness.*" The process of walking in obedience to the Spirit (sanctification by the Spirit) will leave the true believer cleansed and therefore perfect always and forever.

Paul taught that "there is no condemnation for those who are in Jesus Christ… who do not live according to the sinful nature but according to the Spirit." (Rom 8:1…4). John also taught that we will sin but "if we confess our sins God will forgive us our sins and purify us from all unrighteousness." (1Jn 1:9)

Perfection comes through redemption by the sacrifice of Christ followed by justification through the Holy Spirit as he reigns in the believer's life.

perfection. Their practices through obedience will maintain and develop a state of holiness provided they persevere.[41]

> Humans have been given free-will and this characteristic and right will not be taken away.

Humans have been given *free-will* and this characteristic and right will not be taken away. People must *choose* to love and to honor their God if the plan of creation is to bring about the purpose that God desires. Being faithful to God, who is the Spirit, requires proper choices as the believer follows the Spirit's leading. Submission to the Spirit as opposed to the flesh is difficult and will be tested in a person's life experience.[42] God wants to know, and will know, the extent of a person's love for him.

Having been restored to fellowship, God gifts those who have called upon him with the Spirit of Christ. The Spirit is sometimes called the Helper.[43] A helper is someone who gives assistance to another. The Holy Spirit helps the person seeking to satisfy the need for holiness but who cannot accomplish it by himself or herself.

Adam and Eve fell because they chose to defy God's right to exercise his sovereignty. Restoration comes when the contrite or humble person[44] has recognized his or her rebellion, have repented, have declared that Christ is and will be their lord and are once more willing to put God on the throne of their life. Christ can only rule if he is followed. "He [Christ] became the source of eternal salvation for all who obey him." (Heb 5:9) Christ said, "My sheep *listen* to my voice; I know them, and they *follow* me. I give them eternal life, and they shall never perish." (Jn 10:27)

It is through His Spirit, the Spirit of Holiness, that the believer's mind and heart can be changed, and sin defeated. The Spirit enlightens a person's mind concerning sin, leads him or her to avoid its practice, and empowers them for victory.

---

[41] The Lord stated that the believer must "endureth to the end" in order to be saved (Mt 10:22, KJV)

[42] 1 Pet 1:7; "These [all kinds of trials] have come so that your faith-of greater worth than gold, which perishes even though refined by fire-may be proved genuine, and may result in praise, glory, and honor when Jesus Christ is revealed." (NIV)

[43] Jn 14:26, (English Standard Version, New American Standard Version, International Standard Version) Alternately, "Comforter", "Advocate", "Counselor", and "Paraclete" have been used in various translations instead of "Helper."

[44] Ps 34:18; 51:17, 57:15

The redeemed person must be a willing partner in this journey of righteousness. "Therefore, there is now no condemnation for those who are in Christ Jesus...And he condemned sin in sinful man, in order that *the righteous requirements of the law might be fully met in us, who do not live according to the sinful nature but according to the Spirit.*" (Rom 8:1...3-4)

A careful reading of God's Word reveals that eternal salvation is only assured through obedience to the Spirit and through his on-going work and has not been fully accomplished by the sacrificial offering of Christ.[45] It is not his death that saves eternally; it is his life. "The Spirit gives life." (Jn 6:63)[46] The Spirit works from the inside out, sanctifying the believer.[47] Salvation is not by works-the working of the law or the things that a person can do using his or her own resources- but through grace which is the sacrifice of Christ and the gifting of the Spirit, including His work in a person's life. It is not possible for the institution of laws to transform the wicked heart and mind. In order to save humankind and to achieve God's creation plan, Christ had to satisfy the covenant of the law so that the *covenant of the Spirit* could be instituted.

The gifting of the Spirit is not the end of the matter, however. He must be obeyed and permitted to live *living* in the person seeking life. Much of the New Testament deals with the issues of obedience and perseverance. These teachings are important especially since by nature humankind is more prone to rebel than to obey. The "believer" can be recognized by his or her willingness to engage the battle for righteousness and through humility of heart to follow the leading of the Spirit.

1.6 Becoming an Offering Acceptable to God

What is an offering acceptable to God? Perhaps the writer of Hebrews expressed it most clearly: "Without *holiness* no one will see the Lord." (Heb 12:14) Paul taught that "the kingdom of God is not a matter of eating and drinking but of righteousness, peace, and joy in the Holy Spirit, because anyone who serves God in this way is pleasing to God and approved by men." (Rom 14:17-18)

---

[45] 2 Thess 2:13; Titus 3: 5-6; Rom 10:9-10
[46] "I am the way the truth, and the life." (Jn 14:6, KJV)
[47] "From the beginning God chose you to be saved through the sanctifying work of the Spirit." (2 Thess 2:13) "He saved us through the washing of rebirth and renewal by the Holy Spirit." (Titus 3:5)

The only offering acceptable to God is the person who faithfully practices righteousness, peace, and joy and through those practices develops a state of holiness.[48] Some teach that the believer was made eternally holy at the time of his confession of faith; however, Paul taught that righteousness is being "awaited" and that it comes through the Spirit.[49] Although it is true that the believer was legally cleansed of all sin through the sacrificial offering of Christ on his behalf, practical righteousness has not yet been achieved and unrighteous practices will result in his or her removal from the family of God.[50] Paul has made it clear: The righteous requirements of the law are only fully met by those who do not live according to the sinful nature but according to the Spirit.[51] The righteousness that satisfies the law and brings "eternal" salvation comes through life in the Spirit. The life is the life of Christ and is accomplished throughout the duration of the believer's natural life. Life through the Spirit makes the believer an offering acceptable to God.

When the end comes, and Christ has destroyed all dominion, power, and authority he will hand the kingdom over to his Father.[52] The Kingdom of Christ becomes the Kingdom of God. There will be no one in the kingdom of God who harbours evil in their heart or mind or who has allowed the dominion of evil to invade their practices. Paul told his fellow believers *not to be deceived* but that those who live by the evil nature will reap destruction.[53] Every person who will dwell with the Lord in the kingdom that he hands over to the Father must be acceptable in his sight. He or she must be righteous through having been transformed by the sanctifying work of the Spirit. "Neither circumcision nor uncircumcision means anything: what counts is a new creation." (Gal 6: 15) It is the "new creation "of a person, the product created by God, holy in state and practice, which makes him or her acceptable and this is accomplished by *keeping the commandments of God*[54]- through the enlightenment, the leading, and the power of the Spirit.

---

[48] Rom 6: 19, 22
[49] Gal 5:5
[50] Jn 8:35, 15:1
[51] Rom 8:4
[52] 1 Cor 15:24. "Then the end will come, when he hands over the kingdom to God the Father after he has destroyed all dominion, authority and power." (NIV)
[53] Gal 6:8
[54] 1 Cor 7:19 "Circumcision is nothing and uncircumcision is nothing. Keeping

Paul wrote that he was given "the priestly duty of proclaiming the gospel of God, so that the Gentiles might become an offering acceptable to God, sanctified by the Holy Spirit." (Rom 15:16)

Sanctification by the Spirit implies two processes and they both involve the setting apart or the separation of a people for God. The first is marking or distinguishing the believer from the multitude of humanity by "sealing" him with the Spirit. This seal is much like 'stamping' with an identifying mark. The mark in this case is the presence of the Holy Spirit. The second process is the setting aside or the making of the believer distinct from the rest of the evil world through the development of righteous practices that lead to the state of holiness.[55] In the end, it is only the holy (morally pure) who will see the Lord.[56]

To understand the process of sanctification through the Spirit the roles of the believer as priest, the ministry of the Spirit, and that of Christ as High Priest, need to be appreciated.

The priests of Jewish tabernacle worship offered sacrifices for the sins that the Israelite recognized and acknowledged that he or she had committed; under the New Covenant the believer is his or her own priest and is to offer the sacrifice of contrition and repentance through confession of the act of sin that he or she had committed.

The duty of a high priest was to offer sacrifices to God; the Lord Jesus Christ, as High Priest, must do the same.[57] The sacrifices that God accepts are those that are "without blemish" (Lev 1:3, 10) "an aroma pleasing to the LORD." (Lev 1:9) The sacrifice that Christ offers to the Father is to be one that is pure, holy and without defect or blameless; it is the sacrifice of the obedient believer who has been cleansed by the sanctifying work of the Spirit who is an acceptable sacrifice. Paul admonished his readers to "offer their bodies as living sacrifices, holy and pleasing to God" claiming that doing so was their "spiritual act of worship." (Rom 12:1)

The Lord has distinguished the cleansing that comes from a person's initial repentance from the need for cleansing from the sin that follows. Before his crucifixion the Lord washed the feet of his disciples. When Peter protested that Christ would never wash his feet the Lord responded,

---

God's commands is what counts." (NIV)
[55] Rom 6:19, 22
[56] Heb 12:14
[57] Heb 8:3

"Unless I wash you, you have no part with me…A person who has had a bath needs only to wash his feet; his whole body is clean." (Jn 13:8…10) The feet are the part of the body that became soiled as a person passed *through the day*. Christ was teaching that although a person had been bathed at the time of initial repentance and had been made clean, the sins of daily life still had to be dealt with. These are washed away through confession and repentance as they are presented to Christ for cleaning.[58] These acts of confession and repentance are a part of justification through Christ. Also, as Christ washed his disciples' feet so are believers to wash the feet of their brothers. "Therefore, confess your sins to each other and pray for each other so that you may be healed. The prayer of a righteous man is powerful and effective." (Jn 13:8…10)

A dirty, sin-stained, defiled heart is *not* an acceptable offering and will not be accepted as one. Those who present otherwise are deceptive in their words. "Do not be deceived: God will not be mocked. A man reaps what he sows. The one who sows to please his sinful nature, from that nature will reap destruction; the one who sows to please the Spirit from the Spirit will reap eternal life." (Gal 6:7-8) "Without holiness no one will see the Lord." (Heb 12:14)

Paul's priestly duty, and that of all who would claim to be priests of the Lord, is to help others become a sacrifice acceptable to God. The prophet Daniel has recorded, "And they that be wise shall shine as the brightness of the firmament; and they that turn many to righteousness as the stars for ever and ever." (Dan 12:3, KJV)

The distinction between "imputed" righteousness and acquired righteousness must be understood since the hope of many is rested in an erroneous interpretation of the Scriptures. Holiness is "imputed"[59] to the

---

[58] Rev 22:14 states that "blessed are those who have washed their robes, that they might have the right to the tree of life and go into the city." (NIV) Those who will be given the "right" to dwell with God must be cleansed of all sin and holy in His sight. (Heb 12:14)

[59] "imputed" means "counted" or "reckoned." For a person to be brought back to God he or she must be righteous since sin separates the Creator from the created. Christ took the sins of the believer upon himself and suffered death for that person's sins leaving the believer sin free. Christ exchanged his righteousness for the believer's sin, thereby "imputing" his righteousness to the believer. This is only done *once* since doing so requires death and Christ will not be put on the tree again as would be required for cleansing the person who continues to sin.

believer *at the time of confession of faith*;[60] however, following that point it is worked out and maintained through the righteous practices of the believer as he or she is enlightened, led, and empowered by the Spirit. Paul taught the Romans that righteousness leads to holiness.[61] Righteous practices lead to a holy state. Righteousness comes through the Spirit and is being "awaited".[62]

Transformation of the heart of each person who desires to be with the Lord throughout eternity is the great need of every human; a person's eternal hope can *not* be rested in the thought that they had been forgiven for their sin or of having been pardoned. Appreciating this point will clarify Biblical teaching regarding eternal salvation. The believer must be transformed into an offering acceptable to God.

The plan of eternal salvation is to make those who are to dwell with God into the likeness of his Son; God will not dwell *eternally* with the evil-hearted. His purpose was to bring himself pleasure not pain. Consequently, "He also predestined us (in accordance with obedience to His plan) to be conformed to the likeness of his Son." (Rom 8:29) The Lord is not finished his creation because finding a suitable (peculiar) people requires the *re-creation* or transformation of the human heart.

> God will not dwell *eternally* with the evil-hearted.

God's work of grace is misrepresented if its presentation fails to address the heart issue following a person's redemption. Paul wrote, "For it is by grace you have been saved, through faith-and this not from yourselves, it is the gift of God-not by works so that no one can boast. *For [Because] we are God's workmanship*[63]..." (Eph 2:8-10) It is God's grace through faith (persuasion) that allows the redeemed to be made a "product" or "offering" acceptable to him...one that is in the likeness of his Son. It is this 'product' which is the object of God's grace and that cannot be accomplished through "works" or the accomplishment of the law through a person's own efforts. The objective of God's grace in the believer is the creation of a particular *'product'* and it is the transformed believer

---

    (See Heb 6:4-8)
[60] Rom 4:24
[61] Rom 6:19, 22
[62] Gal 5:5
[63] "workmanship" ("masterpiece," NLT) is translated from the Greek *poiema* which means "a product, i.e. fabric (literally or figuratively): —thing that is made, workmanship." From Strong's Greek Dictionary #4161

that is the product of the Spirit's handiwork. Through obedience to the Spirit's leading the believer is made acceptable to his creator as he or she is transformed into the image of the Son of God. It is the product that is important…a soul that is an acceptable offering.

"Neither circumcision nor uncircumcision means anything; what counts is a new creation." (Gal 6:15) According to Paul the issue of circumcision means nothing compared to the need for having become a new creation. Circumcision is an issue of the flesh and that which is needed is a newly created heart-one that is pure in its thoughts and practices and one that honors God. Paul taught the Thessalonians that salvation came "through the sanctifying work of the Spirit." (2 Thess 2:13) And, he encouraged Titus with the same teaching. "He saved us through the washing of rebirth and renewal by the Holy Spirit." (Titus 3:5)[64]

The issue of personal righteousness is a constant theme throughout the New Testament. Believers have been frequently reminded of the need to resist the evil nature and to seek righteousness through the Spirit of Holiness.

---

[64] A person should think cautiously about the teachings that are presented, in the Apostle Paul's name, purporting to offer "eternal security" (surety in the Kingdom of God) through a single confession of faith. Paul, himself did not allow such thinking concerning his own state. He said that he wanted to "know the power of his [Christ's] resurrection and the fellowship of sharing in his sufferings, becoming like him in death, and so *somehow* to attain to the resurrection from the dead," and claimed that he had not already obtained all of this. (Phil 3:10-12)

Chapter 2

The Gospel

2.1 The Gospel of Christ

> The gospel rests in the revelation of an eternal hope through the presence of Christ "in" the believer.

The gospel rests in the revelation of an eternal hope through the presence of Christ "in" the believer. Paul wrote: "God has chosen to make known among the Gentiles the glorious riches of this mystery -that *"which had been kept hidden for ages and generations"*-, which is *Christ in you*, the hope of glory." (Col 1:27) The gospel or good news which manifests God's glorious riches, the "mystery" that has been kept hidden, is Christ "in" the believer which is his or her hope of glory.

This great mystery was revealed following the crucifixion of our Savior. "Christ in you" is the Holy Spirit.[65] Paul wrote: "And we, who with unveiled faces all reflect the Lord's glory, are being transformed into his likeness with ever-increasing glory, which comes from the Lord, who is the Spirit." (2 Cor 3:18)

The Spirit is necessary for a person's eternal salvation. Paul wrote to Titus[66] and to the Thessalonians[67] that God chose them to be saved *through the sanctifying work of the Spirit*. It is not recorded *anywhere* in the Word of God that eternal salvation comes by the sacrificial offering of Christ on the cross. Christ's ministry on the cross redeemed the believer from the consequences of his or her "past sins" and from the jurisdiction of the Old Covenant, completing it for him or her. They were then placed under the

---

[65] See also Eph 2:22; Jn 14:17)
[66] Tit 3:5-6
[67] 2 Thess 2:13

New Covenant, the covenant of the Spirit[68], and have been made *"competent"* to satisfy it *through Christ in them.*

> The believer's eternal hope is not based solely on his being pardoned for sin.

The believer's eternal hope is not based solely on being pardoned for sin, but is based on the sanctifying ministry of Christ in them following their confession of faith and following their confession of the lordship of Christ.[69] In another place Paul also made known the necessity of the life of Christ being lived in and through the believer: "Since we have now been justified by his blood, *how much more* shall we be saved from God's wrath through him… For if, when we were God's enemies, we were reconciled to him through the death of his Son, *how much more*, having been reconciled shall we be saved through his life." (Rom 5: 9-10)

Christ must be allowed to live his life through the believer; his presence in a person is not enough to achieve that person's hope. The Spirit may be quenched, denied, or thwarted. "And if the Spirit of him who raised Jesus from the dead *is living* in you, he who raised Christ from the dead will give life to your mortal bodies through his Spirit, *who lives* in you." (Rom 8:11)

John wrote: "This is how we know we are in him: Whoever claims to live in Christ must walk as Jesus did." (1 Jn 2:6) This requirement is often dismissed out of hand. After all, who can walk as Jesus did? However, this *is* part of the gospel and John has said that the believer *"must"* do this if he or she is to be found living in Christ. The writer of Hebrews has stated that eternal salvation comes through obedience.[70] (This is the *only* passage in the entire Word of God that contains the phrase *"eternal salvation."*) Most challenging of all is John's proclamation: "No one who lives in him keeps on sinning. No one who continues to sin has either seen him or known (understood) him." (1 Jn 3:6) How

> The answer is that *natural person cannot live as Christ did, but the Lord living in him or her can.*

is this writing to be appreciated? The answer is that *natural people cannot live as Christ did, but the Lord living in him or her can.* He accomplished the sinless life in the body that the Father had prepared for him in the womb of Mary, and he can do it in the body of the believer. "How much more shall the blood of

---

[68] 2 Cor 3:6
[69] Rom 10:9-10
[70] Heb 5:9

Christ, *who through the eternal Spirit offered himself without spot to God*, purge your conscience-moral consciousness-from dead works to serve the living God? (Heb 9:14) That is why Paul wrote that *"Christ in you"* was your hope of glory. This is the "good news." The victory has *not* been won for the believer by Christ; that must yet happen. The Spirit must purge the body from interest in, or moral consciousness concerning, acts that would bring about the believer's death. The victory that Christ has won was for himself and gained him the keys to hell and death-gave him authority over or put him in control over decisions concerning hell and death.

> Christ came to fulfill the law through living His life personally and specifically in the body of each believer.

To further develop these truths, we are reminded that Christ came to fulfill the law; not to abolish it. He came to fulfill it through living his life personally and specifically in the body of each believer, if they permit it-God does not over-rule the will of a person. Paul wrote: "For what the law was powerless to do in that it was weakened by the sinful nature, God did by sending his own Son in the likeness of sinful man, *in order that the righteous requirements of the law might be fully met in us who do not live according to the sinful nature but according to the Spirit.*" (Rom 8:4)

Paul also taught that it was those who are led by the Spirit who are not under the law (Gal 5:18), and those who are led by the Spirit who are sons of God. (Rom 8:14) The Spirit's leading comes through conviction of a person's conscience. The Spirit enlightens, leads and empowers for righteousness *leading to holiness* and eternal life.[71]

The Lord has revealed the need for a person to die to self and to the interests of the flesh- the believer's baptism testifies to his or her acknowledgement of this- and to live in obedience to the Spirit. Although there is much to be said concerning the need for obedience and transformation, and the need to "overcome" (Rev 21:7), a singular passage might assert these truths: "Do not be deceived: God cannot be mocked. A man reaps what he sows. The person who sows to please the sinful nature, from that nature will reap destruction; the person who sows to please the Spirit from the Spirit will reap eternal life." (Gal 6:7-8)

The Lord has given the believer all that he or she needs for life and godliness[72] but they must appropriate that provision; they are to live as

---

[71] Rom 6:19, 22
[72] 2 Pet 1:3

Christ lived, and as Christ will live through them if obeyed. The believer is told "to work out [his or her own] salvation with fear and trembling" (Phil 2:12, KJV) and to make "every effort" to enter through the narrow door because many will try to enter and will not be able to. (Lk 13:24)

Judgment awaits the disobedient and rebellious, starting with the household of God.[73] Those who are slaves to sin will have "*no permanent place*" in the family. (Jn 8:35) "He will punish those who do not know (understand or appreciate) God and do not obey the gospel of our Lord Jesus. They will be punished with everlasting destruction and shut out from the presence of the Lord and from the majesty of his power." (2 Thess 1:8)

The judgment that awaits all humankind is also part of the gospel. Paul wrote to the Romans, "All who sin apart from the law -which would include those under the New Covenant-, and all who sin under the law will be judged by the law. For it is not those who hear the law who are righteous in God's sight, but it is those who obey the law who will be declared righteous. This will take place on the day when God will judge men's secrets through Jesus Christ, as my gospel declares." (Rom 2:12-13…16) Those under the New Covenant cannot expect that they will be exempt from judgment. All will be judged according to the provision made for them, starting with the family of God. It is because of this judgment that Paul taught the need for the believer to work out his own salvation with fear and trembling. It is also because of this judgment that he has declared that the glorious riches of God's mystery are availed through *Christ in you, the hope of glory.*

> Those under the New Covenant cannot expect that they will be exempt from judgment.

Does this seem to be an unlikely gospel? Consider it another way. The believer has available all the attributes that Jesus had as he walked this earth except for his soul. Just as Jesus was body, soul, and spirit, so are people. This reality must be appreciated by those who are prepared to excuse themselves from "*walking as Jesus did.*" (1 Jn 3:6)

All people are composed of the trinity of body, soul, and spirit. The body of Christ was the same as that of all men; it was formed in the womb of Mary. "Since children have flesh and blood, he too shared in their humanity…he had to be made like his brothers in every way in order that he might become a merciful and faithful high priest in service to God."

---

[73] 1 Pet 4:17

(Heb 2:14...17) Further, it is written "We have a high priest who has been tempted in every way, just as we are-yet without sin." (Heb 4:15) And to solidify the nature of his humanity the writer has also presented: "During the days of Jesus' life on earth,[74] he offered up prayers and petitions with loud cries and tears to the one who could save him from death, and he was heard because of his reverent submission. Although he was a son, he learned obedience from what he suffered and once made perfect became the source of eternal salvation *for all who obey him.*" (Heb 5:7-9)

> The body prepared for Christ by the Father in the womb of Mary is of the same nature as the one we possess.

The body prepared for Christ by the Father in the womb of Mary is of the same nature as the one we possess. It is the body that brings death[75] and its appeasement subjects a person to temptations and suffering. "Because he himself suffered when he was tempted, he is able to help those who are being tempted." (Heb 2:18) It must be accepted that the "body" of Christ is of the same nature as our own.

But Jesus has a soul and a spirit also. Jesus was given the spirit that humankind had enjoyed at creation; it was in the likeness of God[76] holy in purpose, just as were the spirits of Adam and Eve. However, the spirits that people possess today are far from the nature of the one first given. Adam and Eve had no knowledge of evil but allowed the lies of Satan to infect them with his rebellious spirit. They took on evil spirits desiring to please the flesh rather than God. Jesus, however, maintained the spirit given him and lived a sinless life.[77] "How much more then will the blood of Christ, *who through the Holy Spirit offered himself unblemished to God*, cleanse our consciences -moral consciousness- from acts that lead to death, so that we may serve the living God." (Heb 9:14)

At the baptism of Jesus in the Jordan the *Holy Spirit* descended upon him.[78] The believer is also given the Holy Spirit.[79] Therefore, not only did Christ have a body that suffered the same interests as do those of the rest

---

[74] This passage does not refer only to petition in the Garden of Gethsemane following which he suffered a cruel death; it refers to submission to the temptations that would have brought about his eternal death.
[75] Rom 7:24
[76] Gen 1:27
[77] Heb 4:15
[78] Mt 3:16
[79] Rom 5:5, Jn 7:39

of humankind, the believer, once reborn, has the same Spirit that brought victory to Christ. The believer possesses a body like that of Christ and the Holy Spirit…the very one that enabled Christ to overcome the flesh, the world and the evil one. The believer has been reminded to be *filled* with the Holy Spirit. This is a matter of a person's will…his or her choices; as he or she denies their evil nature, their natural spirit will weaken and become ineffective. A person's eternal hope is availed when he or she is gifted with the Holy Spirit. "But by faith we eagerly await through the Spirit the righteousness for which we hope." (Gal 5:5)

It is the soul of a person that differs from that of Christ and it is their soul that Christ came to transform. A person's soul distinguishes him or her from all others and houses his or her *will*. The soul of a person offers the testimony of a person's faith to God and the world. Their will reacts to their heart interests and determines their choices[80] and practices. The will of Christ was to honor and obey his Father.[81] The person who will be given entrance to God's Eternal Kingdom must also honor and obey the Father.[82] "Thou shalt love the Lord thy God with all thy heart, and with all thy soul, and with all thy mind." (Mt 22:37, KJV)

> It is the soul of a person that differs from that of Christ and it is their soul that Christ came to transform.

In Genesis it is recorded: "The Lord saw how great man's wickedness on the earth had become, and that every inclination of the thoughts of his heart was only evil all the time. The Lord was grieved that he had made man on the earth, and his heart was filled with pain." (Gen 6:5-6) It is not a pardon that is required for eternal salvation, although that is essential, but a transformed heart. A pardon does not transform but relieves the sinner of the consequences of his or her rebellion. Those who cause God pain will not be found in his presence. Paul wrote: "For it is God-the Spirit- who works in you to will and to act according to his good purpose." (Phil 2:13) The Lord must subdue and

> Those who cause God pain will not be found in His presence.

---

[80] The interests of the heart reveal a person's beliefs. Those who believe in Christ will reflect his interests and their will will conform to his. *Belief* in Christ is living as he would.
[81] Jn 5:30
[82] Mt 7:21

convert or transform the soul of people as he is allowed in order to sanctify the evil heart and conform it to the likeness of the Son.[83]

Paul wrote, "You were taught with regard to your former way of life, to put off your old self, which is corrupted by its deceitful desires, to be made new in the attitude of your minds, and to put on the new self, created to be like God in true righteousness and holiness." (Eph 4:22)

The command to live as Christ lived in this world should not be considered an impossibility. The believer has all that Christ had in the body that the Father had prepared for him in the womb of Mary and he is expected to reveal Christ to the world as the Lord lives in his body. He has the same Spirit that can enlighten, lead, and empower for the development and display the nature of the soul of Christ. However, obedience is required- not to the law but to Christ, the Holy Spirit. He or she is truly to become a son of God and a brother of Christ.

Those who excuse the practice of sin will one day have to justify it to the Lord who provided them with all that is needed for life and godliness, who had lived with the same realities of body, soul, and Spirit, and who had made provision of himself to live in the person who had professed him as Lord.

> This is the gospel: *Christ offered himself a sacrifice on the cross, to redeem the believer from his past sins and from the Old Covenant so that he or she might live righteously through the repentant believer and fit that person for the Kingdom of God....*" Christ in you, the hope of glory."

2.2 A Synopsis of Eternal Salvation

For a person to obtain "eternal" salvation the believer must satisfy the requirements of both the Old and the New Covenants. The Old is a covenant of the Law and the New is a covenant of the Spirit.[84] A *covenant* is a compact or an agreement that holds surety of promise between two parties.

The Old Covenant was based on the law and the revelations of the prophets. The fulfilment of God's promises to the Israelites was based upon their ability to satisfy them. They were required "to follow the Lord and keep his commands, regulations and decrees with all their hearts and with all their

---

[83] Rom 8:29
[84] 2 Cor 3:6

souls." (2 Kings 23:3) According to Paul, the covenant "of the letter -the law- kills; but the Spirit gives life." (2 Cor 3:6) It is impossible for any person to keep the Old Covenant, and yet its righteous requirements had to be, and still must be, fulfilled. Through his crucifixion, the Lord brought the Old Covenant to an end for those who are believing in him and has replaced it with the New.

The New Covenant is a covenant of the Spirit and since it is a covenant its terms must also be honored. Its fulfillment also requires the believer's obedience. Obedience is not to the law and the Prophets however, it is to the Spirit. God's righteous requirements as embodied in the Old Covenant will be accomplished by those who live according to the Spirit's leading, "*Christ is you.*" Just as Christ lived a sinless life in the body that the Father had prepared for him in the womb of Mary, he is prepared to live that life in the body of the believer.

The person who through contrition of heart accepts that he or she has offended their sovereign God and confesses their sin and who promises that Christ is and will be their lord will be forgiven their past sins, will be privileged with right to the New Covenant, and will be given the Holy Spirit to enlighten, lead and empower in its completion. This covenant is not written on stone but in the heart; it is accomplished as Christ can live His life in the believer. The *Lord* will complete its terms, if obeyed.

It is obedience to the Spirit that will bring about a person's hope for eternity. The believer must live in the light and confess and seek forgiveness for sin when it occurs. He or she must train themselves through the knowledge of God's Word and the leading of the Spirit to know good from evil, and they must be prepared to resist ungodly temptations as presented by the evil one, the flesh, and the permissions of the world.

The crucifixion of Christ made the believer "perfect" but this perfection only lasts as long as he or she is obedient and walks in the light of the Lord- the Spirit. His or her hope for finding eternal enjoyment in the Lord's presence can be lost through rebellion and disobedience. It is in the process of a person's walk following their redemption that the transformation of their heart and mind is accomplished and through which the believer is made holy in practice; that is, the Spirit will lead the redeemed person in a walk of practical righteousness leading to holiness, and holiness is needed for a person's eternal salvation.

The purpose of a plan for rescuing a people to form "a royal priesthood, a holy nation" is to cull from all of humankind a people who are willing to recognize the Lord's sovereignty, and who through submission to the

Spirit are transformed in heart and mind into the likeness of God's Son... loving, holy, and obedient.

A person's eternal salvation requires that he or she love God with all their heart, soul, mind, and strength. Disobedience and rebellion will not be acceptable. Peter has written that "His divine power (the Holy Spirit) has given us everything we need for life and godliness." (2 Pet 1:3) In addition to a walk of righteousness provision has been made for forgiveness and cleansing when a repentant believer fails.

Those who are considered worthy will enjoy an eternal presence with their Lord in His Royal City, the New Jerusalem. Those who aren't will suffer God's wrath through judgment.

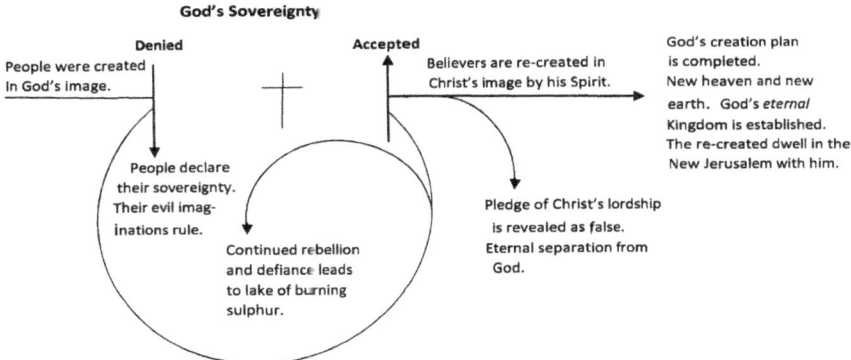

2.3 Putting "Salvation," "Saved," and "Eternal Salvation" into Perspective

The Word of God makes a distinction between "salvation" or "saved" and "eternal salvation."

To be "saved" means that a person has been rescued from some imminent danger. That is, he or she might be saved from drowning by being rescued from the water, or they might be saved from burning by being pulled from a fire.

Like any language, the Greek in which the New Testament was first written, is a means used to convey ideas. The Greek word for "saved" is *'sozo'* which means "to deliver or protect."[85] Its use was not limited to

---

[85] From Strong's Greek Dictionary #4982

Biblical writing but was the common vernacular of the Greeks to convey the ideas of "deliverance" or "protection." Over time many in Biblical study have taken "sozo" to apply to "eternal" salvation only, whereas it has other more limited applications even in the Word of God.[86] To understand the meaning intended by the writer, it is important to gain knowledge of the nature of the danger from which a person is being delivered or protected.

"Eternal salvation" applies specifically to deliverance into God's eternal kingdom. The writer of Hebrews has stated that "eternal" salvation comes through obedience.[87]

When "salvation", "saved" and, "eternal salvation" become confused so do teachings about eternal salvation. There are several issues that must be overcome-from which a person must be saved or delivered-in order that their *eternal* salvation might be accomplished. Paul taught that the end of those who did not live according to the pattern that he had taught would be "destruction."[88] He also presented that those who do not know, or understand, God and those who *do not obey the Lord* are headed for "destruction from the presence of the Lord." (2 Thess 1:9) Paul's epistle to Timothy records that "people who want to get rich fall into temptation and a trap and into many foolish and harmful desires that plunge men into ruin and destruction." (1 Tim 6:9) He told the Galatians that those "who sow to please their sinful nature, from that nature will reap destruction." (Gal 6:8) *False prophets and false teachers who bring in destructive heresies*[89] and those who *distort scriptures* bring destruction on themselves.[90] These teachings reveal that those who fall into temptations, those who do not know the Lord, false teachers and prophets, and those who walk apart from the Spirit's leading are destined to destruction. Those who will dwell with the Lord must be delivered or protected from any such practices.

To be "eternally saved" a person must have overcome the temptations and practices that God condemns. The Lord revealed that the people who

---

[86] Paul used the word *sozo* when he told his Roman guard to throw everything overboard in order to be saved (avoid drowning). Luke also used *sozo* when he spoke of the man who was healed of the many demons that had possessed him and had been cast into the herd of pigs.

[87] Heb 5:9

[88] Phil 3:19, KJV; Paul's testimony to King Agrippa was that people, should "repent and prove their repentance by their deeds." (Acts 26:20, NIV)

[89] 2 Pet 2:1

[90] 2 Pet 3:16

Eternal Salvation

"overcome" (Rev 21:7) will be the ones who will inherit a presence in the New Jerusalem.

Paul has used "saved" apart from "eternal salvation" in several of his writings. "If you confess with your mouth, 'Jesus is Lord,' and believe in your heart that God raised him from the dead, you will be saved. For it is with your heart that you believe and are justified, and it is with your mouth that you confess and are saved." (Rom 10:9-10) That is, when you acknowledge that God exists and that He has the power and authority to, and that He did, raise Jesus from the dead, and when you confess that Jesus is the Lord of creation, and your lord, you will be saved. This salvation or deliverance provides escape from the Old Covenant and deliverance from sins committed while under the Old Covenant. *"For this reason, Christ is the mediator of a new covenant, that those who are called may receive the promised eternal inheritance*-now that he has died as a ransom to set them free from the sins committed under the first covenant." (Hebrews 9:15) The reader must understand that his or her confession of faith frees them from their past sins *only*. It does not mean to indicate freedom from the consequences of sin that he or she will commit, nor does it ensure 'eternal' salvation. The sacrificial offering of Christ is the only means of gaining forgiveness for sin, but following confession of faith each *known* sin is to be confessed for a person to be forgiven and purified.[91] Caution must be taken not to read more into Paul's teaching than he had intended.

> Christ died as a ransom to set believers free from the sins committed under the *first* covenant.

Eternal salvation rests upon a person's being led by the Holy Spirit following his or her gifting. "But if you are led by the Spirit you are not under the law." (Gal 5:18) Salvation from the law and from *past sins* or sins committed under the first covenant sets the grounding so that a person *may*, not *will*, find eternal salvation which is dependent upon the rule of Jesus being practiced in a person's life. It also allows the Spirit to be the

---

[91] Because "being led" implies a requirement of the believer, some accept it as being salvation by "works." Salvation by works is through a person's ability to meet the righteous requirements of the law through his own efforts. A person's confession is for "known" sin since he cannot confess what he doesn't know. Unknown sin is mediated by Christ as High Priest. Confession makes a person conscious of his or her sin and this should help them seek and gain victory over that sin. It is part of the process of a person's transformation. Confession also shows respect for, and humility before, the holy God.

determiner of that which is sinful and that which is not. Eternal salvation is made available through satisfying the New Covenant or the Covenant of the Spirit.[92]

God is building an eternal kingdom of his liking. He is loving and pure in his nature and character and desires to share a relationship with a people that he can enjoy. According to God's Word those who are to dwell with him are to be in the likeness of his Son;[93] they are to be holy.[94] Whatever interpretation a person puts on the Word of God regarding "eternal" salvation it must result in the deliverance of a people who will satisfy God's purpose in creation…the presence of a royal priesthood, a holy nation, a peculiar people."[95]

Although many teach that God's pardon for sin is all that is required, this is not so. A pardoned murder or thief is still a murderer or thief in his or her heart. Having been pardoned only means that a person's lawless act has been forgiven and holds no consequence. The necessary state for dwelling with the Lord and in his kingdom is a *heart* that is loving and holy. "Without holiness no one will see the Lord." (Heb 12:14) The salvation plan that God has put in place is to accomplish a state of holiness in heart, mind and practice. "The Son of Man will send out his angels, and they will weed out of his kingdom everything that *causes* sin and all who *do* evil." (Mt 13:41)

> "The Son of Man will send out his angels, and they will weed out of his kingdom everything that causes sin and all who do evil."

As well, there is more involved with "eternal" salvation than a confession of faith. Confession is a proclamation of a person's convictions, however because a person says something does not mean that he or she will practice what they say. Christ reprimanded, "Why do you call me 'Lord, Lord,' and not do what I say?" (Lk 6:46) Eternal salvation requires that the believer maintain his faith "to the end."[96] Paul taught, "By this gospel you are saved,[97] if you hold firmly to the word I preached to you. Otherwise you

---

[92] 2 Cor 3:6, NIV
[93] Rom 8:29
[94] 1 Pet 1:16
[95] 1 Pet 2:9, KJV
[96] Mt 10:22, 24:13; Mk 13:13; Heb 3:14; Rev 2:26
[97] In this case "saved" would refer to 'eternal salvation' because the condition that Paul applies is the necessity that a person remains faithful to the end. To remain "faithful" requires the practice of faith or obedience to the end.

have believed in vain." (1 Cor 5:2) Christ prophesied that, "At that time (the end of the age) many will turn away from the faith…but he who stands firm to the end will be saved." (Mt 24:10…13) Although some speak of eternal security or the sureness that the confessor has gained "eternal" salvation, the Word of God does not present such; the confessor's name may yet be blotted from the Book through the sins of disobedience and rebellion.

Having a person's name recorded in God's Book of Life is a requirement for *eternal salvation*.[98] "The Lord said to Moses, 'Whoever has sinned against me I will blot out of my book…Whoever has sinned against me I will punish them for their sin.'" (Ex 32:33-34) This is a truth that needs to be understood. When a person confesses that Jesus is his lord, they need to live accordingly.[99] They need to allow the Holy Spirit which is the Spirit of Christ, to lead them. Concerning the righteous, Christ revealed to the church of Sardis that, "He who overcomes-by not soiling his clothes- will be dressed in white. I will never blot his name from the book of life but will acknowledge his name before my Father and his angels." (Rev 3:5) The Lord himself said, "I tell you the truth, everyone who sins is a slave to sin. Now a slave has *no permanent* place in the family." (Jn 8:34)[100]

The Word of God has presented that eternal salvation comes through "obedience" and, obedience is the *practice* of godly faith. It cannot be said that a person has faith if he or she confesses Christ and does not follow him and his teachings. Paul summed up his preaching ministry to King Agrippa, "I preached that they should repent and turn to God and prove their repentance by their deeds."[101]

The way righteousness is achieved becomes extremely important to a person's *eternal* salvation and the book of Hebrews reveals that it comes through *obedience*. "Christ became the source of eternal salvation for all who obey him." (Heb 5:9) And Paul told the Galatians, "But by faith we eagerly await through the Spirit the

> Eternal salvation is accomplished *following* the gifting of the Spirit and it comes through the sanctifying work of the Spirit.

---

[98] Rev 20:15
[99] It may be that a person's name is written in the book of life at his or her confession of faith. However, it may also mean that a person's name is written in the book of life at his birth and "blotted out" according to the Lord's determination.
[100] "Permanence" in the family is the lot of a son, not a slave, and a son must be obedient or led by the Spirit. (Rom 8:14)
[101] Acts 26:20, NIV

righteousness for which we hope." (Gal 5:5) Accordingly, eternal salvation is accomplished *following* the gifting of the Spirit, it comes through the sanctifying work of the Spirit,[102] and it is being *awaited.*

There are a multitude of traps that can bring a person to destruction and from which he or she must be saved. *Eternal salvation,* however, refers to deliverance into God's Eternal Kingdom and it is for all time. Since it comes through obedience, the redeemed person must learn to hear the voice of the Spirit. The Lord said, "My sheep listen to my voice; I know them, and they follow me. I give them eternal life and they shall never perish." (Jn 10:27) Once the leading of the Spirit has been made clear those who desire to be with the Lord for eternity must obediently follow.

People should not accept that their life on earth is the only life they have. To seek much "enjoyment" from it while disregarding God will bring destruction. The Lord admonished, "For whoever wants to save his life will lose it, but whoever loses his life for me will save it." (Lk 9:24) [103]

The eternal salvation of a people should not be considered apart from God's purpose for creation. In a sense, the eternal state of all things is part of the creation story. God created with a specific purpose in mind and is going through a process so that his purpose might be fulfilled. The end state of their[104] (Father, Son, Holy Spirit) creation will not have reached its realization until the Kingdom of God has been established. When this Kingdom has been set up, righteousness has been established, and the Lord is reigning and his holy ones with him, God's creation plan will have been completed. At that time God will dwell in his kingdom with those privileged to be with him. He will be their God and will wipe every tear from their eyes. There will be no more mourning or crying or pain; and, death will have ceased.[105]

When considering a person's eternal salvation, it needs to be understood that God is creator, that he has a purpose in mind and that his motivation is for the accomplishment of his "good pleasure." *Consequently, when pondering the means of the eternal salvation of a people, it should always be considered from God's point of view.* Humankind was formed by God in order that *his* purpose might be accomplished.

---

[102] 2 Thess 2:13; Titus 3:5; Rom 5:12
[103] See also Mt 10:39, 16:25; Mk 8:35
[104] Gen 1:26
[105] Rev 2:13-14, NIV

2.4 The Sacrifice of Christ on the Cross

The sacrifice of Christ on the cross was to complete the requirements of the law for the believer so that he or she might be established in a new covenant, and so that the justice of God's government might be maintained. Although only the House of Israel enjoyed a covenant relationship with God, the law given them contained God's righteous requirements for all people. That is, it is only those who satisfy the righteous requirements of his law who will be suitable to dwell with him eternally; those who have defied his law, and consequently his government, already carry the death sentence.[106]

The writer of Hebrews has revealed the effect of our Lord's sacrificial offering. "Christ is the mediator of a new covenant, that those who are called may[107] receive the promised eternal inheritance-now that he has died as a ransom to set them free from the sins committed under the first covenant." (Heb 9:15)

This passage must be made clear. Christ offered himself as a sacrifice for a person's past *sins*…those committed while under the rule of the first covenant; however, the apostle John has recorded that "if we confess our sins, he is faithful and just to forgive us our sins and to purify us from all unrighteousness," (1 Jn 1:9) and that "if we walk in the light, as he is in the light, we have fellowship with one another, and the blood of Jesus, his Son, purifies us from all sin." (1 Jn 1:7) Both of these statements present a *condition* since they begin with "if." The Word teaches that a person is set free from the consequences of *all* sin committed before their confession of faith *and* sin committed following that occasion, "if" he or she confesses known sin[108] while endeavouring to *walk in the light* or in obedience to him. *The blood offering of Christ is the only means of being set free from the consequences of a person's sins.*

If freedom from the consequences of sin had been the only thing that had been accomplished, humankind's morally corrupt nature would have remained even though they had been cleansed and pardoned for their past sins. It is the transformation of a person's evil nature that results in his or

---

[106] Ezek 18:4; Rom 5:12, 6:23
[107] "may" should not be taken as 'will.' The eternal inheritance is *available* since they are no longer under the first (Old) covenant.
[108] Both known and unknown sin must be mediated. Christ mediates known sin through repentance and confession and unknown sin through his ministry as high priest.

her eternal salvation. The redemption that Christ provided was from "the curse of the law ...so that we might receive the promise of the Spirit." (Gal 3:13, 14) The pardon and cleansing of past sins allows the believer to have fellowship restored with the Father so that he might give the believer the Holy Spirit or the Spirit of Christ. It is the Spirit who saves;[109] the Spirit accomplishes the righteousness for which we hope.[110]

Without the sinless offering of Christ sin would prevail in the believer's life since fellowship with the Father would not have been restored and the Spirit would not have been given. This freedom from sin and from the rule of the law and *restoration to fellowship* with God is a person's *redemption* from the law.

Being redeemed does not give anyone eternal life; it restores him or her to a state *where they can obtain eternal life* since it cleanses them, places them under the jurisdiction of the New Covenant, and allows them to be gifted with the Holy Spirit. The New Covenant is a covenant of the Spirit and he must be obeyed[111] rather than the law having to be obeyed using a person's own resources. The Holy Spirit enlightens, leads, and empowers for righteousness and the requirements of the law.

No one could find a place in God's eternal Kingdom without the horrible and gracious sacrifice of Christ on their behalf; however, his ministry does not stop there. He indwells the believer in the form of the Holy Spirit and if allowed to live out his life in this one's flesh allows for a righteous life resulting in holiness and an eternal hope.

In addition to these accomplishments for humankind, the Lord also gained authority for himself through his death. The Lord has revealed that he now *holds the keys of death and Hades*. "I am the Living One; I was dead, and behold I am alive for ever and ever. And I hold the keys of death and Hades." (Rev 1:18) Like anyone who is in possession of 'keys' they have to power to use them. Christ now has authority to commit those whom he chooses to death and Hades. His judgment will determine the final state of all people.

The resurrection of Christ provides the means that people have of a *living hope*. "Praise be to God the Father of our Lord Jesus Christ! In his great mercy he has given us new birth into a living hope through the resurrection of Jesus Christ from the dead." (1 Pet 1:3) The Lord's

---

[109] 2 Thess 2:13; Titus 3:5-6; Gal 6:8; Rom 8:10, 13; Jn 6:63; 2 Cor 3:6
[110] Gal 5:5; Rom 8:4
[111] Heb 5:9

resurrection has given us a "new birth" and into a "living hope." The new birth is just that…a birth, the beginning of a new life and a new opportunity, and this provision is accompanied with a "living hope" that comes through the resurrection of the Lord.

Before the death of Christ, a person's hope of glory rested in obedience to the law and the Prophets. The law had no life but was etched in stone. Paul said that it kills.[112] The hope that was revealed through the law was no hope at all because "it was weakened through the sinful nature" (Rom 8:3); no person could satisfy it. The "living hope" is the presence of Christ living "in" the believer. As Holy Spirit he enlightens, leads, and empowers for victory over the flesh, the Evil One, and the world. Paul wrote to the Colossians that it was *Christ in them that was their hope of glory.*[113] The righteous requirements of the law must be met for those who will be privileged to dwell with the Lord in his heavenly kingdom and they are met through the ministry of the Spirit as the believer allows the Lord to live through him or her.[114]

The death of Christ on the cross cleansed the believer of his past sins, completed the Old Covenant's jurisdiction over those who have faith in him and who live under his lordship, allowed them right to the New Covenant, and provided them with the resurrected life of Christ in them as Spirit.

OLD COVENANT	NEW COVENANT
The Old Covenant was a covenant based on satisfying the righteous requirements of God through obedience to the Law as given to Moses and the proclamations of the prophets.	The New Covenant is a covenant of the Spirit and is based on meeting the righteous requirements of God through obedience to Christ, who is the Spirit.
The Old Covenant could not be kept because humankind had been weakened by the sinful nature.	"He condemned sin in sinful man, in order that the righteous requirements of the law might be fully met in us, who do not live according to the sinful nature but according to the Spirit." (Rom 8:3-4) Through his divine nature he has given us everything we need for life and godliness. (2 Pet 1:3)

Christ offered himself a sacrifice to complete the Old Covenant and to bring it to an end. To accomplish this he had to take the death of all men in order to relieve them of the death penalty for sin so that some might be saved. He purchased them with his blood-the cost of their redemption- making them his possession. All men are now subject to the New Covenant and those seeking his kingdom must obey him, rather than the law. He is their master and dwells in them as the Holy Spirit. Christ is their lord and is to be their lord.

---

[112] 2 Cor 3:6
[113] Col 1:27
[114] Rom 8:4

2.5 The New Covenant

"The Lord said, 'This is the covenant I will make with the house of Israel after that time,' declares the Lord. 'I will put my laws in their minds and write them on their hearts. I will be their God, and they will be my people.'"

"By calling this covenant 'new,' he has made the first obsolete; and what is obsolete and aging will soon disappear." (Heb 8:10...13)

To understand the means of eternal salvation offered by God, people must first grasp the concept of the "new covenant." The new covenant is not engraved on stone but is in the flesh...the mind and heart. It is not legally based on satisfying the laws as given on stone but is based on a *living relationship* with Christ. It is a relationship that is based on *the life of Christ in the believer*, and the Lord's living through the believer, as allowed by the believer, in order that he might accomplish the requirements of God through that person.

The intimacy of the New Covenant is also revealed as the believer being "in Christ" and Christ being "in the believer." Before his crucifixion the Lord comforted his disciples by stating: "On that day-when the Comforter is given- you will realize that I am in my Father, and that you are in me, and I am in you." (Jn 14:20) The believer's eternal confidence is rested in his or her being "in Christ" and Christ's being in him or her. The Old Covenant was static; it was written on stone. The new covenant is alive; it is the *life* of Christ in a person.

There will be *no* eternal salvation for anyone who prevents the exercise of the Holy One through him or her. He is life and without him there is no hope.

It should not be accepted that a single act of faith (a confession of faith) will accomplish anyone's needs. The Lord has presented a requirement that a person must stand firm "to the end" if he or she wants to be saved. "All men will hate you because of me, but he who stands firm to the end will be saved." (Mt 10:22) The believer has been called to suffer in course of the pursuit for righteousness. "Now if we are children (of God), then we are heirs-heirs of God, *if indeed we share in his sufferings* in order that we may share in his glory." (Rom 8:17) Christ suffered in His denial of the flesh in order that He might not sin.[115] Just as he was victorious in his own body, he will give victory to the believer *as he lives in that person's body* and

---

[115] Heb 2:18

as that person contends for victory through him. Peter taught that, "His divine power has given us everything we need for life and godliness." (2 Pet 1:3) His divine power is the Holy Spirit. Peter did *not* teach that Christ gave life and godliness but that he gave "everything we need *for* life and godliness." They must be appropriated.

There is a life to be lived and a death to be lived and an indifferent and passive relationship with the Lord or weak faith, will not be enough.[116] The believer needs to wholeheartedly and intentionally cling to the Lord. His interest cannot be divided. Paul reminded the Philippians to "work out their own salvation with fear and trembling." (Phil 2:12) The "righteous requirements of the law" are only[117] and fully met in those "who do not live according to the sinful nature but according to the Spirit." (Rom 8:4)

The law cannot be kept without Christ's indwelling presence. For a person to accomplish it on his own he or she would have to overcome the interests and demands of the flesh and they would have to recognize their sin. It was because of the inadequacies of humans that God instituted a "new" covenant, one that they could keep. "He has made us competent as ministers of a new covenant-not of the letter but of the Spirit, for the letter kills, but the Spirit gives life." (2 Cor 3:6) *The sacrifice of Christ on the cross does not give life; it is the gifting of the Spirit following Christ's sacrifice, the completion of the Old Covenant, and Christ's life lived through the believer, that give life.* The fullness of Christ's love and ministry for his Father and for believers must be appreciated.

> The New Covenant is a covenant of the Spirit.

The New Covenant is based on the presence of Christ within the believer[118] with the purpose of purifying him or her, making them an offering acceptable to God.[119] Christ is the one who knows the law and who can lead the believer and empower him or her to obey its righteous requirements. When the writer of Hebrews presented that God would put his laws in a person's mind and write them on his or her heart, he was referencing the presence of the author of righteousness and of salvation

---

[116] It is in this light that the Lord's teaching that if a person's eye causes an offence, he should pluck it out makes sense. (Mt 5:29, 18:9; Mk 9:47) The seriousness of walking righteously before God is revealed in the presentation of this teaching.

[117] Gal 5:18: "But if you are led by the Spirit you are not under the law." (NIV)

[118] Col 1:27: "Christ in you, the hope of glory." (KJV)

[119] Rom 15:16

within a person. It is because Christ indwells the believer that he or she can gain victory over temptations and become "competent" in their walk of righteousness.

Paul disclosed his own battle with the flesh and presented his own "wretched" state. Consequently, he asked, "Who will rescue me from this body of death (body that brings death)?" He concluded with: "Thanks be to God-through Jesus Christ our Lord!" (Rom 7:24)

Christ is the believer's "mediator" between the Father and humankind allowing the believer to meet the righteous requirements of the law. Consequently, he is also the mediator between God and people in the meeting of God's requirements for eternal salvation. A mediator is one who intervenes in order to bring acceptable agreement between two parties. It is the life of Christ in the believer and his ministry as high priest through which he mediates the believer's requirements for righteousness and eternal salvation. It should not be accepted that mediation only requires the application of the blood of Christ for cleansing from sin. "For this reason (to cleanse a person's moral consciousness) Christ is the mediator of a new covenant, that those who are called may receive the promised eternal inheritance-now that he has died as a ransom to set them free from the sins committed under the first covenant." (Hebrews 9:15)

Considering common teaching this verse needs to be clearly understood. Christ offered himself to free the believer from the sins that he or she had committed while subject to the righteous requirements of the Old Covenant. He did this so that the believer would be able, "may," receive the promised eternal inheritance. The writer does not state that he or she "would" receive that inheritance, but that they "may" receive it. Whether or not they do will depend upon how they treat the provision made for them. "His divine power has given us everything we need for life and godliness." (2 Pet 1:3) "He became the source of eternal salvation for all who obey him." (Heb 5:9)

The New Covenant is a covenant made by God through which his provision of the ministry of Christ might accomplish that which humankind could not do. Its purpose is to transform a person into a sacrifice acceptable to God by re-creating him or her in the likeness of his Son…holy in heart and mind.

Chapter 3
Necessary Understandings

3.1 Being "in" Christ

Understanding the teachings of being "in Christ" and Christ being in the believer is vital to understanding the gospel message. It is what distinguishes the Old Covenant from the New Covenant. The former was based on a person's completion of the righteous requirements of the law using his own resources. The latter is based upon *Christ's completion of the law for the believer as He dwells in the believer and the believer dwells "in him."* It brings clarity to the teaching that salvation is by grace through faith as opposed to through "works." In the end a person's eternal state rests on his or her dwelling "in" Christ.

In regard to a person's need for Christ Paul wrote: "Since, then, you have been raised with Christ, set your hearts on things above where Christ is seated on the right hand of God. Set your minds on things above, not on earthly things. For you died, and your life is now hidden with Christ in God." (Col 3:1-3) When you believed and declared Christ's lordship you were "raised with Christ." This should be comforting because the person who is now "in Christ" has the full advantage of the hope that being in Christ provides. He or she has the protection of Christ, the power of Christ, and the state of Christ. These blessings, however, are not under a person's own authority; they are under Christ's.

Being in Christ is a spiritual position and remains if it is honored. The believer still has his or her body since he or she is still alive, but this body must be considered to be dead. The body or the flesh is still the issue over which victory must be attained and this victory has not been achieved. Satan will use it to draw the believer away from Christ. It is the body that Paul states is the body of death or the body that brings death.

Temptation to sin or to defy the Spirit is presented through a person's senses. A person's seeking of earthly pleasures is contrary to the Spirit's leading. John wrote, "Do not love the world or anything in the world. If anyone loves the world, the love of the Father is not in him." (1 Jn 2:15) Those who are lost love the world since that is all that they know. They seek status, fleshly pleasures, or material wealth. The believer is not to get caught up in such distractions. His or her pleasure is in their relationship with the Lord. They are to love the Lord with all their heart, soul, and mind. They are committed to living as Jesus did and are to recognize that they cannot serve two masters… the Lord and the flesh.

Those "in Christ" should *not* consider it their fixed place of residence, however. The Lord stated, "I am the true vine, and my Father is the gardener. He cuts off every branch *in me* that bears no fruit." (Jn 15:1) Some of those "in Christ" will be cut out. Further, He taught that "if" a person remains in him he or she would bear much fruit,[120] that "if" a person remains in him whatever he or she asks will be given them,[121] and that if a person doesn't remain in him they are like a branch picked up and thrown in the fire and burned.[122] The Lord also promised that he would remain in those who remain in him,[123] putting the onus on the believer for some responsibility in maintaining the relationship. Remaining in him is a matter of commitment…the exercise of a person's will.

John summed up his teaching about who is in Christ. "But if anyone obeys his word, God's love is truly made complete in him. This is how we know we are in him: Whoever claims to live in him must walk as Jesus did." (1 Jn 2:5-6)

When Christ returns, Paul has revealed that it is the dead "in Christ" who will be raised first.[124] The believer's love relationship should be so committed, and that to obedience, that he or she remains in Christ. People have been given free-will and may choose to abandon their place in the Lord or to cherish it; in any event, they will reap the reward due them.

---

[120] Jn 15:5
[121] Jn 15:7
[122] Jn 15:6
[123] Jn 15:4
[124] 1 Thess 4:16

3.2 The Path to Eternal Salvation

To understand the path to eternal salvation, it is necessary to appreciate *how* God gifts the Spirit. Paul has written, "If you confess with your mouth that 'Jesus is Lord' and believe in your heart that God raised him from the dead, you will be saved. For it is with your heart that you believe and are justified, and it is with your mouth that you confess and are saved." (Rom 10:9-10)

According to Paul's teaching, belief in the heart and confession of the lordship of Christ with the mouth are needed for salvation.[125] Paul is not speaking of "eternal" salvation but salvation from the law which allows a person greater hope. The salvation provided at the cross frees or delivers the believer from the curse of the law[126] so that by faith he or she might receive the Holy Spirit, given as a gift to help in the achievement of righteousness. The gifting of the Spirit comes by faith or persuasion. Once a person has been persuaded of the reality of God and of his sovereignty and has been persuaded that he or she needs divine help, they are given the Spirit (by the Father) so that they might achieve life and godliness.[127]

The belief that brings the salvation that Paul is addressing does not require a person to understand the fullness of the Word of God. Neither does it mean that they need to appreciate the extent of Christ's love for them or even the way eternal salvation is accomplished. It means that they need to totally accept that Jesus is alive and is therefore able to give life and that Jesus is to be their lord and sovereign. Repentance for a person's offence against God and honoring him by acknowledging Christ's position

---

[125] At this point, it needs to be understood that Paul is not speaking about *eternal* salvation. The confessor is being freed from the jurisdiction of the first covenant and from the burden of his *past sins*. These are both the issues of freedom about which Paul speaks. The writer of Hebrews has clarified the nature of the salvation spoken of by Paul that apply to this occasion. "For this reason [cleansing a person's moral consciousness from acts that lead to death] Christ is the mediator of a new covenant, that those who are called may receive the promised eternal inheritance-now that he has died as a ransom to set them free from the sins committed under the first covenant." (Heb 9:15) Having been satisfied, the first covenant was "cancelled" by God "in order to put the second into effect." (Heb 10:9, 8:13, NLT)

[126] Gal 3:13

[127] 2 Pet 1:3, "His divine power [the Holy Spirit] has given us everything we need for life and godliness."

of authority allows a person to be cleansed of his or her sin and restored to fellowship with God. As Paul says, it "justifies"[128] them.

God gifts the believer with the Spirit following *his confession* that Christ will be his lord. The Father knows that humans cannot make the needed changes by themselves, *so He provides the Holy Spirit to help in the believer's transformation to holiness of mind and of practice.*

> God provides the Holy Spirit to help in the believer's transformation to holiness of mind and of practice.

The presence of the Spirit in a person does not mean that he or she has been granted eternal salvation. The Spirit must *live* in him or her. The Spirit must be allowed to exercise his life-giving ministry in the believer. [129] Once gifted with the Spirit, the believer is to listen to and to be obediently led by him. Listening and obeying become easier with practice and the Lord is patient with those whose ears are insensitive. He persists with the believer even to the point of disciplining and punishing[130] the wayward one, the person who has failed to submit to his leadership. Denying or refusing to accept the Spirit's leading can result in the Spirit being quenched[131] so that his ability to be heard anymore is not possible and with that quenching comes destruction.[132]

Paul has prophesied to Timothy that in the last days many would *deny* the Spirit. That is, they would prevent his work in their lives or even fail to recognize his saving ministry or its need. He says that they will "have a form of godliness but denying its power. Have nothing to do with them." (2 Tim 3:5) They may attend church and participate in the activities of the body. They may even be teachers and pastors but if

---

[128] Paul taught that justification came through the "blood" of Christ. "Since we have been justified by his blood, how much more shall we be saved from God's wrath through his life." (Rom 5:9) He also taught that "He was delivered over to death for our sins and was raised to life for our justification." (Rom 4:24) Accordingly, the resurrected life of Christ is also needed for a person's justification. James explained this further: "You see that a person is justified by what he does and not by faith alone." (Jas 2:24) The resurrected life of Christ provides the ministry of his Spirit in the believer so that what a person does is free of judgment.

[129] A distinction must be understood between the presence of the Spirit in a person and the Spirit "living" in him or her. A living Spirit is active, dynamic, and working. He is not to be ignored or resisted.

[130] Heb 12:6

[131] 1 Thess 5:19

[132] Rom 8:13

Eternal Salvation

they have denied the "power" of the Spirit they have been deceived and may even be deceiving others. The presence of Christ "living" (Rom 8:11) in the believer is a person's hope of glory.[133] "Do not be deceived: God cannot be mocked. A man reaps what he sows. The one who sows to please the sinful nature, from that nature will reap destruction; the one who sows to please the Spirit, from the Spirit will reap eternal life." (Gal 6:7-8) When a person refuses to honor the Spirit's ministry under the false understanding that he or she was eternally saved upon confession of faith is having been deceived. Such an attitude accepts the Spirit's ministry as being unnecessary. Practising sin with the understanding that a person has been given freedom from sin's consequences is being deceived. The Spirit must perform his ministry. To achieve victory over the practice of sin is why he was given, and his ministry is the foundation of the New Covenant.

Wide is the gate that will bring many to sorrow because they have not heard the voice of the Master or have not *followed* him. "Enter through the narrow gate. For wide is the gate and broad is the road that leads to destruction, and many enter through it. But small is the gate and narrow the road that leads to life, and only a few find it." (Mt 7:13-14) Many will find that their self-interest and unrighteousness will lead them down the wide road.

The complete ministry of Christ on behalf of the sinner needs to be recognized. He not only gave his life on the cross to complete the Old Covenant and to provide freedom from the penalty of a person's past sins, he has come to live in the believer as Spirit[134] so that those who have faith in him will allow him to live a godly life through them, meet the righteous requirements of God, and transform their hearts and minds to be of his likeness.

For the Israelites, the standard of righteousness was recorded on stone and as God's chosen people found, it could not be lived. The righteous requirements of the law can only be achieved *through* Christ; God's requirements *have not been accomplished* for the believer by Christ. Christ

> The righteous requirements of the law can only be achieved *through* the life of Christ in a person; they have not been accomplished for the believer by Christ.

---

[133] Col 1:27

[134] "Now the Lord is the Spirit, and where the Spirit of the Lord is there is freedom. And we who with unveiled faces all reflect the Lord's glory, are being transformed into his likeness with ever-increasing glory, which comes from the Lord, who is the Spirit." (2 Cor 3:17-18, NIV)

is righteousness, however, and he indwells anyone who can recognize his need and is willing to accept his presence. The righteous requirements of the law can only be accomplished by his indwelling ministry,[135] the Son of God who defeated sin and temptation while in the body that God had prepared for him as he walked this earth. He can be one's righteousness but only as his sovereignty and authority over a person's life is permitted. It is not the law which a person must satisfy, it is Christ who has gained victory over the law and who wants the believer to enjoy the same victory that he has gained. A person's eyes must be fixed steadfastly on Jesus. Eternal salvation is only granted to those who have crucified themselves of their own interest so that they might obey him in order to defeat sin. "He became the source of eternal salvation for all who obey him." (Heb 5:9)

Understanding the way the Spirit works is helpful. He *convicts* of sin, righteousness, and judgment.[136] He uses a person's conscience (moral consciousness) to inform him or her when sin has been committed. The disquiet or disturbance of a person's soul is intended to notify them of their offence. If the believer is experiencing a guilty conscience, it is expected that he or she will repent and confess their sin to God. "If we confess our sins, he is faithful and just to forgive us our sins and purify us from all unrighteousness." (1 Jn 1:9) It should be noted that satisfying the requirements of God, a person's justification, even following the gifting of the Spirit, is accomplished through the repentance and confession brought about by the Spirit's convicting work, and the application of the blood of Christ for his cleansing.

Responding to the convicting work of the Spirit is part of being "led" by the Spirit. Christ said, "My sheep listen to my voice; I know them, and they follow me. I give them eternal life, and they shall never perish." (Jn 10:27) Eternal life, resulting from eternal salvation, is only promised to those who *listen to* and *follow* Christ, the One that they have pledged or promised to be their lord. "Those who are led by the Spirit of God are sons of God." (Rom 8:14)[137]

A person's transformation to the likeness of Christ is not instantaneous. It is gradually "put on;" (Col 3:10) that is why the Lord taught the need to

---

[135] Rom 8:4

[136] Jn 16:8

[137] Many accept that upon confession of faith they have become a son of God; however, a person's adoption (his or her legal standing as a son) does not happen until "the redemption of our body" and we are "waiting for" this. (Rom 8:23, KJV)

persevere to the end.[138] Paul wrote, "By this gospel -the one that he taught- you are saved, if you hold firmly to the word I preached to you otherwise, you have believed in vain." (1 Cor 15:2) [139] As has been mentioned, Christ also cautioned believers not to sin with the admonition that those who sin are slaves to sin and that a slave has *no permanent place* in the family.[140]

Righteousness, once having been imputed allowing the gifting of the Spirit, is not imputed again, but is worked out through him. "But by faith -persuasion to obey the Spirit- we eagerly await through the Spirit the righteousness for which we hope." (Gal 5:5) The believer waits for the development of righteousness in mind, heart, and practice as he allows the Spirit to minister in his life.

The Spirit is the Spirit of holiness and sonship[141] and for him to accomplish his ministry the believer must fully submit to him, both for righteousness' sake and for the sake of building his kingdom. Life comes to those who have died to self and who continue to remain dead to self-interest. This may sound harsh and is certainly contrary to the natural spirit in people, but the Lord taught death to self as a requirement for life. "The man who loves his life will lose it, while the man who hates his life in this world will keep it for eternal life." (Jn 12:25) Such a teaching is quite contrary to thought that a single occasion of faith at confession is enough for a person to gain God's eternal kingdom.

As has been stated, God requires that the believer be holy in state. "Without holiness, no one will see the Lord." (Heb 12) While holiness is

---

[138] Mt 10:22. Paul, the writer of many of the epistles, has expressed his concern that he might not be qualified if he didn't "beat (discipline) his body." (1 Cor 9:27, NIV) To the Philippians Paul also expressed the sentiment that he must continue to persevere and become like Christ in his death so that "somehow *he might attain to the resurrection from the dead.*" (Phil 3:11, NIV) He did not present that his resurrection was assured.

[139] The need to persevere in righteousness was presented by Peter in another way. He spoke of the "sacred command" that was passed on to them. (2 Pet 2:21) This sacred command is presented by Ezekiel: "But if a righteous man turns from his righteousness and commits sin and does the same detestable things the wicked man does, will he live? None of the righteous things he has done will be remembered. Because of the unfaithfulness he is guilty of and because of the sins he has committed he will die." (Ezek 18:24, NIV)

[140] Jn 8:34-35

[141] Rom 8:15, NIV

the final state of the believer once he submits to the Spirit concerning his transformation, holiness comes through righteous practices.[142]

It should *not* be accepted that once a person makes a commitment to honor Christ as his lord that he is free to walk carelessly through life. Disobedience to the Spirit is an act of rebellion. Deliberate and continued[143] disobedience has eternal consequences. Every person who walks this earth, starting with those of the Lord[144], will be judged for things done while in the body[145] and those who confessed Christ as their lord for their disobedience to the Spirit's leading.

> It should *not* be accepted that once a person makes a commitment to honor Christ as his Lord/lord that he is free to walk carelessly through life.

The believer's transformation takes place as he or she is convicted of sin by the Spirit. As they confess, their sinful activities their sin should become clearly known to them and the distress caused in their heart through conviction should lead them to abandon that practice of sin. The Spirit does not convict of all sin at one time. Some remain unknown to him. Over time, however, the believer will be transformed and will have become God's "masterpiece" (Eph 2:10, NLT), the product of his "workmanship." (Eph 2:10, KJV) The believer should be awed and overwhelmed with gratitude knowing that Christ is working intimately and personally *in him* as an individual. What love and commitment to the person who has pained the heart of God! The Lord has suffered scorn, has given his life on the cruel cross, and then has chosen to minister personally in the life of the person that he is reclaiming. The believer should celebrate daily, not just for what the Lord has done for him, but for what he is continuously doing.

The ministry of Christ as high priest is also essential to accomplishing a person's eternal salvation. The high priest of Jewish tabernacle worship was to offer sacrifices for sins that the people had committed "in ignorance." (Heb 9:7) *Sin is offensive to God!* The Israelites could not offer sacrifices for sins about which they were unaware, neither can those who are subject to the *new* covenant confess and seek forgiveness for sins that are unknown

---

[142] Rom 6:19, 22
[143] Heb 10:26
[144] 1 Pet 1:17
[145] 2 Cor 5:10

to them. As high priest Christ ministers for these offences, pleading his blood for the remission of sins. The man-made sanctuary is a copy of the heavenly sanctuary and being a copy[146] reveals the nature of the ministry of Christ as high priest-the offer of his own blood as a sacrifice for sins committed in ignorance.

The Word of God reveals that there are sins committed *in ignorance* and sins committed about which the believer is aware, which the Spirit has *made known*-often through the troubling of a person's conscience. If sin is revealed before its commission, it is to be avoided. Known sins are to be confessed; those committed in ignorance will be pleaded by Christ with the Father. Since provision has been made for the cleansing of *all* sin, the believer need not bear his sin but may be freed from guilt and sin's consequence provided he or she is striving to "walk in the light." (1 Jn: 1:7)

There are elements in the gaining of eternal salvation that the believer needs to understand. He or she needs to carry their own cross, they need to die to self-interest, and they need to be obedient.

God's grace rests on the redeemed so that they might become conformed to the likeness of Christ *and* so that they might be participants in building his kingdom.[147] Both of these require self-sacrifice. Jesus said, "If anyone would come after me, he must deny himself and take up his cross and follow me." (Mt 16:24) [148]These are the costs that the believer must count and commit to in order to be a follower of the Lord.[149] When self-interest takes over, the Lord is no longer lord or sovereign and he cannot lead. His quiet voice will be drowned out by the clanging of the flesh or the call of the world. In order to gain victory over the evil one, an intentional and committed walk must be entered. As Christ taught, "Love the Lord your God with all your heart and with all your soul and with all your mind and with all your strength." (Mk 12:30)

---

[146] Heb 8:5, NIV
[147] Eph 2:10
[148] See also: Mk 8:34, 10:21; Lk 9:23
[149] Lk 14:28

This kind of "love" does not leave room for a person to engage his or her own interests. Judgment will come to the person who neglects either righteousness in his or her walk[150] or service for the kingdom.[151]

> Judgment will come to the person who neglects either righteousness in his or her walk or service for the kingdom.

As quoted earlier, Jesus said that those who are to be his disciples are to take up their cross and follow him. The cross is an instrument of death and according to the Lord his disciples are to carry this instrument in order to put to death their earthly bodies. Of course, he is speaking figuratively. The body was reckoned[152] to have been crucified with Christ when a person came to him to be redeemed from his sinful state.[153] However, the body did not actually die and can try to exercise its evil nature once again. When this happens, the believer is to figuratively set up his or her cross and crucify that emerging life once again. If they are carrying their cross it is always in proximity. If a person's old nature has been crucified and Christ is indwelling him or her, only the godly nature of Christ will be present so that he might live and reveal himself in the crucified believer.

---

[150] In speaking of the narrow gate Jesus said, "Not everyone who says to me 'Lord, Lord,' will enter the kingdom of heaven, but only he who does the will of my Father in heaven…Then I will tell them plainly, "'I never knew you. Away from me, you evil-doers.!" (Mt 7:21…23) The Lord revealed to John that, "Blessed are they that do his commandments, that they may have right to the tree of life." (Rev 22:14, KJV) See also Heb 12:14.

[151] The parable of the talents can be found in Mt 25:14-28. Christ issued the following command concerning the worthless servant: "And throw the worthless servant outside, into the darkness, where there will be weeping and gnashing of teeth." (v. 30) Paul revealed that a person's "work will be shown for what it is… if what he has built survives, he will receive his reward. If it is burned up, he will suffer loss." (1 Cor 3:13…14)

[152] "Crucifixion with Christ" is not a bodily event, but a spiritual one. Christ literally died in the flesh and the believer is to accept that state for his own body. If he has, the body and its interests have been put to death in his mind and by conviction. The believer must be careful not to weaken in this conviction, or to change his mind. Paul wrote, "If we have been united with him like this in his death, we will certainly also be united with him in his resurrection. For we know that our old self was crucified with him so that this body of sin (that causes sin) might be done away with so that we should no longer be slaves to sin." (Rom 6:5-6)

[153] Rom 6:6

Eternal Salvation

As well, the redeemed person has been purchased by Christ and has become his servant, not just for the sake of righteousness, but for service in building his kingdom. When self-interest takes over and service for a person's Master is being denied, that person needs to plant his or her cross firmly and mount it so that their fleshly pursuits might be put to death.

The eternal Kingdom will be established both through love and obedience. That is, only those who love God and who are committed to him through their appreciation of who he is will dwell with him. Love is always chosen and never forced. He could have made a people through his power and authority who would have displayed the characteristics of love, but had it been forced love would not really have been the basis of the relationship and at some time the motivation of the hearts of those compelled to "love" him would have revealed their true nature. Instead, God will select those who according to their own free-will, have chosen to love Him. Their love will be sincere, and their devotion committed and proven through obedience in recognition of his grace and mercy to them.

When his Kingdom is finally established all evil will have been removed; the hearts of those present will be totally pure. Love and kindness will reign. As Christ has revealed, "He will wipe every tear from their eyes. There will be no more death or mourning or crying or pain, for the old order of things has passed away." (Rev 21:4) All who do evil and all who cause sin will have been weeded out of his Kingdom.[154] The process of finding a people who have freely chosen to love their Lord and Savior requires a separation, the saving of some and a destruction of others. This does not mean that some are more deserving than others of his blessing, but that some will have been made to recognize their sinful state, will have repented of it, and will have responded to the Spirit in order to make them products fit for his Kingdom.

It is worth repeating that only the victorious will find life in the New Jerusalem.[155] Victory comes by engaging the battle for righteousness and by allowing Christ to live through them so that he might defeat the evil one, the interests of the flesh, and the permissions of the world.

From the beginning it needs to be understood that pardon for sin does not bring about a person's eternal salvation; it is that pardon followed by a

---

[154] Mt 13:41
[155] Rev 21:7; 22:14

transformation of the heart and mind by the Spirit of Christ that provides 'eternal' salvation.

3.3 More About Gaining the Spirit

Since the ministry of the Holy Spirit is vital to a person's gaining "eternal" salvation, the way the believer comes into his possession needs to be made clear.

The Spirit is a *gift* of the Father[156] following the believer's confession that Christ is and will be his lord. He was not even made available, except for specific purposes and to specific individuals, prior to the atoning work of Christ and his accession on high. The Holy Spirit is the Spirit of Christ in the believer.[157] Just as He lived righteously in the body that the Father had prepared for him, he will live righteously in the believer, if followed. The Holy Spirit is essential to a person's eternal hope and is not given through the believer's authority. He comes from the Father *according to his will and for the accomplishment of his purposes*. He is a Helper or Counsellor on the path of righteous living and for building God's Kingdom. Some are of the thought that the gifting of the Spirit is in response to their profession of faith, however the Father knows the heart of a person and its motivations[158] and gifts the Spirit as *he* wills to the confessor. The Holy Spirit is given for a purpose and is essential to a person's eternal salvation and for effective service. He is to be honored in the life of the believer; he is to be obeyed.

> The Holy Spirit is the Spirit of Christ in the believer. Just as he lived righteously in the body that the Father had prepared for him, he will live righteously in the believer, if followed.

In addressing a crowd Peter made the declaration: "Repent and be baptized, every one of you, in the name of Jesus Christ for the forgiveness of sins. And you will receive the gift of the Holy Spirit."[159] His understanding was that the Holy Spirit was gifted upon repentance and baptism.

---

[156] Lk 11:13; Jn 15:26
[157] Col 1:27; 2 Cor 3:17, 19; Gal 4:6
[158] Ps 44:21; Jer 17:10
[159] Acts 2:38, NIV; In another passage he taught that some should not be refused baptism since they had received the Holy Spirit. This is the only occasion (Acts 10:47) revealed in God's Word where the Spirit was given before a person's baptism. This occasion took place at the beginning of the church and would seem to be a special event.

Eternal Salvation

"Repentance" reveals the presence of faith and the awareness and acknowledgment of a person's sin. The psalmist wrote, "The sacrifices of God are a broken spirit; a broken and a contrite heart you will not despise." (Ps 51:17) Repentance is an act of contrition. If a person is not prepared to humble himself or herself before God, he or she will not be given the Spirit. God is sovereign and he is creator; he will not give his glory to another. In this vein, the person seeking salvation needs to recognize who God is by existence and nature, and must also recognize, in truth, who he is…created and sinful. It is a person's heart and his or her disposition towards their creator that are used to determine whether the Spirit is given. Paul wrote, "If you confess with your mouth, 'Jesus is Lord,' and believe in your heart that God raised him from the dead, you will be saved. For it is with your heart that you believe and are justified and with your mouth that you confess[160] and are saved." (Rom 10: 9, 10) [161] A person's "confession" is his *promise* that Christ is and will be his lord.

According to Peter, the baptism that saves is *"the pledge of a good conscience toward God. It saves you by* [through] *the resurrection of Jesus Christ…"* (1 Pet 3:21) The Lord's resurrection allows for his Spirit to be given to the believer in order that he might enlighten, lead, and empower for righteousness and a good conscience. The significance of water baptism is in its "pledge" [162] to God and to people. It is because of this pledge or promise and because of the believer's repentance that the Holy Spirit is given to the believer.

> The baptism that saves you is *"the pledge of a good conscience toward God."*

Paul taught that "Christ redeemed us from the curse of the law…so that by faith we might receive the promised Holy Spirit." (Gal 3:13…14) This thought reveals the gifting of the Spirit from another perspective. He presented that "faith" is required. That is, the person who receives

---

[160] "confess" is translated from the Greek *homologeo* which means "to assent, i.e. covenant, acknowledge: —con- (pro-)fess, confession is made, give thanks, promise." –from Strong's Greek Dictionary # 3670

[161] Although the confessor is "saved," this does not amount to his or her 'eternal' salvation.

[162] The word "pledge' as used in the NIV is translated from the Greek *eperotema* which means "an inquiry: —answer. - Strong's Greek Dictionary #1906. Various translations use different words for 'eperotema.' ASV: "interrogation"; KJV: "answer"; Darby's: "demand"; Young's Literal Translation: "question"; New Living Translation: "response."

the Spirit does so based on his or her having been morally convicted or persuaded of their unrighteousness and of their need.[163] Their mind and their heart have changed regarding their offences towards their creator. They understand that God is the creator and that they are the created. They appreciate their rebellion and disobedience regarding the sovereignty of God. When they recognize these truths, their heart will be broken, and they will become contrite just as anyone would who truly recognizes an offence against another. Because of this persuasion or conviction and because of their commitment to live righteously, the Holy Spirit is given them. God makes us "competent"[164] to live a godly life.[165] The Lord requires the believer to make both the contrition of his or her heart and the confession of their heart public and to him in the form of a pledge of their commitment to honor their lord. *It is according to this pledge that the Spirit is given* so that a person's promise of a righteous walk might be enabled.

The accounts of the disciples showed that those converted desired to be baptized immediately upon confession of faith; they wanted the Spirit's help, counsel, and power for the new life that they were determined to live. They recognized their need and valued the Spirit's ministry in their lives.

> Paul taught that a person had to be redeemed from the curse of the law before or in order that that he might receive the Holy Spirit.

Paul taught that a person had to be redeemed from the curse of the law before or in order that he might receive the Holy Spirit. Accordingly, the believer must first be relieved from the law before the Spirit is given. This is so because two different covenants exist and they both involve eternal salvation. The covenant of the law must be satisfied before the covenant of the Spirit can be started. The writer of Hebrews has recorded a conversation that Christ had with the Father. "Here I am; I have come to do your will." He sets aside the first to establish the second." (Heb 10:9) The second covenant is better. It is one that the believer is competent to satisfy. "He has made us competent as ministers of a new covenant-not of the letter but of the Spirit; for the law kills, but the Spirit gives life." (2 Cor 3:6)

Christ had to complete the righteous requirements of the first or Old Covenant in order to make available the new. The writer of Hebrews has

---

[163] Rom 8:4
[164] 2 Cor 3:4-6
[165] 2 Pet 1:3

made this very clear. "Christ is the mediator of a new covenant, that those who are called may (not "will") receive the promised eternal inheritance-now that he has died as a ransom to set them free from the sins committed under the first covenant." (Heb 9:15) In order that the believer might be given access to the New Covenant, Christ had to free him or her by cleansing them from the sins committed while under the first covenant. The death of Christ satisfies the Old Covenant for the believer once he believes and has professed his "faith" in the Lord. He will be given the Holy Spirit, the presence of Christ in him or her[166] when he confesses that Christ will be his lord.

The Spirit is given when a person repents of the hurt or pain that he or she has caused God through their rebellion, professes their faith in Christ and confesses that they are going to make Christ their lord.

---

[166] Some seem to accept that Christ completed his ministry through his sacrificial offering. The Spirit who indwells the believer is Christ. "Now the Lord is the Spirit...And we, who with unveiled faces all reflect the Lord's glory, are being transformed into his likeness with ever-increasing glory, which comes from the Lord, who is the Spirit." (2 Cor 3:17-18)

Chapter 4

The Life of Faith

4.1 Understanding "Faith"

The believer is expected to live a "life of faith." Paul stated: "For in the gospel a righteousness from God is revealed, a righteousness that is by faith from first to last, just as it is written: 'The righteous will live by faith.'" (*Rom* 1:17)

It is easy to trivialize Paul's teaching that the righteous will live "by faith" and to dismiss that "life" with the understanding that "belief in Christ" or mental acceptance, even profoundly rooted in a person's heart, is all that is required. The meaning of "belief" is often defined uniquely from person to person and is often confined to the notion that belief in the existence of Christ and in his atoning sacrifice, along with a person's "trust" in him to do all that is required for deliverance, satisfies Biblical teaching about belief. This is not what the life of faith requires. Neither is it confined to the single act of confession that a person made at the time of conversion. Christ taught: "All men will hate you because of me, but he who stands firm *to the end* will be saved." (Mt 10:22 "Belief" requires obedience,[167] and to the end. It is revealed through a deep commitment -loving God with all a person's heart, body, soul, and strength.

> "Belief" requires obedience, and to the end.

The writer of Hebrews has written concerning the Jews who did not enter God's rest at the time of the Exodus, "the message they heard was of no value to them, because they did not share the faith of those who obeyed." (Heb 3:18-4:2)

---

[167] Heb 3: 18-19

Since anyone who desires to be delivered into the Kingdom of God[168] must maintain their faith, it is important to understand what "faith" means. Its sense cannot be left vague and undefined allowing the believer to apply his or her own interpretation. "Faith" means "persuasion."[169] It should not be confused with 'trust' which is not the Biblical meaning or intention of the Greek 'pistis' from which "faith" originates. Applying "faith" to mean "persuasion" will make a person's study much more meaningful.

> "Faith" means "persuasion." It should not be confused with 'trust.'

The Greek word for "trust" is elpizo which means "to expect or confide."[170] If you trust someone you *expect* that person to respond according to some known or disclosed understanding. That is not what Paul is presenting since he uses the Greek "pistis." Consequently, "faith" should not be confused with "trust."

Some would say that they trust in Christ and that they know that salvation only comes through him. They rest in these confessions or professions as being their faith. Faith requires having confidence in or being persuaded about something to the point that a person is willing to obey the object of their faith regardless of what might be demanded of them. Faith does not rest in a profession but in a *practice*. Obedience is faith in practice.[171]

> Faith does not rest in a profession but in practice.

When true faith is rested in someone, the faithful person will respond in obedience to the requirements of that one and he or she will fearlessly adhere to their conviction. Faith is proven by a person's practice of it, especially when testing occurs. When a person fails in honoring either the Word or the Lord, he or she cannot be said to have faith. *Eternal* salvation comes through obedience,[172] which is the *practice* of faith.

---

[168] Mt 10:22; 1 Cor 15:2

[169] "faith" is translated from the Greek *pistis* which means "persuasion, i.e. credence; moral conviction (of religious truth, or the truthfulness of God or a religious teacher), especially reliance upon Christ for salvation; abstractly, constancy in such profession; by extension, the system of religious (Gospel) truth itself: — assurance, belief, believe, faith, fidelity." –from Strong's Greek Dictionary #4102

[170] Strong's Greek Dictionary #1679

[171] Heb 4:2

[172] Heb 5:9

To say that you have placed your trust in God would mean that you expect him to respond according to his Word or promises. Although this may be true, it is not through trust that you are given grace or even by trust that you are saved; it is because you have been persuaded of the truth of the gospel and from your response to the persuasion that by God's graciousness through Christ and His Spirit, and your obedient response to him, you will be saved. This "persuasion" is *revealed* in the believer's heart, attitude, and actions. A person's *practices are a better indication of his or her faith than are their professions.*

Faith is not passive; it is not confined to a person's mind. The faith demanded by God requires a lifetime commitment to Christ and to his teachings. It requires death to self-interest[173] and obedience to the Lord. The result will be a transformation of the ever-present evil inclinations of a person's heart[174] into the conformation of a heart that is in the likeness of Christ's,[175] the image in which humankind had been created. Faith allows Christ to *live* in a person with a commitment to seek his will rather than the believer's own. The life of faith saves. Jesus said that he was the way, the truth, and that he was also the life.[176]

Faith must be placed in something or someone for a particular purpose. That is, a person must be persuaded that something can accomplish a recognized need. For example, according to Paul the believer must be persuaded that he "was dead in his trespasses and sins," (Eph 2:1) and that he was "by nature an object of wrath." (Eph 2:3) [177] The believer must also have been persuaded that because of God's "great love for him or her, God who is rich in mercy, made them alive with Christ." (Eph 2:5)

The faith that a person exhibits through persuasion *at the time of confession* results in *marking* or sealing him or her with the Holy Spirit. That "sealing", however, does not necessarily result in his or her eternal salvation. It puts them in the position where they can have it and gives them the resources that they might have it. Because a person is persuaded of something once, does not mean that his or her persuasion will not

---

[173] Mt 16:25
[174] Gen 6:5
[175] Rom 8:29
[176] Jn 14:6
[177] "by nature" refers to his natural spirit and soul…these will bring down God's wrath.

weaken or even disappear. The Lord requires a life of faith to the end. The life of faith or of having been persuaded causes a person to view God and humans in a new light and with different convictions.

The life of faith is accomplished through the Spirit and is not of "works" (obedience to the law). Paul stated that he was "crucified with Christ; nevertheless, I live; yet not I, but Christ liveth in me: and the life which I now live in the flesh I live by the faith of the Son of God, who loved me, and gave himself for me." (Gal 2:20, KJV) He revealed that he or she *"no longer lived"*, that their own interests had no draw upon themselves and due to their persuasion (faith) they allowed Christ to live in them. The life of Christ being lived in a person is his or her *hope of glory*. The Lord's life *being lived in a person* is the life of faith. Paul encouraged Timothy to "fight the good fight of [strive for] faith" and to seize eternal life. (1 Tim 6:12)

The life of faith is not as easy as is often presented. To die to self and to live through Christ requires submission of a person's earthly goals and aspirations, their earthly pleasures and often comforts, to the will of Christ. The command given to all who will dwell with their Lord and Savior is to love him completely or to submit to him fully-with all their heart, soul, and mind.[178] Eternal salvation only comes through obedience.[179]

The faith that a person exhibits through persuasion *at the time of confession* results in marking or sealing him or her with the Holy Spirit and releases them from the jurisdiction of the Old Covenant. The sacrificial death of Christ does not provide the believer with eternal salvation but makes provision so that he or she may have it. Therefore, a walk of righteousness cannot be abandoned.

Neither is the righteousness of Christ imputed to the believer following his or her redemption. It must be lived out through a person's life. This truth is too frequently left unrecognized. Paul taught, "For what the law was powerless to do in that it was weakened by the sinful nature, God did by sending his own Son in the likeness of sinful man to be a sin offering. And so, he condemned sin in sinful man, *in order that the righteous requirements of the law might be fully met in us, who do not live according to the sinful nature but according to the Spirit.*" (Rom 8: 3-4) Because this is so, it is extremely important for the believer to understand the nature of the Spirit's sanctifying work as accomplished through living the life of faith.

---

[178] Mt 22:37
[179] Heb 5:9

Christ came to dwell in the believer and to live his righteous life through the believer. The Lord has the knowledge and the power necessary to live a sinless life as he indwells a person just as he did as he walked this earth in the body that the Father had provided him in the womb of Mary. The believer needs to recognize that Christ lives through him or her only by permission. He does not force the redeemed person to comply with him. A person's exercise of free-will as given at creation will always be honored. Obedience to the Lord, chosen and practiced by the believer, is an act of honor and an act of love. Defiance of the Holy Spirit, however, is rebellion or blasphemy and to defy the Spirit's leadership will not allow a person to live righteously. The Lord has presented the need for death to self, and for a person to carry his or her cross[180] so that they might crucify the flesh when it begins to take on life once more.

> Christ came to dwell in the believer and to live his righteous life through the believer.

The Holy Spirit is to take control. The aspect of letting go will probably be the most difficult challenge facing the believer. Many teach that such sacrifice is not necessary. Teaching that permits the believer to live a life free of sacrifice is an act of deception.[181] Humankind's evil nature would encourage him or her in opposing the need to relinquish control and Satan would discourage such a need. During Eve's discourse with Satan she told him that she was not to eat of the fruit from the tree in the middle of the garden or she would die. Satan responded, "You will not surely die, for God knows that when you eat of it your eyes will be opened and you will be like God." (Gen 3:4-5) There will be many who offer the encouraging words of Satan; that is: "You *don't really need to give up right to your life. God does not expect that of those He loves. There may be some things that you shouldn't do but you were given life to enjoy. So, enjoy!*"

> The Spirit is given to change the believer's heart and practices.

The Spirit is given to change the believer's heart and practices. Paul taught that the fruit of the Spirit or that which He produces is "*love, joy, pace, patience, kindness, goodness, faithfulness, gentleness and self-control.*" (Gal 5:22-23) The believer will be transformed into a person who desires and practices these attributes if he or she is obedient. The Lord also cautioned that those who do not

---

[180] Mt 16:24; Mk 8:34; Lk 9:23;
[181] Gal 6:7-8

produce such fruits would be "cut off" from him. "I am the true vine, and my Father is the gardener. He cuts off every branch in me- the redeemed person-that bears no fruit, while every branch in me that does bear fruit, he prunes so that it will be even more fruitful." (Jn 15:1-2)

Concerning the death of Christ Paul taught, "We died to sin; how can we live in it any longer? Or don't you know that all of us who were baptized into Christ Jesus were baptized into his death. We were therefore buried with him through baptism into death in order that, just as Christ was raised from the dead through the glory of the Father, we too may live a new life. If we have been united with him like this in his death, we will certainly also be united with him in his resurrection. For we know that our old self was crucified with him so that the body of sin might be done away with, that we should no longer be slaves to sin-because anyone who has died has been freed from sin." (Rom 6:2-7)

> Being baptized into Christ's death symbolizes that a person's old self was crucified with their Savior.

Being baptized into Christ's death means that a person has identified himself with the death of Christ and it *symbolizes* that his or her old self was crucified with their Savior. The purpose of being united in the Lord's death is so that a person's earthly body, the body of sin or that causes sin, might be done away. It should be noted, as well, that "*If*" we are united in his death we will be united in his resurrection. This is a conditional statement. Paul struggled with his death so that he might be resurrected;[182] he did not presume that his confession would achieve his eternal hope.

A person's faith or commitment will be tested.[183] Satan is not through with the person who confesses belief. He will strive to lead the Christ-follower to his persuasions and will deceive and lie relentlessly for that to happen. It is not without reason that Paul taught his followers to put on the full armour of God.

The believer is to fight the good fight by standing against the devil's schemes.[184] The evil one is still trying to destroy the believer who has committed himself or herself to practicing the lordship of Jesus Christ. He or she is to know and to practice

> The devil is still trying to destroy the person who has committed himself to practicing the lordship of Jesus Christ.

---

[182] Phil 3:10-11
[183] 1 Thess 2:4
[184] Eph 6:11

truth, to protect his or her heart through righteous living, to flee from conflict, and to live in peace. Their faith or persuasion of the truth compels them to extinguish the attacks of the evil one. They are to protect their mind through the study of the Word of God and to be faithful in prayer so that they might be victorious.

4.2 Death to Self

Paul told the Romans, "We know that our old self was crucified with Christ so that the body of death -that causes death- might be done away with, so that we should no longer be slaves to sin." (Rom 6:6)

It should not be accepted that in a "mystical" sense the believer has died- a death without dying. Paul is not teaching that a death took place in our bodies about which we are unaware, that our bodies have been crucified. A crucified body has no life; hence, it cannot sin. Observation would affirm both that our bodies are very much alive and that they can relent to sin's draw even following baptism. However, when it comes to the body's enticement to sin, if allowed to exercise his power, Christ can gain victory for the believer. If the believer acknowledges that his or her body with its interests has been put to death, he or she will not allow (will) its demands to be satisfied. It has been crucified and is dead after all. As well, if the "body of sin" had literally or spiritually died the Lord would not require a person to take up his or her cross and to crucify it on a daily basis or as necessary. The walk in the Spirit is a serious business with grave outcomes.

If the body has been crucified with Christ, only a person's soul and spirit remain. The spirit who directs the believer's life is to be the Holy Spirit. The natural spirit is to be re-trained or transformed and with it, a person's soul. This transformation can *only* take place as the believer relents to the Spirit's leadership of his or her life so that Christ *can* take control. When a person's natural spirit has been put to death or has been crucified he or she has become *filled* with the Holy Spirit. They have become Christ-like and an offering acceptable to God.

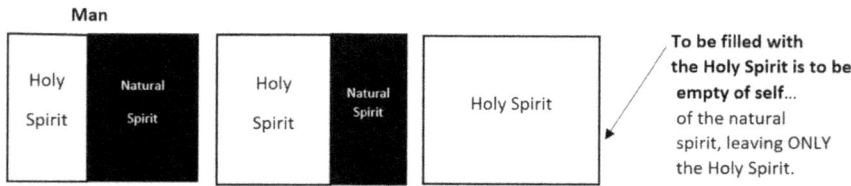

Eternal Salvation

However, God will not over-rule the free-will that he has allowed humans to enjoy; consequently, a very real battle is engaged between the believer's evil nature and the Holy Spirit. It is those who "overcome" who will dwell eternally with the Lord.[185] Those who fall prey to Satan's lies and deceptions will not see the Lord but will dwell apart from him.[186] As long as a person claims right to his being, he or she cannot find eternal salvation. They remain the spiritual offspring of their parents Adam and Eve.

> God will not over-rule the free-will that He has allowed humans.

Disobedience brought on by the flesh leads to death; accordingly, the flesh must be crucified. John has recorded, "Do not love the world or anything in the world. If anyone loves the world, the love of the Father is not in him." (1 Jn 2:15) And it is with this reality in mind that Paul told the Philippians "continue to work out your own salvation with fear and trembling, for it is God who works in you to will and to act according to his good purpose." (Phil 2:12-13)

The body, through its senses, is enticed and tempted by the "pleasures" offered by the world, but joy and peace come through Christ. The body is only temporal, and interest spent on accommodating it leads a person's focus and attention away from that which is eternal-a person's soul and spirit- and fosters their evil imaginations. The body informs a person's soul; and, a body that is persuaded to entertain unrighteous interests also leads the soul in that regard.

The devil is still trying to destroy the person who has committed himself or herself to practicing the lordship of Jesus Christ.[187] In Proverbs it is recorded, "Above all else guard your heart [soul], for it is the wellspring of life." (Prov 4:23) A person must choose his or her master carefully.

Paul reminded his Christian brothers of the need to gain victory over the sinful nature. "For when we were controlled by the sinful nature, the passions aroused by the law were at work in our bodies, so that we bore fruit to death. But now, by dying to what once bound us, we have been released from the law so that we serve in a new way of the Spirit and not in the old way of the written code." (Rom 7:5-6)

---

[185] Rev 21:7
[186] Rev 22:15
[187] Heb 12:14

Release from the law comes through the sacrificial offering of Christ and remains as long as a person allows Christ to rule through the crucifixion of his or her flesh. The redeemed person has confessed their sin and rebellion and, through baptism into Christ, has *affirmed* death to his or her bodily interests through obedience to Christ-the lordship of Christ. The person who lives a lie, abandons his or her pledge of Christ's right to rule, will be found outside the walls of the holy city, the New Jerusalem,[188] and forever separated from the Lord. The only way for a person to gain victory over the sinful nature is through the life of Christ in him or her. He enlightens, leads, and empowers for its defeat. Paul taught that "*now we* serve (are in bondage) *in a new way of the Spirit*"-that is, we must obey.

> The person who lives a lie will be found outside the walls of the holy city, the New Jerusalem, forever separated from the Lord.

If a person accepts that Christ died for him or her or in their place, they cannot also claim that their body may act as though it was alive. That is, they cannot say that they have died with Christ or are in Christ but that they still live or have right to life in their body. *It is dead*! If not, they have *not* died. If they have not died, they have not died in Christ.

The believer is to be baptized into the *death* of Christ. "Or don't you know that all of us who were baptized into Christ Jesus were baptized into his death. We were therefore buried with him through baptism into death in order that, just as Christ was raised from the dead through the glory of the Father, we too may live a new life." (Rom 6:2-5) A body that is dead and buried has *no life*. However, a new life has been given through the Spirit and as Christ was resurrected, so will those be who live a life of faith through him;[189] they will be physically raised at his return if their faith is maintained.[190] Their natural spirit will have effectually died, and

---

[188] Rev 22:15
[189] "faith" as pertaining to the teaching that "faith has come" (Gal. 3:25) and that "For it is by grace you have been saved, through faith" is translated from the Greek pistis which means "persuasion, i.e. credence; moral conviction (of religious truth, or the truthfulness of God or a religious teacher), especially reliance upon Christ for salvation; abstractly, constancy in such profession; by extension, the system of religious (Gospel) truth itself: —assurance, belief, believe, faith, fidelity." From Strong's Greek Dictionary #4102
[190] Mt 10:22; Rom 11:22; 1 Cor 15: 1-2;2 Tim 2:12; Heb 10:36-39; Rev 2:26

the Spirit of Christ will be their life. In the meantime, the believer's body must be dead and must be treated, concerning its interests, as if it was dead.

Paul has called those who continue to sin "while they seek to be justified", "lawbreakers." (Gal 2:18) [191] He has stated that they have "rebuilt" that which they had destroyed-namely, the law. If they have rebuilt it, they are again subject to it. It is those who "with fear and trembling" (Phil 2:12) walk in obedience[192] to the Spirit who are freed from the law[193] and who are considered "sons of God." (Rom 8:14) If a person allows the sinful nature to have life in his or her mortal body, they will reap destruction.[194] That body must be put to death.

> Freedom from the law has been provided by the sacrificial death of Christ; but, it is *conditional*.

Freedom from the law has been provided by the sacrificial death of Christ; but it is *conditional*. Paul has presented that a person must be led by the Spirit in order to be freed from the guardianship of the law. The domain of the law is over a person's body and his old nature. If these have been crucified, life must exist in his or her spirit and soul. If the believer treats their body as if it has been put to death, they are no longer subject to the law but are freed from it. If by faith a person's body is considered dead, the Spirit becomes his life. Christ's Spirit is to become the believer's spirit. We know that we all have bodies that have life functions and interests; however, spiritually and practically, these must be continuously put to death or subdued so that the spirit and soul may be saved. As long as a person is led by the Spirit and denies the flesh, righteousness which leads to holiness[195] will be practiced. "The Spirit gives life." (Jn 6:63)

---

[191] In order to eliminate confusion in understanding, a person is justified through faith (Rom 5:1, 3:28, Galatians 2:16, 3:24), but he or she is also justified through Christ's resurrected life (Rom 4:24), and by what they do and not by faith alone (James 2:24). They are justified concerning past sins, but they also require justification through submission to the exercise of Christ's life in them.

[192] Heb 5:9

[193] Gal 5:18

[194] Gal 6:8

[195] Rom 6:19, 22

4.3 Slavery and the Believer

Every person must either work out the righteousness demanded by the law using his or her own resources, or he or she can have it accomplished through the grace and gifting of the Spirit[196] as they are obediently led. If they reject the ministry of the Spirit, they are left to their own devices; they must "work" out the righteousness demanded by the law by themselves.

It is the ministering Spirit in a person that leads to eternal life. "But now that you have been set free from sin and have become slaves to God, the benefit you reap leads to holiness, and the result is eternal life." (Rom 6:22) [197] The blood of Christ has set the believer free from his *past sins* and has allowed him or her the Holy Spirit so that they might become a slave to God as opposed to a slave to sin.

The need to be a slave to God is very real. Paul told his readers to "work out[198] their own salvation with fear and trembling." (Phil 2:12, KJV) A slave only has interest in his master's business and rewards will be given based upon a person's dedication as a servant. In working out a person's own salvation Paul is addressing the need for the believer to be a slave to the Holy Spirit in the pursuit of righteousness so that he or she might have eternal life.

> In working out a person's own salvation Paul is addressing the need for the believer to be a slave to the Holy Spirit in the pursuit of righteousness.

Concerning "slavery" Paul wrote, "Don't you know that when you offer yourselves to someone to obey him as slaves, you are slaves to the one whom you obey-whether you are slaves to sin, which leads to death, or to obedience which leads to righteousness?" (Rom 6:16) Jesus also spoke on slavery. "I tell you the truth, everyone who sins is a slave to sin. Now a slave has *no permanent place* in the family, but a son belongs to it forever." (Jn 8:34) And, Paul clarified that it is the "sons of God" who submit to the Spirit's leadership. "Therefore brothers, we have an obligation-but it is not to the sinful nature, to live according to it. For if you live according

---

[196] Gal 5:5
[197] See also 2 Thess 2:13, Titus 3:5-6; Rom 5:9-10
[198] "work out" is translated from the Greek "*katergazomai*" which means "to work fully, i.e. accomplish; by implication, to finish, fashion: —cause, to (deed), perform, work (out)." –from Strong's Greek Dictionary #2716

to the sinful nature you will die, but if by the Spirit you put to death the misdeeds of the body you will live, because those who are led by the Spirit of God are sons of God." (Rom 8:12-14) The Holy Spirit is the special gift, the gift of grace, given to those who confess that Jesus is Lord-their lord- so that they might live righteously and be transformed into a state of holiness, and through that state to find eternal life. The believer who desires to dwell eternally with Christ must live slavishly to the Spirit, as a slave to Christ.

4.4 Eternal Salvation through Relationship

A person's eternal salvation is accomplished through his or her relationship with the Lord; it is not accomplished through belief in Christ's sacrificial ministry on the cross. Neither is it accomplished through church attendance, adherence to religious practices such as baptism or even to a warm 'feeling' of love towards the Lord. Certainly, the believer must love the Lord, but that love is to show itself through commitment to the practice of *obedience*. Jesus said, "If you love me, you will do what I command." (Jn 14:15) [199]

Jesus taught that he had come to fulfil the Law.[200] That is, he had come to fulfil the Law through *his life in the believer* and the one who is going to have him or her fulfil it for them through his enlightenment, leading and power must be led. He or she must obey! The righteous requirements of the Law are still in place and it is concerning righteousness that Christ will judge his children in the end. The writer of Hebrews has recorded that, "he [the Lord] became the source of eternal salvation for all who obey him." (Hebrews 5:9)

Modern concepts of "love" have often reverted to feeling or sentiment and have cast aside the idea of commitment. "Love" has become self-gratifying and emotional; such thinking will not result in a person's eternal presence with their God.

The prophets presented the nature of the relationship that a person is to develop and practice with his or her creator. "He requires only that you fear the lord your God, and live in a way that pleases him, and to love him

---

[199] See also verse 21. "Whoever has my commands and obeys them, he is the one who loves me."
[200] Mt 5:17

and serve him with all your heart and soul." (Deut 10:12)[201] The Lord Jesus also confirmed this nature of the relationship in his teaching.[202]

The heart that God requires cannot be established in the heart of humans without committed and humble obedience to the Spirit of Christ. Under a person's own rule, his or her evil nature and self-interest will prevail.

God told the Israelites that they were to "cling" to him. "You must fear the Lord your God and worship him and cling to him." (Deut 10:20, NLT) Some translations use, "cleave to" or "hold fast to." "Clinging to" is not a passive activity. It has intent and it has action that keeps another close. The person clinging does not want there to be distance between him or her and the one to which they are clinging. They cling for security-for protection, for maintenance of the relationship. God does not condone independence but as creator demands that his created people submit to his sovereignty. Christ said, "My sheep listen to my voice; I know them, and they follow me. I give them eternal life and they will never perish." (Jn 10:27-28)

Christ presented the nature of the relationship that he and the Father will have with the believer in another way. He told his disciples that he would never leave them as orphans but that the Counsellor -Holy Spirit or the Lord, Jesus Christ- would come to them and that they would realize "that I am in my Father, and you are in me and I am in you." (Jn 14:20) In this teaching he has presented the nature of the intimacy that the believer's relationship with him is to take on. However, such a thought can be confusing. How is a person to be in the Lord and yet he to be in that one?

If the believer is "in Christ" that person cannot be seen; *only Christ will be observable.* The revelation or expression of Christ will prevent the believer's evil nature from being visible. Likewise, if Christ is not visible when the redeemed person is viewed, it cannot be said that that person is *in* him. Remaining in Christ demands death to self, the believer's crucifixion for the sake of his or her Lord. Of course, this requires a *very intimate, obedient, and sacrificial walk.* This is your act of worship. "Offer your bodies as living sacrifices, holy and pleasing to God-this is your spiritual act of worship." (Rom 12:1) It is those who offer their bodies that he has promised will bear much fruit[203] and who will gain eternal salvation.

---

[201] See also: Deut 11:13; 13:3; Josh 22:5; 1 Sam 7:3, 12:20, 12:24; Joel 2:12
[202] Mt 22:37, 38
[203] Jn 15:5

Eternal Salvation

At the same time, Christ is in believers. That is, his Spirit is in them in order to defeat sin's call upon their lives. *Christ did not remain on the cross!* He is very dynamically ministering in the lives of all of those that he has redeemed from their past sins and from the law. He is alerting them to sin, encouraging them to victory, and empowering them for it. He is actively developing righteousness and is building his kingdom through them.

Many accept that once they have made a confession of faith, they are considered to be in him and that they will remain in him for eternity. Being "in Christ" is not necessarily a permanent status. A person may choose not to remain there. Christ told his disciples, "Remain in me and I will remain in you." Jn 15:4) [204] And later he taught, "If you remain in me and my words remain in you, ask whatever you wish, and it will be given you." (Jn 15:7) This is a conditional statement allowing that a person might not remain in him and that his promise rests on those who do. John has explained that the requirement "of remaining" in Christ requires the believer to maintain the truths which he or she had heard from the beginning.[205]

> Being "in Christ" is not necessarily a permanent status. A person may not choose to remain there.

The position of *remaining* "in Christ" is a matter of a person's will and *only* his will. He or she may die to their flesh-become a servant of righteousness- and remain in Christ or they may take over control of their life and live apart from Christ. The revelation of the need for obedience or to practice faith to the end in order to gain eternal salvation is presented in several places in the Scriptures,[206] Christ stated, "I am the true vine, and my Father is the gardener. *He cuts off every branch in me* that bears no fruit, while every branch that does bear fruit will be even more fruitful." (Jn 15:1) Permanence in the family of God comes with obedience to the Spirit.

> It is those who are "in" Christ who will enjoy his deliverance, not those who "claim" to be in him.

It is those who are "in" Christ who will enjoy his deliverance, not those who "claim" to be in him, but those whose walk is according to

---

[204] He also taught: *"Remain in me and I will remain in you…If a man remains in me and I in him, he will bear much fruit. If anyone does not remain in me, he is like a branch that is thrown away and withers; such branches are picked up, thrown into the fire and burned."* (Jn 15:5, NIV)
[205] 1 Jn 2:24
[206] Mt 10:22; Jn 8:34; Rom 11:22; 1 Cor 15:1-2; Gal 6:7-8; Phil 3:18-19; Col 1:21-23; 1 Tim 4:16; 2 Tim 2:12; Heb 6:4-6, 10:26-31, 36-39; 2 Pet 2:20-21; Rev 21:7

Christ's leadership. If they are "in him" they go where he goes and do what he wills. A person cannot remain "in" him and take a different path. John has written, "We know that we have come to know him if we obey his commands. The man who says, 'I know him,' but does not do what he commands is a liar, and the truth is not in him. But if anyone obeys his word, God's love is truly made complete in him. This is how we know we are in him: Whoever claims to live in him must walk as Jesus did." (1 Jn 2:3-6) The believer no longer must satisfy the law by himself or herself in order to be righteous in God's sight and prepared for his Kingdom; Christ came to dwell in him or her for that purpose. "I have not come to abolish them (the law and the Prophets) but to fulfill them." (Mt 5:17) According to Paul, "Christ condemned sin in sinful man, in order that the righteous requirements of the law might be fully met in us, who do not live according to the sinful nature but according to the Spirit." (Rom 8:3-4)

The reality of being "in Christ" requires that a person be led by Christ. It is through obedience and submission to him that a person's relationship with God is maintained. The Lord's leadership is both for righteousness leading to holiness[207] and for service.

---

[207] Rom 6: 19, 22

Eternal Salvation

Moral Relationship in Eternal Salvation

GOD

People were created in the image of God... morally pure, righteous.	The constant evil imaginations of people grieved God and pained his heart. (Gen 6:5-6) Sin separates people from God so that he will not hear. (Isa 59:2)	The sacrificial offering of Christ redeems the believer and restores him and her to fellowship with God. (Rom 5:10)	God gives the Holy Spirit (Spirit of Christ) * to enlighten, lead, and empower for righteousness. (Christ "in" the believer and the believer in Christ.)	Obedience to the Spirit is required. The believer must remain** "in Christ" and die to self so that Christ lives through him or her.*** The believer is returned to the likeness of Christ. (Rom 8:29)	Judgment awaits all for things done in the flesh, whether good or bad...for obedience to, or rebellion against, the Holy Spirit.

*2 Cor 3:6; Col 2; Col 1:27; 2 Cor 3:17-18) The Holy Spirit is Christ in the believer. His ministry of reconciliation and salvation was not completed by his sacrifice on the cross. He indwells the believer to complete his work of holiness making the believer acceptable to dwell in God's presence. (Rom 15:16; Eph 2:10). Willing obedience is necessary to accomplish this.

** Mankind has been given free-will...the ability and privilege of making his own choices. Consequently, he may not choose to remain "in Christ" (Jn 15: 4, 5, 7).

***As Christ lived in the flesh given him by the Father without sin, he will live in the believer without sin, if obeyed. If the believer sins he or she is not "in" Christ at that time because Christ would not sin. If Christ is "in" the believer, that person has the ability through the power of Christ to defeat sin's practice. However, Christ must be permitted to live, not merely be present, in the believer.

4.5 The Practice of Being Led by the Spirit

The importance of being *led* by the Holy Spirit cannot be overstated. Because a person has the presence of the Holy Spirit his or her eternal salvation is not guaranteed. The believer was given the Spirit on the basis of his or her confession or pledge that Christ would be their *"lord,"-their sovereign and their life.* The person who confessed faith may yet not honor that pledge and may abandon the righteous walk that the Spirit would avail. Christ presented that those who do not walk in the light "love and practice falsehood" (Rev 22:15) and says that they will be found outside the walls of the New Jerusalem separated from him.

Paul taught, "From the beginning God chose you to be saved through the sanctifying work of the Spirit and through belief in the truth." (2 Thess 2:13) He repeated this to Titus, "He saved us through the washing of rebirth and renewal by the Holy Spirit." (Titus 3:5) This truth cannot be missed by the person whose heart is set on dwelling in his presence. "But if through the power of the Spirit you put to death the misdeeds of the flesh, you will live." (Rom 8:13) While freedom from the penalty of past sin can be obtained through the sacrifice of Christ, it is the sanctifying work provided by his indwelling Spirit that is the means of "eternal salvation" (Col 1:27)[208] and escape from his wrath. Paul taught that the believer must co-operate with the Spirit when he stated that *"you"* have to put to death the misdeeds of the flesh. The Spirit has the ability to give victory over the temptation to sin and to transform the wicked heart so that it is acceptable to God.

> It is the sanctifying work provided by his indwelling Spirit that is the means of "eternal salvation."

Paul told the Galatians, "But if you are led by the Spirit, you are not under law." (Gal 5:18) And to the Romans he stated that "those who are led by the Spirit of God are sons of God." (Rom 8:13-14) It needs to be noted that Paul has required the believer to be led by the Spirit in order to live apart from the law and to be a son of God. The believer is not to be passive in the fight for righteousness but is to engage the battle for victory over the flesh. Victory is not something that is given him or her but is made possible for him or her and available to them; it requires a person's life to be lived through the enlightenment, leading, and power of the Holy Spirit.

---

[208] "Christ in you, the hope of glory."

Eternal Salvation

Jesus said, "I am the way and the truth *and the life*. No one comes to the Father except through me." (Jn 14:6) It is the "life" of Jesus in a person that is his or her hope. The Lord must be allowed to live his life through the believer, and he does that through his Spirit. Anyone who prevents the Spirit from doing his work has no eternal salvation. The Spirit was gifted for the very purpose of allowing the believer to live a righteous life and for the transformation of the heart.

It is obvious that a person needs to obediently follow Christ-the Holy Spirit- if he is to be led. All revelation and knowledge of the will of God for a person's life comes through the Holy Spirit.[209] Before the Lord was crucified, he promised that he, as well as the Father, would dwell in those who love him and that he would teach them. "But the Counsellor, the Holy Spirit, whom the Father will send in my name, will teach you all things and will remind you of everything I have said to you." (Jn 14:26) Later he stated, "When he comes, he will convict the world of guilt regarding sin and righteousness and judgment" (Jn 16:8), and "But when he, the Spirit of truth, comes, he will guide you into all truth." (Jn 16:13) He stated, "If anyone loves me, he will obey my teaching. My Father will love him, and we will come and make our home with him." (Jn 14:23) Paul identified this indwelling to be that of the Holy Spirit who would minister to them. It is the Spirit who leads for the development of truth and righteousness,[210] in the understanding of the Word of God, and in ministry. "No one knows the thoughts of God except the Spirit of God." (1 Cor 2:11)

The Spirit is presented as the source of "power"[211] *for the accomplishment of God's purposes in the believer's life*. It is he who *saves* through his sanctifying work. This sanctifying work is the achievement of holiness in a person's body. Only those whose bodies are sanctified-redeemed from evil interests- will be adopted as sons.[212]

> The believer not only has the Spirit, he or she also has Satan, the world's permissions, and their own evil natures that are attempting to guide them.

A person must be cautious however, in his or her pursuit for obedience. The believer not only has the Spirit, he or she also

---

[209] 1 Cor 2:14, NIV, "The man without the Spirit does not accept the things that come from the Spirit of God, for they are foolishness to him, and he cannot understand them because they are spiritually discerned. "
[210] Gal 5:5
[211] Rom 15:13, 19, 1:4; Lk 4:14
[212] Rom 8:23

has Satan, the world's permissions, and his or her own evil nature that are attempting to guide them. Satan is known as the deceiver[213] and a liar[214] and often uses half-truths and worldly wisdom to sooth a person's conscience. Also, a person must be certain that his or her understanding is from the Lord and not the manifestation of his or her own desires. Some claim to have received a vision, but not all visions are from the Lord. Audible voices have also been used by the Lord; however, many unspeakable crimes have been perpetrated by those who have claimed to have heard the Lord speaking to them. The Spirit will only lead a person in paths and understandings that agree with his revealed Word.

Although it is often practiced, it is dangerous to accept the leading of a person's heart or to be led by intuition. The Word of God often speaks of the wickedness of the heart of natural humans. "The heart is deceitful above all things and beyond cure. Who can understand it?" (Jer 17:10) Before responding to such leading it would be wise to be constant in prayer on the matter and to meditate on the Lord's teaching through his Word. Also, advice from another faithful servant of the Lord might be sought. Of course, the heart is *curable*, but only through the extensive ministry of the Spirit as a person submits to his sanctifying ministry so that his heart is transformed into that of the likeness of his Savior.

Just before his crucifixion, the Lord reminded his disciples that he would not leave them as orphans but would give them the Spirit who would teach them everything that he had said.[215] Neither does he teach anything contrary to that which Christ has taught because the Spirit is Christ.[216]

The Word of God is truth and it is the revelation of righteousness for humankind. The appropriateness of most actions can be discerned through knowledge of the Scriptures. However, humankind is weak and can easily be led astray. Not only does a person need the knowledge of truth but he or she needs the revelations and the promptings of the Spirit to protect him or her from the evils that would seek to devour their soul. The Spirit, the indwelling presence of Christ, is God's great gift to the redeemed, his hope of glory.[217]

---

[213] Rev 20:3, 8
[214] Jn 8:44
[215] Jn 14:26
[216] 2 Cor 2: 17-18
[217] Col 1:27

Awareness of sin's proximity and practice often comes through the promptings of the Spirit. This prompting is presented through unrest in a person's conscience and the believer should be guided by it.[218] A person's conscience is a measure of his or her moral consciousness. It is the Spirit's ministry to bring God's Word to memory so that the believer is conscious or convicted of his or her offence toward their creator. Peter addressed the issue of moral consciousness concerning knowledge and action in the following manner: "Anyone, then, who knows the good he ought to do and doesn't do it, sins." (Jas 4:17)

It is through a person's conscience that conviction of sin comes. Paul has revealed the role of the conscience in his own life. "Now this is our boast: Our conscience testifies that we have conducted ourselves in the world, and especially in our relations with you, in the holiness and sincerity that are from God. We have done so not according to worldly wisdom but according to God's grace." (2 Cor 1:12) [219] It was Paul's boast that he had kept a good conscience according to God's grace (the conviction of the Spirit). Further, John taught. "If our hearts do not condemn us, we have confidence before God...because we obey his commands and do what pleases him." (1 Jn 3:21-22)

The conscience, of course, can be denied or as Paul has recorded in his letter to Timothy. "The Spirit clearly says that in the later times some will abandon the faith and follow deceiving spirits and things taught by demons. Such teachings come through hypocritical liars, whose consciences have been seared as by a hot iron." (1 Tim 4:1-2) It is dangerous for a person to defy his or her conscience and the leading of the Spirit. Over time a person will not be able to hear the righteous call of God upon his or her life at all and the result will be destruction.[220] Those whose consciences have been seared are vulnerable to being deceived by hypocrites and deceiving spirits and may eventually abandon their faith.

The searing of the conscience results when a person has been persuaded to pursue his or her own interests and to abandon the Spirit. A person's conscience is not seared by others, or by the Spirit. Searing comes about through each person's own choices as he or she submits to their will in

---

[218] "conscience is translated from the Greek *suneidesis* which means "co-perception, i.e. moral consciousness: —conscience." –from Strong's Greek Dictionary #4893

[219] An example of the conscience as a convicting agent is given in Jn 8:9.

[220] 2 Thess 1:8-9; See also Phil 3:18-19

order to engage in unlawful activities which callous or harden his or her heart against the prompting of the Spirit. When the redeemed person made a confession of faith, they declared that Christ would be lord of their life[221] and that means hating his or her life for the sake of the Lord. "The man who loves his life will lose it, while the man who hates his life in this world will keep it for eternal life." (Jn 12:25) The Spirit was gifted to help the redeemed accomplish holiness, to become a sacrifice acceptable to God.[222] God knows the mind of the Spirit[223] and those changes that the Spirit is trying to bring about in a person's life, and he may work through punishment, discipline[224], and blessings, to accomplish his will. The holy ones will be God's workmanship, *his* re-creation, so that no person can boast.[225] The need of everyone is the transformation to holiness and only those who are prepared and committed to obeying him will accomplish that state.

Paul told the Galatians, "But by faith we eagerly await through the Spirit the righteousness for which we hope." (Gal 5:5) Our necessary righteousness comes through the Spirit's leading. The way this is accomplished is through a person's knowledge of the Scriptures and through the Spirit's *convicting* followed up with an obedient response. If the believer is "awaiting" this righteousness, it must not yet be his or hers, as some would present. As Paul told the Colossians, the mystery that had been hidden for so long is, "Christ in you, the hope of glory." (Col 1:27)

It is not complicated to be led in the path of righteousness. God has provided all that is necessary[226] through the knowledge of his Word and the enlightenment, leading, and power of the Spirit. This, however, requires the reading of his Word and sensitivity to the Spirit. Through time, exercising

---

[221] Rom 10: 9-10
[222] Rom 15:16
[223] Rom 8:17
[224] Hebrews 12:6, NIV. "The Lord disciplines those he loves, and he punishes everyone he accepts as a son." Heb 12: 10, NIV. "God disciplines us for our good, in order that we may share in his holiness."
[225] Eph 2:9; Paul has frequently referred to his readers as "sons" of God. In doing so he is presuming that they are practicing obedience to the gospel. Not all who read his writings would have made a confession of belief, so not all readers are "sons of God." Paul has stated that adoption as a son occurs when *the body has been redeemed* and that we are eagerly waiting for this to happen. "Belief" implies obedience and is not merely mental assent of something. (See Heb 2:18-19)
[226] 2 Pet 1:3

Eternal Salvation

the Spirit's leadership,[227] and humility of attitude, attending to the Spirit becomes easier. The Lord spoke to the masses, "Take my yoke upon you and learn from me, for I am gentle and humble in heart, and you will find rest for your souls. *For my yoke is easy and my burden is light.*" (Mt 11:28-30) And, John has written, "This is love for God: to obey his commands. And his commands are not burdensome." (1 Jn 5:3) The Lord did not say that the believer would not have any burden but that the burden would not be heavy.

> The greatest error that a redeemed person can make is to deny the leadership of the Spirit in his or her life.

The greatest error that a redeemed person can make is to deny the leadership of the Spirit in his or her life. To do so will prevent their transformation into the likeness of Christ and without this change, they will not "see"[228] the Lord.[229] They will not be in a place of proximity to their Savior. In fact, Paul states that if, through the Spirit, a person does not overcome their evil nature they will die.[230] He wrote that "He will punish those who do not know [understand] God and do not obey the gospel of our Lord Jesus. They will be punished with everlasting destruction and shut out from the presence of the Lord and from the majesty of his power. On the day that he comes to be glorified in his holy people and to be marvelled at among those who have believed." (2 Thess 1:8-10)

Some will abandon the faith[231], and deny the Spirit[232], while others will quench the Spirit[233], or grieve the Spirit[234], and all have been cautioned not to blaspheme the Spirit.[235] To deny the Spirit does not mean that a person

---

[227] The writer of Hebrews refers to this as "training" oneself (Hebrews 5:14, NIV), and states that it is accomplished through "constant use" of the Word of God "to distinguish good from evil."

[228] "see" is translated from the Greek *optanomai* which means "to gaze (i.e. with wide-open eyes, as at something remarkable; and thus differing from 991, which denotes simply voluntary observation; and from 1492, which expresses merely mechanical, passive or casual vision; while 2300, and still more emphatically its intensive 2334, signifies an earnest but more continued inspection; and 4648 a watching from a distance): —appear, look, see, shew self." –from Strong's Greek Dictionary #3700

[229] Heb 12:14, NIV

[230] Rom 8:13-14

[231] 1 Tim 4:1

[232] 2 Tim 3:5

[233] 1 Thess 5:19

[234] Eph 4:30

[235] Mk 3:28

mentally asserts that the Spirit does not exist but that he or she prevents or denies the Spirit's ministry in their life. Those who quench or grieve the Spirit do not follow his leading; they have relented again to directing their own path and to ruling their own lives.

Some take blaspheming the Spirit to mean speaking demeaning or degrading insults, however it also refers to the abandonment of his ministry. God told the prophet Ezekiel, "…your fathers blasphemed me by *forsaking me*." (Ezek 20:27) Christ cautioned his listeners, "But, whoever blasphemes against the Holy Spirit will never be forgiven; he is guilty of an eternal sin." (Mk 3:29)

To deny the Spirit's leadership, or to be ignorant of his ministry in a person's life, leads to grave consequences. God is sovereign and the believer has confessed that Christ is his or her Lord;[236] for a person not to allow the Spirit to direct their life is to deny the majesty and glory of God and to walk in darkness.

Paul enlightened his readers concerning the relationship between the one who searches our hearts and the Spirit. He has recorded, "And he who searches our hearts knows the mind of the Spirit, because the Spirit intercedes for the saints in accordance with God's will." (Rom 8:27) The one who searches our hearts[237] gets to "know" us. Through the Spirit's "intercession" the Father becomes more familiar with us because the Spirit communes with him. In this regard the Lord stated, "Not everyone who says to me 'Lord, Lord,' will enter the kingdom of heaven, but only he who does the will of my Father who is in heaven. Many will say to me on that day, 'Lord, Lord, did we not prophesy in your name, and in your name drive out demons and perform many miracles?' Then I will tell them plainly, 'I never knew[238] you. Away from me you evil-doers!' Therefore, everyone who hears these words of mine and puts them into practice

---

[236] Rom 10:9

[237] "he who searches our hearts" is the Father (Ps 139:1). Much is made about the Lord's teaching that it is the Father's will that He should lose none of those that the Father has given him. (Jn 6:39) and that "no one can come to me unless the Father draws him." (Jn 6:44) It should be considered that he who searches our hearts works with the Spirit to achieve his will. "Everyone who listens to the Father and learns from him comes to me." (Jn 6:45) This "learning" may come from punishment and discipline among other sources.

[238] "Knew" in this instance means *certainty* of understanding. That is, although these people had professed Christ as lord, and had been given the Holy Spirit, the testimony of their lives created uncertainty about their commitment to Him.

is like a wise man who built his house on the rock." (Mt 7:21-24) Even though some may be used for God's purposes, because of their denial of his sovereign rule regarding righteousness they will be cast from him. The claim of Christ will be that he had never known them.

God's Word is clear that the redeemed person is to be holy as he is holy,[239] and that without holiness no one will see the Lord.[240] A person can either use God's provision to accomplish the transformed mind and heart that leads to this state, or he or she can attempt to accomplish it, as revealed in the law and the prophets, using their own resources. Those "in Christ" have been redeemed from the law and enjoy the presence of Christ in them, the Holy Spirit, to meet this great need. God is holy and all who are privileged to dwell with him must be and will be, as well.

4.6 The Leading of the Spirit for Righteousness

The law, if it could have been honored would have led the obedient person in a righteous walk. It could not be kept. A person's evil nature will always demand appeasement. Paul taught, "For what the law was powerless to do in that it was weakened by the sinful nature, God did by sending his own Son in the likeness of sinful man to be a sin offering. And so he condemned sin in sinful man, in order that the righteous requirements of the law might be fully met in us, who do not live according to the sinful nature but according to the Spirit." (Rom 8:3-4) Rather than having to obey the law and the prophets, the believer has been provided the better means of attaining holiness in mind and heart, and that is through living according to the Spirit who will lead and empower him in meeting the righteous requirements of the law.

> The clearest way to hear the Spirit concerning issues of righteousness is to become familiar with what is good and what is evil through God's Word.

The clearest way to hear the Spirit concerning issues of righteousness is to become familiar with what is good and what is evil through God's Word. The Spirit uses the Word of God to bring knowledge and understanding to the believer. Peter has written, "His divine power has given us everything we need for life and godliness through our *knowledge*

---

[239] 1 Pet 1:16
[240] Heb 12:14

of him who called us by his own glory and goodness. Through these he has given us his very great and precious promises, so that *through them you may participate in the divine nature* and escape the corruption in the world caused by evil desires." (2 Pet 1:3-4) The Bible is the Word of God and was given so that his people might participate in his divine nature. The righteousness of his nature is revealed in his Word and victory for it is empowered through his Spirit.

If the Spirit is to bring to remembrance the teachings of Christ, a person must *read* or otherwise become knowledgeable concerning his Word; he or she must know it. The Spirit cannot bring to remembrance those things about which a person has not first been informed. It is essential that the believer is faithful in his or her study. The achievement of righteousness leading to holiness is important. Proverbs records, "The discerning heart seeks knowledge." (Prov 15:4)

Not only does the Spirit bring God's Word to the believer's awareness, he *teaches* through the reading and the hearing of the Word. A person should be open and prepared to allow the Lord to direct his or her understanding and to inform their heart concerning the truths that he would have them gain. These can be very person specific since each person is an individual in which Christ is working to achieve holiness. The believer is *God's "masterpiece"* (Eph 2:10, NLT) or *"workmanship"* (Eph 2:10, KJV) and He works individually in each of his redeemed to achieve the state of holiness.

The way a person is "led" is dependent upon the method which the Spirit chooses, but it is always the Spirit who leads for the accomplishment of God's purposes. The Spirit may convict a person's conscience-he may disturb his moral consciousness- he may lead directly through the Word by bringing a teaching to a person's attention, he may bring others or circumstances into a person's life to direct him or her to his will, and he may use visions or dreams. Some have even heard the voice of God speaking directly to them which was a common procedure in the time of the prophets.

4.7 The Leading of the Spirit for Service

Although the believer was called[241] and gifted for service[242] at the time of his profession of faith, the Lord may not be able to use him, at least for noble purposes. Righteous practices as developed by the Spirit are the first need of the believer for the provision of his eternal salvation and to fit him for service.

Although the Spirit leads for building the kingdom, failure in service does not in itself lead to condemnation to the lake of burning sulphur, although it will lead to severe judgment. Paul stated that fire (judgment) will test each man's service. "If what he has built survives, he will receive his reward. If it is burned up [of no worth], he will suffer loss; he himself will be saved, but only as one escaping through the flames." (1 Cor 3:14) He may be cast outside the walls of the New Jerusalem.[243]

It is Paul's teaching that those whose walk is unrighteous are unfit for doing anything good. "They claim to know God, but by their actions they deny him. They are detestable, disobedient and unfit for doing anything good." (Titus 1:16) He has also presented that a person needs to cleanse himself or herself if they desire to be used for noble purposes. "In a large house there are articles not only of gold and silver, but also of wood and clay; some are used for noble purposes and some for ignoble. If man cleanses himself from the latter, he will be an instrument for noble purposes, made holy, useful to the Master and prepared to do any good work." (2 Tim 2:20-21) He told the Philippians that they were to "be blameless in a crooked and depraved generation" in which they are to shine as lights in the world.[244] Christ said that his disciples were to let their light shine so that humankind would see their good works and glorify God in heaven.[245]

> God cannot honorably use those whose conduct would misrepresent him and defame his good name.

God cannot honorably use those whose conduct would misrepresent him and defame his good name. That is, the believer is to reveal Christ to those around him. Because of his great name, he leads first

---

[241] Eph 2:10
[242] 1 Cor 12: 7-11
[243] Mt 25:30
[244] Phil 2:15
[245] Mt 5:16

towards righteousness and then into ministry. All believers have been redeemed for ministry and will be judged according their work in regard to their calling.[246]

Paul told the Romans, "Do not conform any longer to the pattern of this world but be transformed by the renewing of your mind. *Then you will be able to test and approve what God's will is-his good, pleasing and perfect will.*" (Rom 12:2) God's will for the believer can only be discerned by the person who clings to him and develops a "renewed" mind; that person will be able to recognize the will or mind of God.

Many claim that they do not know the gift for service that they have been given. However, the person who is bent on obedience will understand what he is being called to when the need arises.

There are ways to discern a person's gifting and God's will regarding that gifting. It needs to be appreciated that God gifts for a purpose and he will endeavour to use the believer in the capacity of the gift that he or she has been given. As a person looks back over the ministry opportunities presented to him or her and considers those occasions where they have been most fruitful, they should gain some idea of the gift that they possess. The ministry should bring that person joy as well. Of course, a person might also gain knowledge of his gifting from other believers.

Personal ministry is more individually specific than corporate ministry. Concerning individual ministry, the Spirit is more apt to prompt a person to use the gifting that he has determined for his servant according to the needs of the church body than to direct him to minister in another way. Accordingly, a person might be particularly sensitive to discernment of ministry opportunities according to the use of his gifting. For example, the person with the gift of "helps" should be especially sensitive to the Spirit's ministry leading in this regard.

Some readily profess that they have been called by God into a certain ministry. To say that a person has been called by "faith" to pursue a ministry means that he or she has been "persuaded" by the Spirit of their calling. If such is the case, they need to pursue it with their whole heart, otherwise they risk being rebellious or demonstrating a lack of faith. If a person has not been called, their efforts will soon reveal themselves.

Seeking corporate direction is somewhat different than gaining direction for personal ministry. However, both require discernment

---

[246] 1 Cor 3:11-15

through faith or persuasion. There is no biblical record of God calling a body to undertake a certain course other than through an individual who has been called to take leadership in the matter. Moses, Joshua, David, Nehemiah and the husband of the family[247] come to mind. The person who has been called for corporate leadership needs to use their gifting to enlist the assistance of others according to their gifting in order to accomplish the Lord's will.

4.8 Facing Trials

Many believers are of the opinion that once they have expressed faith in Christ only good things are to come their way. Not only do they think it but they pray to that end and get discouraged when their prayers are not answered. Such thinking is based on the understanding that God is love and that love always accommodates their perceived need. The Scriptures do not reveal this to be true. People are not being brought into the Kingdom to have their needs met; they are being brought in to satisfy God's plan which is the building of a righteous Kingdom, a "kingdom of priests and a holy nation." (Ex 19:6) [248] It is true, however, that the Lord will bless those, even according to their immediate *needs*, who are humble before him and who walk in obedience to his Word and will. Nevertheless, blessings must be seen from an eternal perspective. In the eyes of the Lord, discipline and punishment are to be considered *blessings* and acts of love. The Christian life is not about having a person's worldly interests satisfied; it is about honoring God through the building of his kingdom and through righteous practices making the believer *"an offering acceptable to God, sanctified by the Holy Spirit."* (Rom 15:16)

> Purging the mind, heart, and body of its sin-interests does not come without discomfort and even pain.

Purging the mind, heart, and body of its sin-interests does not come without discomfort and even pain. The practices that a person has developed are those that have appealed to him or her. Their practices have satisfied them in some manner. Evil practices have pleased

---

[247] Eph 5:22-23; 1 Pet 3:1
[248] See also 1 Pet 2:9

their evil nature, and these must be defeated since only those who are *victorious* will enjoy the presence of God.[249]

Trials come to prove and to build a person's faith. It is easy to be persuaded of the gospel when things are going well; however, it is during adversity that a person's faith proves itself and is built. James wrote, "Consider it pure joy, my brothers, whenever you face trials of many kinds, because you know that the testing of your faith develops perseverance. Perseverance must finish its work so that you may be mature and complete, not lacking anything." (Jas 1:2)

It is not uncommon for confessors to abandon their faith when trials present themselves or when the Lord does not respond according to their wants and wishes. Strong faith is the possession of those who have rested in the Lord and his promises during times of tribulation. They have proven his faithfulness and their faith has grown. It must be remembered that it is those who have given their lives in testimony to the Lord who will be most highly honored; the "cowardly" will be given a place in the fiery lake of burning sulphur.[250]

Christ praised the church in Ephesus because of their perseverance. "You have persevered and have endured hardships for my name and have not grown weary." (Rev 2:3) The believer *will* face trials and tribulations. Satan has not finished his work. He will lie and mislead, distract and discourage; however, the true believer must stand[251] strong and rest their confidence in the Lord. Paul encouraged, "And we know that in all things God works for the good of those who love him, who have been called according to his purpose." (Rom 8:28) Sometimes it is God's intent and purpose to cleanse the believer from unrighteous practices so that he or she might become an offering acceptable to him[252] and cleansing can be uncomfortable.

Although in a person's pride they might find it hard to accept, he or she begins their spiritual walk as a child-a new birth, a new creation- and the Lord often deals with him or her as a parent might a child. For the sake of their own eternal welfare, the Lord will bring discipline and punishment in order to train a person so that he or she might learn to distinguish good from evil.[253] "My son, do not make light of the Lord's discipline, and do

---

[249] Rev 21:7
[250] Rev 21: 8
[251] Eph 6:10-18
[252] Rom 15:16
[253] Heb 6:14

not lose heart when he rebukes you, because the Lord disciplines those he loves, and he punishes everyone he accepts as a son. God disciplines us for our good that we may share in his holiness. No discipline seems pleasant at the time, but painful. Later, however, it produces a harvest of righteousness and peace for those who have been trained in it." (Heb 12:5-6, 10-11) This training is an act of love because those who relent to it will become suitable to dwell with their Lord eternally. Those who rebel and reject it will be eternally separated from him.[254]

> The believer is *not* called to a life of ease and pleasure; he is called to a life of suffering and persecution and is required to persevere for righteousness' sake and for the kingdom.

The believer is *not* called to a life of ease and pleasure but to a life of suffering and persecution and is required to persevere for righteousness' sake and for the kingdom. Standing strong and remaining faithful will provide rewards in the end. Paul clearly presented the need for perseverance: "By this gospel you are saved, if you hold firmly to the word I preached to you. Otherwise you have believed in vain." (1 Cor 15:2) Christ taught that only a few would find the gate that leads to life.[255] The Lord expects a person to remain faithful even though faithfulness might lead to death.

Discontentment with what a person has or his state in life often leads to abandoning faith and commitment. The believer is not to entertain such a heart attitude. The Lord knows the *needs* of his children and will provide for them.[256] There is no place for greed in the Christian life. "Put to death, therefore, whatever belongs to your earthly nature: sexual immorality, impurity, lust, *evil desires and greed, which is idolatry*. Because of these things the wrath of God is coming." (Col 3:5-6) John has written, "Do not love the world or anything in the world. If anyone loves the world, the love of the Father is not in him." (Jn 2:15) As long as a person focuses on satisfying his or her need for comfort, however that is envisioned, their commitment cannot be to the Lord. Contentment with godliness

---

[254] Heb 12:14; 2 Thess 1:8-9 (NLT) "He will come with his mighty angels, in flaming fire, bringing judgment on those who don't know God and on those who refuse to obey the Good News of our Lord Jesus. They will be punished with eternal destruction, forever separated from the Lord and from his glorious power.
[255] Mt 7:14
[256] Mt 6: 31-33

brings peace to a person's life and great gain eternally. The Lord wants his children to pursue a relationship with him rather than to grovel for the manna of the world. "Keep your lives free from the love of money and be content with what you have, because the Lord has said, 'Never will I leave you; never will I forsake you.'" (Heb 13:5)

Trials may be put in a person's path for the Lord to "train" him or her, or even because of the ungodly decisions that they have made as they have chosen to exercise control of their lives. The Lord desires to keep them but he will not over-ride a person's God-gifted right to exercise free-will. Satan also wants to reclaim them.

James has written, "Blessed is the man who perseveres under trial, because when he has stood the test, he will receive the crown of life that God has promised to those who love him." (Jas 1:12)[257] Trials are a part of the true believer's life and he or she must cling to their Lord and persevere through them for their own eternal welfare.

4.9 The Fight for Victory

Once the Holy Spirit has been gifted, the redeemed person has both the Spirit of Holiness and the spirit of his or her evil nature contending for their attention. The fight is on! The believer's flesh is still very much with him or her demanding appeasement and comfort. The world gives them permission to act in ways that are contrary to God's will, and the evil one is still trying to reclaim another soul who is escaping from his grasp. The person who continues to sin or who loves darkness will *not* be a "permanent" member of the family of God.[258]

Paul told the Ephesians to put on the full armour of God.[259] The believer is to put on the "*belt of truth,*" "*the breastplate of righteousness,*" to have "*feet fitted with the readiness that comes from the gospel of peace,*" to carry "*the shield of faith,*" to be covered with "*the helmet of salvation,*" and, to buckle on "*the sword of the Spirit, which is the word of God.*" He or she

---

[257] In Hebrews it is recorded: "You need to persevere so that when you have done the will of God, you will receive what he has promised." (Heb 10:36, NIV)
[258] Jn 8: 34-35. "Jesus replied, 'I tell you the truth, everyone who sins is a slave to sin. Now a slave has no permanent place in the family, but a son [the person led by the Spirit, Rom 8:14] belongs to it forever.'" (NIV)
[259] Eph 6:10-18

is to stand strong and to resist the temptations that they encounter. There will be many challenges and the struggle for victory will cause suffering for the person who would be victorious; it did for Christ in his own walk in the flesh.[260] The walk in the Spirit is not an easy one but the person who perseveres in the Lord will be victorious. The Lord has revealed that it will be those who overcome who will enjoy the promise of his eternal presence.[261] The Spirit's ministry is to make the believer *an offering acceptable to God*. This truth should never be lost.

> The believer is *not* called to a passive or an indifferent life; it is purposeful and is to be committed.

The believer is called to put to death the deeds of his or her sinful nature,[262] to purify themselves from everything that contaminates body and spirit, perfecting holiness,[263] to put off their old selves,[264] to not grieve the Holy Spirit by their actions,[265] to live a life filled with love,[266] to have the same attitude that Christ had,[267] to work at living in peace,[268] to get rid of all moral filth and evil,[269] to live as God's obedient children,[270] to avoid evil,[271] to live a holy life,[272] and to obey God's

---

[260] The writer of Hebrews states. "During the days of Jesus' life on earth, he offered up prayers and petitions with loud cries and tears to the one who could save him from death, and *he was heard because of his reverent submission*. Although he was a son he learned obedience from what he suffered and once made perfect became the source of eternal salvation for all who obey him." (Heb 5:7) Jesus could have suffered death (This "suffering" references the "days of Jesus' life on earth" and does not specifically refer to the agony He suffered before his crucifixion because He was not saved from this death.) if he had not continued to work out his own salvation through obedience to the Father. Destruction also awaits those who do not use his provision to defeat sin and to live righteously.
[261] Rev 21:7
[262] Rom 8:13
[263] 2 Cor 7:1
[264] Eph 4:22
[265] Eph 4:30
[266] Eph 5:2
[267] Phil 2:5
[268] Heb 12:14
[269] Jas 1:21
[270] 1 Pet 1:14
[271] 1 Thess 5:22
[272] 2 Tim 1:9

commandments.[273] These things cannot be accomplished without engaging the battle against the flesh, society, and the evil one. The believer is *not* called to a passive or an indifferent life; it is to be purposeful and is to be committed. Christ must be allowed to live in him or her and through them.

It is often suggested that Christ has won the victory, and he has for those "in him." However, to claim that victory a person must "remain" in him. Christ did not sin while on this earth and he will not while in the believer. If a person chooses to sin, he or she is no longer in the Lord, because the Lord would not sin. The Lord has been victorious over all things that could have prevented him and could prevent those "in him" from entering his eternal kingdom. However, he must fight the life of faith for righteousness with each person who would dwell with him. Peter has clearly presented, "His divine power has given us everything we need for life and godliness." (2 Pet 1:3) The believer must engage the battle for righteousness through fellowship with the Lord. "God, who has called you into fellowship (partnership, NLT) with his Son Jesus Christ our Lord, is faithful - *"to keep you strong to the end. (v. 8)"* (1 Cor 1:9)

The ministry and mission of Christ is to defeat the works of Satan[274] and to restore fallen humankind so that God's Kingdom and plan could be brought to fullness. Understanding eternal salvation might be easier to grasp if the full ministry of Christ as teacher, sacrifice, Lord, Holy Spirit, and High Priest is appreciated.

4.10 Gaining Victory

The importance of "walking in the light" or of being "led by the Spirit" cannot be overstated. Paul told the Galatians, "But if you are led by the Spirit, you are not under law." (Gal 5:18) And to the Romans he stated, "For if you live according to the sinful nature, you will die; but if by the Spirit you put to death the misdeeds of the body you will live, because those who are led by the Spirit of God are sons of God." (Rom 8:13-14) Paul has required the believer to put to death the misdeeds of the body in order to live and be a son of God. The redeemed person is not to be passive in the fight for righteousness but is to engage the battle for victory.

---

[273] 1 Jn 5:3
[274] 1 Jn 3:8

Eternal Salvation

Victory is not something that is given a person but is made possible for him or her and is available to them; it requires a person's lifetime to be lived through the enlightenment, leading, and power of the Holy Spirit. The Lord stated that it would be those who overcome[275] who would inherit his kingdom. It is Paul's teaching that there is a way to victory over all temptations. "No temptation has seized you except what is common to man. And God is faithful; he will not let you be tempted beyond what you can bear. But when you are tempted, he will also provide a way out so that you can stand up under it." (1 Cor 10:13) And Peter taught that "God's divine power-the Holy Spirit- has given us everything we need for life and godliness." (2 Pet 1:3) Victory is very possible for those living in Christ[276]; he gained it for himself and he will attain it for the obedient believer. Some would excuse their sins and sinning on the basis that they are fallible human beings but allowing themselves such permission can only be entertained if they fail to appreciate the ministry of the Lord "in" them.

> The *requirement* for life, as Paul has presented, is that in conjunction with the Holy Spirit the believer must put *"the misdeeds of the body to death"*, or be finished with them.

The *requirement* for life, as Paul has presented, is that in conjunction with the Holy Spirit the believer must put *"the misdeeds of the body to death"* or be finished with them. Because the issue of the Spirit's leadership is vitally important, an understanding of how His leadership is achieved in a person's walk and transformation needs to be made clear for each one who desires to escape the death of the law and to be called a "son" of God.

The believer's walk of righteousness is based on his or her "knowledge" of the glory of God and this is firstly revealed in the "face" of Jesus. "For God, who said, 'Let light shine out of darkness,' made his light shine in our hearts to give us the light of the knowledge of the glory of God in the face of Christ." (2 Cor 4:6) Christ, through the Spirit, is shining in the hearts of those who have been redeemed and only through him can the veil that separates the believer from God be taken away allowing the believer to know him. Knowledge comes through the Spirit. Not only is the veil taken away so that the redeemed one can see the Lord, but it is removed allowing his life and righteousness to be *displayed* in the believer's life for the benefit of others.

---

[275] Rev 21:7
[276] "greater is he that is in you, than he that is in the world." (1 Jn 4:4, KJV)

The *"knowledge of the glory of God in the face of Jesus"* is that which allows a person to be like his or her Lord and Savior. The "face" of Jesus is the person of Jesus. His person is revealed both directly by the Spirit and as the Spirit leads through the study of his heart through the Word.

Even through the Spirit the redeemed person cannot fully discern the image of Christ. Paul says that the believer sees it as a *poor reflection*. "Now I see but a poor reflection as in a mirror; then we shall see face to face. Now I know in part; then I shall know fully, even as I am fully known." (1 Cor 13:12) Since knowledge of God's glory is not fully understood, those walking this earth will never be fully conformed to Christ's likeness. His glory is only reflected through his Word and by His Spirit, and possibly in the lives of other saints. When he returns, however, those who have remained "in him" *will be like Him* because they will see him as He is.[277] They will not be seeing a poor reflection, but they will rest their eyes on him and will see him in his glory-his image will be clear and perfect. This does not mean that that "looking at" the Lord will automatically transform a person into his likeness, but that those seeing him will have full knowledge of his glory and through his power and their submission will be able to appropriate it.

The new person -rescued from the misdeeds of the body- is not put on instantaneously. Paul taught that it is put on through the "knowledge" gained from Christ according to his revelation of himself in a person's heart. Like any relationship, the closer that relationship the better one person knows another. That is, as the believer comes to "knowing" what Christ is like in his purity and holiness, he or she is able to become like their Lord.[278] "But we all, with unveiled face beholding as in a mirror the glory of the Lord, are changed into the same image from glory to glory, even as by the Spirit of the Lord." (2 Cor 3:18, KJV2000) As we "behold" the glory of the Lord and gain knowledge through the Holy Spirit, he leads us into conformity with him. Christ is in the believer, and as he lives through that person, the person who has died to self and is alive with Christ is *one* with Him-he or she takes on the Lord's image. He or

---

[277] 1 Jn 3:2

[278] 2 Cor 3:18 Paul spoke of there being a veil hiding the glory of God from the sight of the Israelites. That veil remains for those under the law but is made visible by those in Christ. "It has not been removed because only in Christ is it taken away." (2 Cor 3:14)

she comes to know the Lord's heart. Only through Christ is confusion and blindness removed and God's glory made visible. "And we, who with unveiled faces all reflect the Lord's glory, are being transformed into his likeness with ever increasing glory, which comes from the Lord, who is the Spirit." (2 Cor 3:18)

Paul has also admonished that even though some have gained knowledge, they will not like to retain that knowledge and the Lord will turn them over to a "depraved mind." (Rom 1:28) He encouraged his readers by saying that they have put off the old self with its practices and have put on the new self that is being renewed in the knowledge of the image of its creator.[279] The old self has only been put off when its interests have been defeated and victory has been gained over practices such as sexual immorality, impurity, lust, evil desires, greed, anger etc. The Spirit transforms and sanctifies and this accomplishment takes time; it is being *awaited*.[280] It also takes commitment to a person's faith, including "obedience", which is *faith in practice*[281] and a clinging to the Lord, gazing into his glory, for the person who desires to know him.

There is a righteous walk to be lived through the Spirit. "If we claim to have fellowship with Christ and yet walk in darkness, we lie and do not live by the truth. If we walk in the light, as he is in the light, we have fellowship with one another, and the blood of Jesus, his Son, purifies us from all sin." (1 Jn 1:6-7) And Jesus had revealed that "everyone who loves and practices falsehood" (Rev 22:15) will find himself or herself separated from God's presence and outside the walls of the New Jerusalem. "He will punish those who do not know -*understand*- God and do not obey the gospel of our Lord Jesus. They will be punished with everlasting destruction and shut out from the presence of the Lord and from the majesty of his power on the day he comes to be glorified in his holy people." (2 Thess 1:8-9)

The blood of Jesus purifies from all sin only those who walk in the light. "But *if* we walk in the light, as he is in the light, we have fellowship with one another and the blood of Jesus, his Son, purifies us from all sin." (1 Jn 1:7) The inclusion of "if" in John's teaching makes a person's access to the cleansing by the blood of Jesus *conditioned to* his or her walking in the light, or as the writer of Hebrews has stated, conditioned to "obedience."

---

[279] Col 3:9-10
[280] Gal 5:5
[281] Heb 4:2

The body must be considered dead along with a person's earthly nature. Paul told the Colossians, "Put to death, therefore, -so that you can appear with him in glory- whatever belongs to your earthly nature: sexual immorality, impurity, lust, evil desires and greed, which is idolatry. Because of these the wrath of God is coming...You must rid yourselves of all such things as these: anger, rage, malice, slander, and filthy language from your lips. Do not lie to each other." (Col 3:5-9) Paul presented a similar list in his letter to the Ephesians but added a caveat: "No immoral, impure or greedy person—such a man is an idolater-has any inheritance in the kingdom of Christ and of God. Let no one deceive you with empty words, for because of such things God's wrath comes on those who are disobedient." (Eph 5:5-6) Ridding oneself of the evil that constitutes his "earthly nature" is a *command* given to *every believer*.[282]

> Paul has stated that a person can re-build that which he has destroyed. That is, the law.

Paul has stated that a person can re-build that which he has destroyed. That is, the law.[283] It should be noted that he was speaking to those who are "seeking to be justified[284] through Christ's resurrected life. These people have been graced with his Spirit-his resurrected life[285]- but have rejected his leadership.

Escape from the law, or death to the law, came through the body of Christ. "So, my brothers, you also died to the law through the body of Christ so that you might belong to another, to him who was raised from the dead, in order that we might bear fruit to God." (Rom 7:4) [286] Paul told the Galatians, "He redeemed us ...so that by faith we might receive

---

[282] In his great commission Jesus stated that his disciples were to "go and make disciples of all nations, baptizing them in the name of the Father and of the Son and of the Holy Spirit, *and teaching them to obey everything that I have commanded you*. (Mt 28:19-20) The obedience portion of this commission is often ignored as a part of the Lord's commission but is essential to a person's salvation.

[283] Gal 2:17-18

[284] A person should not confuse the justification that comes at confession of faith through the blood of Christ and which allowed for his or her redemption (Rom 5:9) with the justification that comes through the Lord's resurrection by allowing his presence-the Holy Spirit- in them. In Romans, Paul stated, "He was delivered over to death for our sins and was raised to life for our justification." (Rom 4:24, NIV) James has made it clear that a person's justification requires obedience to the Spirit. "You see a person is justified by what he does and not by faith alone." (Jas 2:24, NIV)

[285] 2 Cor 3:17-18; Col 1:27

[286] See also Heb 9:15

the promise of the Spirit." (Rom 4:24)[287] Accordingly, the believer was redeemed *so that he or she might receive the Spirit* and bear fruit to God.

Paul presented the nature of his ministry to King Agrippa, "I preached that they should repent and turn to God and *prove their repentance by their deeds.*" (Acts 26:20) Paul did not allow his listeners to rest in a profession of repentance but required its proof by their actions.

Victory must be attained by the person who would dwell with the Lord. He or she is to engage the fight through the ministry of the Holy Spirit-Christ in him or her. The spiritual life that would bring eternal salvation cannot be lived passively regarding the things of God but must be actively and committedly pursued.

---

[287] See also Jas 2:24

Chapter 5

Putting Issues into Perspective

5.1 Repentance and Salvation

There can be no hope of salvation without repentance. It is humankind's evil imaginations that brought the wrath of God on his created people, even bringing to destruction most of humankind through the great flood of Noah's day. The history of Israel, and of all nations, has revealed stubbornness and pride and a failure to acknowledge God and his government. Those who continue in the state of disregard of their creator and of rebellion against him will also face destruction. However, the Psalmist has written, "The sacrifices of God are a broken spirit; a broken spirit and a contrite heart, O God, you will not despise." (Ps 51:17, KJV) [288] Pride of heart prevents the lost from repenting, but a broken spirit and a contrite heart are pleasing to God.

God created the world and everything in it; it belongs to him. Those who finally recognize this truth and repent of the sorrow that they have brought to him, and who desire to live under his authority will be given right to his eternal kingdom if pride and arrogance do not once more separate them from him. The Lord taught the need for repentance: "Unless you repent, you will all perish." (Lk 13:3)

Pride before the Lord is a most detestable sin. It indicates that a person considers himself or herself to be equal to, or superior to, their creator and that their sin should be acceptable. God will not give his glory to another and will not suffer his being to be defamed or belittled. An attitude of humility that recognizes the sovereignty and majesty of God needs to pervade a person's soul. Humility is a truthful attitude that appreciates God as creator and provider

---

[288] "The Lord is close to the broken-hearted and saves those who are crushed in spirit." (Ps 34:18) See also: Isa 55:7

and people as created and needy. Repentance is an act of contrition before an awesome and holy God. It acknowledges the creator's superiority and right to govern as well as a person's contravention of God's righteous standards.

> Repentance is an act of contrition before an awesome and holy God.

Repentance is not a one-time act. Whenever the believer is convicted of sin he is to repent. John wrote, "If we confess our sins, he is faithful and just and will forgive us our sins and purify us from all unrighteousness." (1 Jn 1:9) This admonition is addressed to those "in Christ," not to those who have yet to recognize him. Repentance and confession are to take place throughout the course of a person's life, otherwise he or she cannot be fitted for the kingdom. Everyone who will be privileged to dwell with God must first become "an offering acceptable to God, sanctified by the Holy Spirit." (Rom 15:16)

5.2 The Issue of "Works" and "Grace"

The nature of works and grace when it comes to salvation needs to be well understood.

At creation, humans had been formed in the likeness of God. They had been made pure and regular in their hearts and in their imaginations. This state of God's likeness is the state that would have brought the creator pleasure in fellowship, but it was soon destroyed. Shortly after the creation of humans God's heart was revealed concerning the condition of people. "The Lord saw how great man's wickedness on the earth had become, and that every inclination of the thoughts of his heart was only evil all the time. The Lord was grieved that he had made man on the earth, and his heart was filled with pain. So the Lord said, 'I will wipe mankind whom I have created, from the face of the earth.'" (Gen 6:5-7) The tendency for wickedness of his created people had become painful to the heart of their creator.

> The issue that eternal salvation has to address is the formation of a people who would be holy in heart and practice and who would not bring "pain" to the heart of God.

The issue that eternal salvation has to address is the formation of a people who would be holy in heart and practice and who would not bring "pain" to the heart of God. Paul revealed to the Romans that those who would dwell with their creator must be once more "conformed to the image of his Son." (Rom 8:29, KJV) It is this transformation or reformation that will result in the achievement of the believer's eternal hope. The sovereign God will not dwell eternally with those who bring him pain.

At first God wiped all people, except for righteous Noah and his family, from the face of the earth in the Great Flood. However, evil surfaced again, even in Noah's family. Following the Flood, the Lord tried to separate a people for himself through Abram. Again, his sovereignty and holiness were not recognized, and these people drifted from him and were subjected to bondage in Egypt. Those who were prepared to recognize his being and authority were redeemed at the Passover and led by Moses and by the flame and cloud on a journey that was intended to test their hearts.[289] Once more they rebelled. The evil of the human heart had prevailed. The Lord could not gain a people who would bring him pleasure.

Through Moses the Lord gave *his people* the Law, the Ten Commandments, written on stone. He also introduced the tabernacle system of worship and the offering of sacrifices for the forgiveness of sin. At this point, understanding of the term, "the works of the law," can be gained. It is not obedience to the law that should be the focus, although that is necessary, but the nature of the work *that the law could do in the hearts of people*-the works or working of the law in transforming the evil imaginations of people- if they could be obedient. It is like trying to change the heart and mind of a rebellious child through the implementation of rules or of adults by the laws of the land. Even with rules and laws that bear consequences, unless the defiant person accepts the penalties entailed for disobedience and is willing to consistently endeavour to obey the rules, no change will result. This approach seldom fully meets with success. History has proven that *the works of the law*, which would result in acceptable behaviour could not be accomplished by the Israelites and neither can it be for any of humankind today. The believer cannot work out or live the law; consequently, the law cannot do its transforming work in the life of a person. Since God's government requires perfect obedience, a person's hope can not be placed in his or her "works" or doing.

Paul wrote of the insufficiency of the law and the inadequacy of people to the Romans: *"For what the law was powerless to do in that it was weakened by the sinful nature, God did by sending his own Son in the likeness of sinful man to be a sin offering."* (Rom 8:3) It is a person's sinful nature that prevents the law from *doing* what it might have done if obeyed. People do not have the capacity to accomplish the righteous requirements of the law so their evil imaginations must prevail if they are left to their own resources. Paul asked the question: "What a wretched man I am! Who will

---

[289] Deut 8:2

rescue me from this body of death (that brings death)?" And responded with, "Thanks be to God-through Jesus Christ our Lord!" (Rom 7:24-25)

The righteous hearts that God seeks must be produced *in a way other* than through the Law and the Prophets. The new way came through Christ and through faith in him. Paul has clarified that "we are God's workmanship." (Eph 2:10, KJV) ("masterpiece," NLT) His workmanship or masterpiece refers to the *product* that he is making of the believer. Paul referred to this product as being "an offering acceptable to God." (Rom 15:16) No one can brag about accomplishing his or her own heart transformation; the Spirit must complete this work.

The sacrificial offering of Christ redeemed the repentant believer *so that he might obtain the Spirit*. "*He redeemed us* in order that the blessings given to Abraham might come to the Gentiles through Christ Jesus, *so that by faith we might receive the promise of the Spirit.*" (Gal 3:14) Both the sacrifice of Christ which provides the believer's redemption[290] and the gifting of the Spirit are expressions of God's *grace*. It is the Spirit who brings about the believer's transformation and eternal salvation. The Spirit does not work by imposing behaviours from the outside, by use of the written code, but by the living Word inside the believer. "God has chosen to make known among the Gentiles the glorious riches of this mystery- "*which had been kept hidden for ages and generations*" (v. 26)- which is Christ in you, the hope of glory." (Col 1:27) The gospel or good news which manifests God's glorious riches, the "mystery" that has been kept hidden, is Christ "in" the believer and it is his ministry that accomplishes a person's hope of glory.

It is with this understanding that "grace" and "works" must be considered. When "works" or "law" is referenced, the idea should be understood as meaning "works of the law." Some biblical translators have left out "*of the law*" when referencing works and this has resulted in some confusion. The law has proven unable to accomplish God's righteous requirements in the hearts, souls, and practices of people and it is because of this that no one can be saved by works of the law. The sinful nature of people prevents them from living the law; their evil imaginations must persist if they are left to their own resources.

---

[290] "Redemption" is from the consequences of sin and release from the domain of the Old Covenant's jurisdiction. (Heb 9:15)

God used the law in order that people could see their own inadequacies, *and to point them to Christ*[291] who could accomplish a person's great need. The working of Christ in the believer and for the believer in order to do that which no person could do for himself or herself is the expression of God's grace. It is Christ who must rid people of their evil imaginations and practices. As stated above, "*God sent his Son in the likeness of sinful man to become a sin offering*" but the passage does not end there. It concludes with, "And so he condemned sin in sinful man, in order that the righteous requirements of the law might be fully met in us, *who do not live according to the sinful nature but according to the Spirit.*" (Rom 8:4) Escape from the body of death is only provided to those who overcome the sinful nature by living according to the Spirit who is Christ in them.

The righteous requirements of the law must be accomplished but their completion necessitates the Holy Spirit's ministry for that purpose. When the Word of God speaks of salvation as not being accomplished through works, it is referring to the works of the law. It does not mean that the believer need not be obedient or that he or she is not required to walk righteously or in the light of Christ. It means that the covenant of the law, of works, cannot bring about a person's eternal salvation. The covenant of the law "kills."[292] That which can bring about the believer's eternal salvation is the appropriation of the ministry of the Spirit in order to satisfy the righteous requirements of the law and the Prophets; but the Spirit *must be obeyed*.[293]

When considering "grace," the sacrifice of Christ was *an act of grace* which allows the believer escape from the consequences of the sinful acts that he had committed while under the ministry of the law. The sacrifice of Christ also provided redemption and the gifting of the Holy Spirit-an act of grace- making the believer competent to satisfy the New Covenant.[294] The ministry of Christ as High Priest is *an expression of God's grace and mercy so that confessed sin might be forgiven.* Complete provision has been made by Christ for the person who would honor him through obedience.[295] Eternal salvation is *not* a gift of grace but must be worked out through the provision God has made in Christ.

---

[291] Ga 3:24
[292] 2 Cor 3:6
[293] Heb 5:9
[294] 2 Cor 3:6; 2 Pet 1:3
[295] Heb 5:9

Eternal Salvation

The gift of grace is twofold. It is the sacrifice of Christ that freed the believer from the consequences of his or her sins while under the jurisdiction of the first covenant so that he or she might enjoy the second and *Christ's presence in the believer.*[296] *He has come to fulfil the law in the believer and for the believer.* He does not over-rule the will of a person but will allow it to be exercised. Paul taught that you must die to self and live for Christ. Obedience is *faith in practice* and the faithful will obey their lord.

> The gift of grace is Christ's presence in the believer. He has come to fulfil the law in the believer and for the believer.

The righteousness for which the believer hopes and requires is being awaited.[297] Eternal salvation comes through God's grace and the believer's allowance of the Spirit being lived through him or her; it is not by the works of the law. However, the believer is to put every effort into obeying the Spirit. "*Make every effort* to enter through the narrow door, because many, I tell you, will try to enter and will not be able to." (Lk 13:24) When the Lord encouraged his listeners "*to make every effort,*" he was requiring just that. They are to hear his voice- the Spirit- and they are to follow.

> When the Lord encouraged His listeners "to make every effort," He was requiring just that.

They are to *do* something.[298] Later in the passage Christ made it clear that those who are *evildoers*[299] will be condemned and cast from him even though they had walked in his presence-they had not been led or had not put forth the "effort" to walk righteously. The writer of Hebrews offered the same admonition.[300] Paul cautioned the Philippians to "work out their own salvation with fear and trembling." (Phil 2:12, KJV)

When Paul spoke of being saved by grace, he identified that grace as being the divine power that creates an acceptable product-God's *workmanship*-, a person's transformed being. In the end, the person who would enjoy the Lord's eternal presence must be in the likeness of his Son.[301] The expression of God's grace through the power of the Holy Spirit makes a person an offering acceptable to God allowing him or her entrance

---

[296] Col 1:27
[297] Gal 5:5
[298] The need to apply effort is also shared in Heb 12:14, 2 Pet 1:5, 10; 2 Pet 3:14.
[299] Lk 13:27
[300] Heb 4:11
[301] Rom 8:29

into God's eternal kingdom. The works of the law cannot accomplish a person's sanctification and transformation.

5.3 The Law and Salvation

Those "in" Christ are not under the Old Covenant or the Covenant of the Law. The law of sin and death has been brought to completion and done away with for those enjoying right to the New Covenant.[302] The requirement for the believer is not to obey the law *but is to obey the Spirit of life*, holiness, and sonship and through him to satisfy the righteous requirement that God has placed upon those who will dwell with him.[303]

The new compact or agreement that has been made, the New Covenant, is a covenant of the Spirit[304] and it has displaced the Old. The completion of the Old does not mean that there is no covenant in place or that there is no righteous requirement for eternal salvation. Holiness is to be a person's state but the means of accomplishing it has changed.

Concerning the law Jesus stated, "Anyone who breaks one of the least of these commandments and teaches others to do the same will be called least in the kingdom of heaven." (Mt 5:19) The law cannot be de4liberately broken, nor can it be permitted to be disregarded by teachers, because it is good even though the believer is not subject to its rule. Paul recorded, "But now dying to what once bound us-sinful passions- we have been released from the law so that we serve in the new way of the Spirit, not in the old way of the written code." (Rom 7:6) He affirms that, "The law is holy, and the commandment - that aroused sin in us- is holy and righteous and good." (Rom 7:12) The law is to be respected and it is to be honored in a person's life, but the believer is not subject to the covenant that embodies it-provided he *is being led* by the Spirit.[305] That is, the person who is being led by the Spirit, by Christ, will not suffer death as the law prescribed. He or she can repent of their sin when they fail and will be cleansed of their transgression.[306] However, a person can re-build the law's dominion, or fall under judgment, if they deny the Spirit's rule even though the rule of the law

---

[302] Rom 8:2
[303] Rom 8:4
[304] 2 Cor 3:6
[305] Gal 5:18
[306] 1 Jn 1:9

had been destroyed. Paul wrote, "If, while we seek to be justified in Christ, it becomes evident that we ourselves are sinners, does that mean that Christ promotes sin? Absolutely not! If I rebuild what I had destroyed, I prove that I am a lawbreaker." (Gal 2:17-18) The person who is not obedient to the Spirit must necessarily be subjected to the law and to his or her own resources.

Since Christ came to fulfill the righteous requirements of the law through his presence in the believer, it should *not* be accepted that the righteousness that he possessed is imputed to believers once they have been cleansed of past sins and have been redeemed. Such thinking will lead many into damnation through separation from the Lord. The believer is to work out his own salvation through the Spirit.

The believer is to meet the righteous requirements of God but he or she is to accomplish that through the ministry of the Spirit. There can be no valid justification for righteousness not having been achieved since God's divine power, the Holy Spirit has provided all that is necessary to satisfy God[307] and provision for forgiveness has been made if the believer should sin.[308]

The freedom that has resulted through escape from the Old Covenant's jurisdiction has allowed many to accept that since the law has been completed, they are free of any encumbrance that would prevent entrance to the kingdom of God. The Lord has also revealed humanity's attitude toward the law and the prophets concerning the treatment of his good news: "The Law and the Prophets were proclaimed until John. Since that time, the good news of the kingdom of God is being preached, and everyone is forcing his way into it. It is easier for heaven and earth to disappear than for the least stroke of a pen to drop out of the law." (Lk 16:16-17) The point that he made was that many, and the teachings of many, allow for, promote, or "force" a variety of ways to get into the kingdom of God. Then he brought it right back to the Law and made it clear that there was no way to circumvent the law for the person who would find the Kingdom. God's "grace" provides all that is necessary to satisfy the law through Christ in the believer. When he says that "everyone is forcing his way into it," He is implying that people are trying to find a way into the kingdom of God without regard to his law or his righteous requirements. The doors of the kingdom of God cannot be opened through any other means than Christ in you, the hope of

---

[307] 2 Pet 1:3
[308] 1 Jn 1:9

God's Government and Eternal Salvation

The Father gives the Spirit →

God has decreed that all who sin must die. (Ezek18:4; Rom 6:23) Sin is rebellion against his government. He has revealed that all have sinned (Rom 3:23) and warrant death. The world was created holy in nature and without holiness no one will see Him. (Heb 12:14)	Christ offered Himself as a sacrifice* for all who would believe. The believer is cleansed and all sin while under the first covenant— he or she has been pardoned and placed under the New Covenant which must be honoured. (Heb 9:15)	The New Covenant is a covenant of the Spirit (of Christ).** The Spirit enlightens, leads, and empowers for righteousness and must be obeyed in order for the righteous requirements of the law to be met. (Rom 8:4)	Judgment takes place for things done in the flesh, whether good or bad.*** As a result the redeemed will be: 1. with God eternally. 2. separated from God eternally. 3. in the lake of burning sulphur eternally.

*The sacrifice of Christ applies firstly to sins committed prior to the gifting of the Holy Spirit…those committed under the jurisdiction of the Old Covenant (Heb 9:15) and secondly, to confessed sin following that point (1 Jn 1:9) The Holy Spirit has been given so that the believer may have victory over sin. It should not be taken that victory for the believer has been accomplished, but that all that is needed for life and godliness has been given the one "in Christ." (2 Pet 1:3) The believer must use all that has been made available to him or her to work out their own salvation. (Phil 2:12; Gal 6: 7-8; Heb 5:9; Mt7:21; Rev 7:21)

** 2 Cor 3:6, 3:17-18; Col 1:27; 2 Cor 3:17-18) The Holy Spirit is Christ in the believer. His ministry of reconciliation and salvation was not completed by his sacrifice on the cross. He indwells the believer to complete his work of holiness making the believer acceptable to dwell in God's presence (Rom 15:16; Eph 2:10) and free of negative judgment.

***2 Cor 5:10. Since all that is necessary for life and godliness has been given to the believer (2 Pet 1:3; Rom 8:4) a lack of obedience, or rebellion, will result in judgment and possibly eternal separation from the Lord. (2 Thess 1:8-9; Rev 22:14-15) Those who have resisted acknowledging the Lord's sovereignty will be cast into the lake of burning sulphur. (Rev 21:8)

glory,[309] and of the law being fulfilled through his Spirit. He is "the way, the truth, and the life." (Jn 14:6) He alone can satisfy the law. The intent of the law was to reveal a person's need for Christ and his righteous life in the believer.

Paul wrote that by dying to sinful passions we have been released from the law.[310] Victory must be gained over sinful passions; that is why a person is to carry his or her cross and why he or she is to die to self. Those who do not allow the Spirit, with their co-operation, to accomplish righteous practices will remain under the law. "But if you are led by the Spirit you are not under the law." (Gal 5:18) This is a conditional statement. The person who will not humble himself in obedience to the Lord must remain under the law. There is no other alternative.

> Those who do not allow the Spirit, with their co-operation, to accomplish righteous practices will remain under the law.

It is worth noting that God is going to destroy the world when the time comes because people will have "twisted his instructions, violated his laws, and broken his everlasting covenant." (Isa 24:5, NLT)[311] The accomplishment of instructions, laws, and the covenant is not a gift of grace as is often taught; their accomplishment is *through* the gift of grace, the Holy Spirit, and the believer's commitment to obedience. Paul told his readers not to be deceived; they would reap what they sow…receiving either life or destruction.[312]

5.4 Conditions Applied to Eternal Salvation

There are several conditions presented in the Word of God concerning the gaining of a person's eternal salvation.

Condition 1. The redeemed person must be led by the Spirit.

The Word of God speaks a great deal about the necessity of being led by the Spirit for those who have ears to hear. Paul taught that it is those who are led by the Spirit of God who are sons of God[313] and calls the Spirit "the Spirit of sonship." (Rom 8:15) He also wrote that it is those who are

---

[309] Col 1:27
[310] Rom 7:5
[311] The NIV reads, "disobeyed the laws, violated the statutes and broken the everlasting covenant."
[312] Gal 6:7-8
[313] Rom 8:14, NIV

led by the Spirit who are not under the law.[314] Those who are not willing to be led by the Spirit, if they are to achieve the state of holiness, must accomplish it through their own works, which is not possible. There are many other passages that address the requirement of being led.[315] It was Paul's teaching that salvation comes through the sanctifying work of the Spirit which is accomplished through obedience to him.[316]

Condition 2. The redeemed must persevere to the end.

The believer must accept that a commitment to the lordship of Christ is to be a very real commitment and requirement that is to be pursued to the end of his or her life. The promise of eternal salvation is only given to those who stand firm in their faith to the end.[317] The Lord admonished, "All men will hate you because of me, but he who stands firm to the end will be saved." (Mt 10:22) [318] If a person is not diligent in his or her walk, sin will creep in and the walk of righteousness will be abandoned.

Paul taught, "By this gospel you are saved, if you hold firmly to the word I preached to you. Otherwise you have believed in vain." (1 Cor 15:2) [319]

The Lord also admonished his disciples that they were to remain in him. "Remain in me and I will remain in you." (Jn 15:4) Accordingly, it must be understood that something is required of the believer for him or her to remain in Christ. The blessings of producing much fruit are attached to the believer's remaining in Christ. Do not accept that because a person was in Christ once that he or she will always remain in Christ. The Lord taught that the believer must obey his commands in order to remain in his love.[320]

Paul has stated that a person can re-build that which he had destroyed. That is, the law. He was speaking to those who are "seeking to be justified[321]"

---

[314] Gal 5:18, NIV
[315] Rom 8:9, 11, 13; Eph 5:5, 6; Heb. 5:9, 10:14, Heb 10:26-27, 29; Jn 5:28, 29, 8:34-35, 15:6; Rom 8:4; Mt 7:21, 13:41
[316] Heb 5:9
[317] Mt 10:22, 24:13; Mk 13:13; Heb 3:14; Rev 2:26
[318] This statement by the Lord also affirms that person's eternal salvation is not "gifted" as an act of grace at the time of his confession.
[319] For other references see Heb 3:6, 14; 1 Jn 3:6; Col 1: 22-23
[320] Jn 15:10. This thought should make a person question his or her understanding of God's "unconditional" love. It is expansive, but not unconditional.
[321] The believer should not confuse the justification that comes at confession through the blood of Christ and which allowed for the sinner's redemption

through Christ's resurrected life.[322] These have been graced with his Spirit,[323] but those who are not being led will have rejected his leadership.

Paul presented the nature of his ministry to King Agrippa, "I preached that they should repent and turn to God and *prove their repentance by their deeds.*" (Acts 26:20) He did not allow his listeners to rest in a profession of repentance but required its proof by their actions.

The Apostle Paul said, "I discipline my body like an athlete, training it to do what it should. Otherwise, I fear that after preaching to others I might be disqualified. (1 Cor 9:27, NLT)" Even Paul did not rest his hope in a single confession of faith but felt the need to pursue righteousness to the end. Further, he confessed that he wanted "to become like Christ in his death, and so, somehow to attain to the resurrection from the dead." He concluded by saying, "Not that I have attained all of this, or have already been made perfect, but I press on to take hold of that for which Christ Jesus took hold of me." (Phil 3:10-12) Accordingly, Paul was under the conviction that he had not yet achieved right to resurrection with Christ, but that he had to "press on" to achieve that goal. His life was not completed so neither was his striving for righteousness and for the resurrection.

The Lord admonished his listeners "to make every effort to enter through the narrow door, because many will try to enter and will not be able to." (Lk 13:24)

There is a death to be lived and a life to be walked and they must be pursued to the end.

Condition 3: The believer must share "in Christ's sufferings."

Paul taught," Now if we are children (of God) then we are heirs—heirs of God and coheirs with Christ, *if indeed* we share in his sufferings in order that we may also share in his glory." (Rom 8:17) [324]

(Rom 5:9) with the justification that comes through the Lord's resurrection by allowing his presence (Holy Spirit) in the believer. In his letter to the Romans, Paul stated, "He was delivered over to death for our sins and was raised to life for our justification." (Rom 4:25, NIV) And James has made it clear that a person's justification requires obedience to the Spirit. "You see a person is justified by what he does and not by faith alone." (Jas 2:24, NIV)

[322] Rom 4:24; Jas 2:24
[323] 2 Cor 3:17-18; Col 1:27
[324] Paul presented this truth in Romans 6:5 also.

This is another "conditional" statement. A person's position of becoming an "heir of God" rests on his or her willingness to share "in Christ's sufferings." The writer of Hebrews has revealed that "he [Christ] suffered when he was tempted." (Heb 2:18) Consequently, it needs to be understood that the believer's becoming an heir is conditioned to accepting and becoming victorious over the suffering that temptation brings. Because Christ was made like us "in every way" (Heb 2:12) He knows our suffering and temptations and will help those who rest in him to gain the victory.

Paul spoke of this matter concerning his own eternal state. He has presented: "I want to know Christ and the power of his resurrection and the fellowship of sharing in his sufferings, becoming like him in his death, and so somehow, to attain to the resurrection from the dead." (Phil 3:10-11) The power of his resurrection is the power of the Holy Spirit who led him to victory over the flesh that his Father had given him and the temptations through which he had faced and had suffered.[325] Paul understood that he was to share in Christ's sufferings in order that he might share in his resurrection. He was not satisfied at the time of his writing that he had achieved the state where he would be resurrected. There is no glory available to those who practice sin.

5.5 How Can You Know that You Enjoy the Hope of Eternal Salvation?

It is comforting for the believer to know that he or she has the hope of eternal salvation or that they are "in Christ." If a person cannot place confidence in their *confession* of faith how can they gain confidence of their eternal state? The apostle John addressed this issue in his epistle. "I write these things to you who believe in the name of the Son of God so that you may know that you have eternal life." (1 Jn 5:13)

A person's hope is secure if he or she:

---

[325] The writer of Hebrews states, "During the days of Jesus' life on earth, he offered up prayers and petitions with loud cries and tears to the one who could save him from death, and he was heard because of his reverent submission. Although he was a son, he learned obedience from what he suffered and once made perfect became the source of eternal salvation for all who obey him." (Heb 5: 7-9, NIV)

1. enjoys fellowship with Christ and the Father.[326]
2. is sensitive to sin.[327]
3. obeys God's Word.[328]
4. rejects this evil world.[329]
5. eagerly awaits Christ's return.[330]
6. sees a decreasing pattern of sin in his life.[331]
7. loves other Christians.[332]
8. experiences answered prayer.[333]
9. experiences the ministry of the Holy Spirit.[334]
10. can discern between spiritual truth and error.[335]
11. suffers rejection because of his faith.[336]
12. loves others, including the unlovable.[337]
13. has concern about the material needs of others.[338]
14. is like Christ in this world.[339]
15. has a clear conscience.[340]

No person can "work" adequately in order to achieve what is required for eternal life. Without the Spirit a person does not have the capacity to accomplish that which is needed. Without the Spirit, a person is left with his or her own sinful nature and a demanding body. The only power for victory that they have is their own. The life that produces holiness of mind, heart, and spirit is being worked on by the Spirit of Christ in order that our Lord might be the *first-born among many brothers and sisters*. Humankind's work is to "believe" which requires submission to the

---

[326] 1 Jn 1: 3, 2:24
[327] 1 Jn 2:29, 3:6, 9
[328] 1 Jn 2:3, 3:24; 5:3
[329] 1 Jn 2:15, 16; 5:4
[330] I Jn 3:2, 3
[331] 1 Jn 3:3, 6, 9; 5:18
[332] 1 Jn 2:9, 10; 3:10, 14; 4: 7, 11, 12, 4:19-20
[333] 1 Jn 3:22; see also Lk 11:9; Jn 14:14, 15:7
[334] 1 Jn 2:27, 3:20, 24, 4:13
[335] 1 Jn 3:6; 2:21
[336] 1 Jn 3:13
[337] 1 Jn 1:1:5, 4:7, 16
[338] 1 Jn 3:17
[339] 1 Jn 4:17
[340] 1 Jn 3:21

leadership of the Holy Spirit so that they might become like God's Son. The transformed believer is *God's* masterpiece, not the result of a person's own efforts.

> Christianity involves a person, Jesus Christ, the Son of God, and one's faithful *relationship* with him.

Christianity is *not* an institution, not a list of rules, not a religious experience, and not a certain type of service. Neither is it superficial "belief" that lacks commitment and obedience. Christianity involves a person, Jesus Christ, the Son of God, and a person's faithful *relationship* with him. Christianity-faith in Christ- is the practice of obedience so that Christ might live in and through the person who claims his name. The relationship that develops must lead a person into a holy walk because that is the only walk accepted by the Lord.

Chapter 6
Judgment

The thought of judgment is fearful to most. It is always a time of accountability. With judgment comes the dreadful expectation of some form of punishment. Modern western teaching would dispose of any concept of judgment leading to punishment for those who have confessed faith in Christ. It is readily accepted that Christ has taken any punishment due the "believer" and that upon death of the body a state of eternal bliss will be entered in the presence of the person who has relieved him or her of God's wrath.

To many the thought of God's judgment is too harsh a concept to even be given consideration. Most would quickly dismiss it from their thought life and from their spiritual understanding. Paul's writing should dispel such thinking. "Since we have now been justified by his blood, how much more shall we be saved from God's wrath through him! For if, when we were enemies, we were reconciled to him through the death of his Son, *how much more shall we be saved from God's wrath through his life*! (Rom 5:9-10) It is Paul's teaching that God's wrath exists but can be avoided through the exercise of the Lord's life in a person.

In the end, judgment is promised for all.[341] The issue of judgment cannot be understood without grasping God's purpose and his desires for creation.

The Word reveals that God created for his "good pleasure"-for his own purposes-and it is revealed that he created to have a people in his image[342]…a royal priesthood and a holy nation.[343] They were created to fellowship with him in a righteous and honorable manner, according to the

---

[341] "For we must all appear before the judgment seat of Christ, that each may receive what is due him for the things done while in the body, whether good or bad." (2 Cor 5:10)
[342] Gen 1:26, 27
[343] Ex 19:6; 1 Pet 2:9

likeness of the fellowship that he enjoys with his Son. Paul has recorded that it will be those who have been "conformed to the image of his Son" (Rom 8:29) who will enjoy his presence. Those whose hearts are inclined to evil bring him "pain" (Genesis 6:7) and will not be part of his eternal kingdom.

In order to have a people who could relate to him honestly and through conviction, God allowed humanity the right to exercise *free-will*. That is, people have been created to exercise choice according to the leading of their spirit and soul. They can choose either to develop a relationship with God or to reject their creator. They can choose either to honor their Lord through obedience, or they can rebel and choose to take their own path as in the manner of Adam.

> People have been created to exercise choice according to the leading of their spirits and souls.

The good news or gospel reveals that God has made provision through Christ so that people might cast aside their evil thoughts and practices and might truly be *transformed* into the likeness of Christ. This transformation required the sacrifice of the Son of God on the cross and necessitates his on-going ministries as Holy Spirit and High Priest. The needed transformation cannot be accomplished without a person's willingness to humbly submit to the sovereign leadership of Christ as his or her Lord while they live out their lives. Those who are willing to be led must be obedient[344] and it is on this basis that judgment will be applied by Christ to those who have 'claimed' him as their Lord.[345] "My sheep listen to my voice; I know them, and they follow me. I give them eternal life and they shall never perish." (Jn 10:27)

Since it is the obedient or those who "hear" and "follow" who will find eternal salvation, a separation of people is required, and the separation requires a *judgment* and a *judgment call* resulting in the choosing of some -election[346] or selection- and the rejection of others. It is for this purpose that judgment will take place. All who dwell with God must be holy[347] just as He is holy.

---

[344] Heb 5:9, "He became the source of eternal salvation for all who obey him."
[345] Rom 10: 9-10
[346] "election" is translated from the Greek *ekloge* which means "(divine) selection (abstractly or concretely): —chosen, election." –from Strong's Greek Dictionary #1589
[347] Heb 12:14, "without holiness no one will see the Lord."

If there is an election or selection of some, there must be a rejection of others. The rejection or selection will be based on a person's state of holiness or on his or her willingness to allow Christ to rule or lead in the transformation of the body of sin.[348] The believer's hope of glorification comes through the life of Christ or ministry of Christ in him or her. The Lord revealed, "Blessed are those who wash their robes ("do his commandments", KJV), that they may have the right to the tree of life and may go through the gates into the city (the New Jerusalem)." (Rev 22:14) [349] It is those who have *"washed their robes"* from sin through his blood *and* as they walk righteously according to the Spirit's leading, who confess and repent of sin when they are convicted, who will enter the city to dwell with him. However, few will be present with the Lord. Christ said, "Enter through the narrow gate. For wide is the gate and broad is the road that leads to destruction, and many enter through it. But small is the gate and narrow the road that leads to life, and only a few find it." (Mt 7:13-14)

Judgment is an evaluation of a person's obedience, of his or her willingness to die to self, to humble themselves to the Lord's rule following confession of faith. Unless Christ lives in and through the believer righteousness leading to holiness cannot be achieved. Many will follow the way of Adam and will seek to satisfy their own desires; consequently, their evil imaginations and actions will not fit them to dwell in the presence of the Holy One. Paul revealed that he was given "the priestly duty of proclaiming the gospel of God, so that the Gentiles might *become an offering acceptable to God*, sanctified by the Holy Spirit." (Rom 15:16)

Judgment rests on the Biblical teaching that when Christ returns the

---

[348] Paul wrote: "What a wretched man I am! Who will rescue me from this body of death? Thanks be to God- through Jesus Christ our Lord!" (Rom 7:24-15, NIV)

[349] Note: According to the Lord a person must *do* something…he must wash his robes. A person's robes or covering of righteousness becomes spotted by sin and needs cleaning. This cleaning takes place as the believer confesses his or her sins and seeks forgiveness. (1 Jn 1:9) The Greek does not translate into "wash their robes" but translates into "do his commandments."

redeemed person is to be held accountable for the things done while in the body. His or her actions will come under evaluation followed by the possible consequence of God's wrath[350] being visited upon him or her for defiance and rebellious behaviours considering all that has been provided for them.

The thought of judgment can be disturbing. It requires the scrutiny of a person's life and most know of their weaknesses and failures. We do not like these revealed to another or to the world. The righteous façade that has been built up might crumble with the real person being exposed. Judgment will reveal absolute truth and is frightening to contemplate, especially for the hypocrite.

Because of the unpleasantness associated with judgment, much modern theology has tried to exempt the "believer" from any hint of its reality and has devised ways to explain the "believer's" freedom from being subject to any judgment that might bring negative consequences. The writer of Hebrews states, "Man is destined once to die, and after that to face judgment." (Heb 9:27) Such teaching would suggest that *all* people face judgment. Paul taught, "For we must all stand before the judgment seat of Christ, that each one might receive what is due him *for the things done while in the body, whether good or bad.*" (2 Cor 5:10)

Concerning those who deliberately continue to sin after having received the knowledge of the truth, God's Word presents: "How much more severely do you think a man deserves to be punished who has trampled the Son of God under foot, who has treated as an unholy thing the *blood of the covenant that sanctified him*, and who has insulted the Spirit of grace? For we know him who said, 'It is mine to avenge; I will repay,' and again, 'The Lord will judge his people.' It is a dreadful thing to fall into the hands of the living God." (Heb 10:29-31) This warning is applied to those who have been sanctified *by the blood of the covenant*, to believers.

6.1 The Basis of Judgment

Judgment will be based on "the law of the Lord," or "the law of liberty."

Judgment will be based on "the law of the Lord" (Jas 2:12) [351], or

---

[350] Paul taught that a person is saved from God's wrath through him [Christ] after he had been justified by His blood. (Rom 5:9-10) It is the Lord's "life" lived through the believer that saves him from God's wrath.

[351] See also Ps 19:7 "The law of the Lord" (NIV) -The meaning is, that in all our

"the law of liberty." (Jas 2:12, KJV) Great freedom has been given to those who live in Christ; however, the plan of salvation requires obedience to the Lord[352] with the defeat of sinful practices.

Jesus was incarnated for a purpose… "The reason the Son of God appeared was to destroy the devil's work." (1 Jn 3:8) The Father has given to his Son the responsibility of preparing a holy people for his eternal kingdom.[353] Although some take this to mean that he came to atone for the sins of humankind, this singular aspect of his ministry does not "destroy the devil's work." Conformity to the likeness of Christ is necessary.[354] The redeemed person may have been washed of *the sins committed under the first covenant*" (Heb 9:15, KJV) at his confession of faith, however his heart and his actions must be changed, and this is accomplished by Christ or the Holy Spirit in him or her. Satan continues to work on the heart of the believer following his redemption at confession of faith. The battle of the redeemed person has not ended. The Lord told his followers that in order to be saved they had to "stand firm to the end." (Mt 10:22) Satan will try to reclaim the person that he has lost and turn him into one who will live a lie[355] concerning his or her proclamation of Christ's lordship. Paul admonished his readers to "put on the full armour of God so that they can take their stand against the devil's evil schemes." (Eph 6:11)

> It is *not* the Lord's teaching that all the redeemed will gain "eternal" salvation.

It is *not* the Lord's teaching that all the redeemed will gain "eternal" salvation. This

---

conduct we are to act under the constant impression of the truth that we are soon to be brought into judgment, and that the law by which we are to be judged is that by which it is contemplated that we shall be set free from the dominion of sin. In the rule which God has laid down in his word, called "the law of liberty," or the rule by which true *freedom* is to be secured, a system of religion is revealed by which it is designed that man shall be emancipated not only from one sin, but from *all*. Now, it is with reference to such a law that we are to be judged; that is, we shall not be able to plead on our trial that we were under a necessity of sinning, but we shall be judged under that law by which the arrangement was made that we might be free from sin. If we might be free from sin; if an arrangement was made by which we could have led holy lives, then it will be proper that we shall be judged and condemned if we are not righteous -Albert Barnes Notes on the Bible

[352] Heb 5:9; Mt 7:21
[353] 1 Pet 2:9
[354] Rom 8:29
[355] Rev 22:15

privilege belongs to the "obedient." (Heb 5:9) [356] Paul taught, "Do not be deceived: God cannot be mocked. A man reaps what he sows. The one who sows to please the sinful nature, from that nature will reap destruction; the one who sows to please the Spirit, from the Spirit will reap eternal life." (Gal 6:7-8) The Lord also revealed, "Not everyone who says to me 'Lord! Lord!' will enter the kingdom of heaven, but only he who does the will of my Father who is in heaven." (Mt 7:21) A person's choices and actions following his or her redemption will determine the nature of the judgment that will be rested upon them and these choices may be influenced by the evil one and be testimony to his work in a person's life, even a redeemed person's life.

Some might harbour the thought that their sins will pass unnoticed; however, Paul wrote to Timothy that, "the sins of some men are obvious, reaching the place of judgment ahead of them; the sins of others trail behind them. In the same way, good deeds are obvious, and even those that are not cannot be hidden." (1 Tim 5:24-25) A person's bad or evil deeds will be noticed even in the presence of many good deeds. In the same manner his or her sins might be buried in the process of an otherwise well-lived life but at the judgment these will be revealed.

Jesus clarified, "I tell you the truth, everyone who sins is a slave to sin. Now a slave has *no permanent place* in the family, but a son belongs to it forever." (Jn 8:34-35) A "son" is one who has been led by the Spirit.[357] Paul also taught that a believer is not adopted into the family until redemption of the body[358] has been accomplished.

The believer need not be burdened with sin and consequently, need not fear judgment for its practice. The provision that the Lord has made for purity is complete and is remarkable. All "the sins committed under the first covenant" (Heb 9:15) were washed away at confession of faith and following that "God's divine power has given us everything we need for life and godliness." (2 Pet 1:3) It is expected that the person who has claimed belief and has confessed the lordship of Christ will demonstrate that belief by living in obedience to him. Sin committed after that point can be washed away through confession. The Lord did not sin while in his earthly body and he *will not* sin while in the believer; however, a person might choose to go his or her own way. Disobedience is rebellion against

---

[356] "He became the source of eternal salvation for all who obey him."
[357] Rom 8:14
[358] Rom 8:23

Eternal Salvation

the Spirit, the "divine power," and it reveals a person's subjugation to the rule of the evil one- his slavery to sin.

The issue of obedience to the Holy Spirit must not be taken lightly. "He will punish those who do not know[359] God and do not obey the gospel of our Lord Jesus. They will be punished with everlasting destruction and shut out from the presence of the Lord and from the majesty of his power on the day he comes to be glorified in his holy people and to be marveled at among all those who have believed." (2 Thess 1:7-8)

Daniel prophesized that following the Great Tribulation, at Christ's return, "multitudes who sleep in the dust of the earth will awake: some to everlasting life, others to shame and everlasting contempt." (Dan 12:2) Those who have failed to submit to the Lord in obedience will awake to *shame and everlasting contempt*."

> Those who have failed to submit to the Lord in obedience will awake to "shame and everlasting contempt."

They will not be cast into the lake of burning sulphur[360] but will feel eternal shame for their failure to honor their Savior's love and provision and will suffer everlasting contempt from those who have foregone the pleasures of this world, many having chosen death, for the sake of loving and honoring their God. These are not momentary conditions but are "everlasting." They will be ruled with an iron scepter and by those from within the city (the New Jerusalem). They will not be the rulers that they had anticipated but will be separated from the Lord[361] and will be the ruled.

---

[359] "know" is translated from the Greek *eido* which means "properly, to see (literally or figuratively); by implication, in the perfect tense only) to know: —be aware, behold, X can (+ not tell), consider, (have) know(-ledge), look (on), perceive, see, be sure, tell, understand, wish, wot. "–from Strong's Greek Dictionary #1492. To "know" God is "to see" Him as He is and "to know" or appreciate him in this sense. It does not mean to know about him, but to have knowledge of His holiness and of his awesomeness to the point of being fully persuaded concerning both his holiness and awesomeness. That knowledge demands an appropriate response which will require a person to be molded through God's workmanship (Eph 2:10, NIV) into a sacrifice acceptable to him. (Rom 15:16)

[360] Rev 21:8

[361] 2 Thess 1:8-9: "He will punish those who do not know God and do not obey the gospel of our Lord Jesus. They will be punished with everlasting destruction and shut out from the presence of the Lord and the majesty of his power on the day he comes to be glorified in his holy people and to be marveled at among those who have believed." (NIV) This should *not* be taken to be those who have not been redeemed.

6.2 Destruction of the World

The basis of judgment will be a person's commitment to Christ as revealed through obedience to the Holy Spirit who was given to meet the righteous requirements of the law.[362] Christ has made it clear that he did not come to "abolish the Law or the Prophets...but to fulfil them." (Mt 5:17)

Many have made light of the need for righteous living and have felt the freedom to disregard the rule of Christ who came to fulfill the law by his presence in them. Isaiah prophesied however, "See, the Lord is going to lay waste the earth and devastate it...The earth will be completely laid waste and totally plundered. The Lord has spoken this word. The earth dries up and withers, the world languishes and withers, the exalted of the earth languish. The earth is defiled by its people; they have disobeyed the laws, violated the statutes and broken the everlasting covenant. Therefore, a curse consumes the earth; its people must bear their guilt. Therefore, earth's inhabitants are burned up, and very few are left." (Isa 24:1...3-6) God takes his Covenant very seriously; it is "everlasting" and those who take God's grace as means of escape from the Law will one day reap the rewards of their folly.

> Those who take God's grace as means of escape from the Law will one day reap the rewards of their folly.

6.3 Abuse of God's Grace

Mistreating God's grace through the freedom that many suppose they have, has been labelled by Dietrick Bonhoeffer as "cheap grace" and he has defined it as follows:

> *"Cheap grace is the grace that amounts to justification of sin without the justification of the repentant sinner who departs from sin and from whom sin departs. Cheap grace is not the kind of forgiveness of sin which frees us from the toils of sin.*

---

[362] Rom 8:3-4 (NIV), "For what the law was powerless to do in that it was weakened by the sinful nature, God did by sending his own Son in the likeness of sinful man to be a sin offering. And so, he condemned sin in sinful man, in order that the righteous requirements of the law might be fully met in us, who do not live according to the sinful nature but according to the Spirit."

Cheap grace is the grace we bestow on ourselves. Cheap grace is the preaching of forgiveness without requiring repentance, baptism without church discipline, communion without confession, absolution without personal confession.

Cheap grace is grace without discipleship, grace without the cross, grace without Jesus Christ, living and incarnate."[363]

Those who trample the blood of Christ with such disregard will not experience the full Christian life and will suffer the discipline of the Lord. God will not be trivialized and has created humankind "for his good pleasure" which involves bringing glory to his name.

Paris Reidhead has observed that many Christians see God's grace as a blank credit card to be honored by the Lord. *"People take the grace of the blood of Christ as if it were a blank credit card and charge their sins to Jesus and live as they will."*[364]

The world will be destroyed because God's law and his everlasting covenant have been abused; judgment will rest on all those who treat them with disdain and his covenant with contempt.

Christ lived on this earth in a body just as all humans have and was victorious over the flesh and the devil. Just as he did not sin in his incarnated body he will not sin while living in the body of the redeemed; however, his ministry in a person can be denied so that his or her evil nature can wilfully submit to the rule of Satan and bring destruction. The victory that was his can be that of the redeemed person provided he or she allows it.

Major Ian Thomas has presented the nature of the Lord's ministry within a person:

"On the third morning after His crucifixion, the Lord Jesus Christ rose from the dead and appeared to His disciples. He instructed them for some forty days and then ascended to the Father. On the first day of Pentecost He returned, not this time to be with them externally--clothed with that sinless humanity that God had prepared for Him, being conceived of the Holy Spirit in the womb of Mary--but now to be in them, imparting

---

[363] Van Dyke, Michael, <u>DIETRICH BONHOEFFER Opponent of the Nazi Regime</u>, Barbour Publishing, Inc., Uhrichsville, Ohio, 2001, pages 110-111

[364] Reidhead, Paris, Sermon: <u>The Grace of God Brings Repentance</u>

> to them His own divine nature, clothing Himself with their humanity, so that they each became "members in particular" of a new, corporate body through which Christ expressed Himself to the world of their day. He spoke with their lips. He worked with their hands. This was the miracle of new birth, and this remains the very heart of the gospel!
>
> "Faithful is he that calleth you, who will do it." The One who calls you to a life of righteousness is the One who by your consent lives that life of righteousness through you! The One who calls you to minister to the needs of humanity is the One who by your consent ministers to the needs of humanity through you! The One who calls you to go into all the world and preach the Gospel to every creature, is the One who by your consent, goes into all the world and preaches the Gospel to every creature through you!"[365]

The ministry of the Lord in a person is by that person's allowance or permission. Humankind was given free-will and this special provision will not be over-ruled. "Because he himself suffered when he was tempted, he is able to help those who are being tempted." (Heb 2:18) It is to be noted that "he is able to *help;*" The Lord does not unilaterally assure victory. "For we do not have a high priest who is unable to sympathize with our weaknesses, but we have one who was tempted in every way, just as we are-yet without sin. Let us then approach the throne of grace with confidence, so that we may receive mercy and find grace *to help us* in our time of weakness." (Heb 4:15-16) The believer is to put on the full armour of God,[366] to be faithful in prayer, and to stand strong.

> The Lord does not unilaterally assure victory.

"Those who do not know God and who do not obey the gospel" (2 Thess 1: 7-8) and "everything that causes sin and all who do evil" (Mt 13:41) will be weeded out of his Kingdom. "Those who practice magic arts, the sexually immoral, murderers (those who hate their brothers), idolaters (those "believers" who love the things of the world or other gods), and everyone who loves and practices falsehood" will be cast outside the city (the New Jerusalem). (Rev 22:15)

---

[365] Thomas, Major W. Ian, <u>The Saving Life of Christ</u>, Zondervan Publishing House, Grand Rapids, Michigan, 1961, pages 14-15.
[366] Eph 6:10-18

The issue of judgment is serious and needs to be earnestly considered by all who would claim the name of Christ. Those who desire to fellowship eternally with their God have been told to "work out their own salvation with fear and trembling." (Phil 2:12)

6.4 Judgment for Service

The believer has been redeemed not only for his own eternal sake, but also for ministry in building the kingdom. "For we are God's workmanship, created in Christ Jesus to do good works, which God prepared in advance for us to do." (Eph 2:10) Concerning the distribution of "gifts" Paul wrote, "Now to each one the manifestation of the Spirit is given for the common good." (1 Cor 12:7)

Neither should a person's neglect of the gifting that he has been given be dismissed. Concerning the "worthless servant" Christ spoke, "And throw that worthless servant outside into the darkness, where there will be weeping and gnashing of teeth." (Mt 25:30) The believer's commitment to Christ must be taken seriously.

According to Paul, believers will be judged according to their participation in building the kingdom: "For no one can lay any foundation other than the one already laid, which is Jesus Christ. If any man builds on this foundation using gold, silver, costly stones, wood, hay or straw, his work will be shown for what it is, because the Day will bring it to light. It will be revealed with fire, and the fire will test each man's work. If what he has built survives, he will receive his reward. If it is burned up, he will suffer loss; he himself will be saved, but only as one escaping through the flames." (1 Cor 3:11-15) When Paul speaks of fire and flames, he is speaking of judgment. The lazy and neglectful will undergo great loss and although they might not dwell with him, they will not be cast into the lake of burning sulphur.

6.5 Christ, the Judge

The responsibility of establishing the final kingdom was given to Christ and it is he who will elect those who will be permitted entry. "The Father judges no one, but has entrusted all judgment to the Son, that all may honor the Son just as they honor the Father." (Jn 5:22) The Father would have his Son honored and one day all will bend the knee to him.³⁶⁷ He is the one who offered himself a sacrifice to restore people to fellowship with the Father. He is the one who indwells the believer³⁶⁸ to transform him or her and to allow them victory over Satan and his evil nature. He is the one who mediates between the believer and the Father.³⁶⁹ And, he is the one who will judge a person's commitment and heart, and no one knows them better than he who is within them.

> Christ is the one who will judge a person's commitment and heart, and no one knows them better than the one who is within them.

When his judgment is finalized, and his enemies have been defeated Christ will hand over his holy kingdom to the Father. "Then the end will come, when he hands over the kingdom to God the Father after he has destroyed all dominion, authority and power. For he must reign until he has put all his enemies under his feet." (1 Cor 15:24-25)

6.6 Reward Following Judgment

Those who have committed to honoring their Lord will be rewarded. Christ has revealed to the seven churches in Revelation some of the rewards that will be given to those who *"overcome"* issues. Among the rewards are:

1. Fruit from the tree of life in the paradise of God.³⁷⁰
2. Protection from the second death.³⁷¹
3. Some of the manna that has been hidden away in heaven, and a white stone with a new name that no person understands except the person who receives it.³⁷²
4. Authority over all the nations. The victorious will rule the nations with an iron rod and smash them like clay pots. They will receive the same authority Christ received from his Father. And, they will also get "the morning star."³⁷³

---

[367] Rom 14:11
[368] 2 Cor 3: 19, 20; Col 1:27
[369] 1 Tim 2:5; Heb 8:6, 9:15, 12:24
[370] Rev 2:7
[371] Rev 2:11
[372] Rev 2:17
[373] Rev 2:26-28

Eternal Salvation

5. White clothing accompanied by the promise that their names will never be erased from the Book of Life. Christ will announce before his Father and his angels that they belong to him.[374]
6. They will become "pillars in the Temple of God, and they will be citizens in the New Jerusalem." (Rev 3:12)
7. They will sit with the Father on his throne.[375]
8. A promise is also given to those who persevere. *"Because you have obeyed my commands to persevere, I will protect you from the great time of testing that will come upon the whole world to test those who belong to this world."* (Rev 3:10, NLT)

6.7 The Millennium and Judgment

The Millennium must be considered when judgment is being considered. The Millennial period takes place following the Great Tribulation and prior to the judgment of "unbelievers." The millennium is the *time* or *era* of judgment. Through the great revelation of Christ to John it is presented: "The time[376] has come for judging[377] the dead, and for rewarding your servants the prophets and your saints and those who reverence your name, both small and great-and for destroying those who destroy the earth." (Rev 11:18) In the previous verse John has recorded the angel's reference to the time as being the point at which Christ began his reign.[378] His reference is to the *era* of God's judgment having begun with its continuation until the completion of the Great White Throne judgment,

> The millennium is the *time* of judgment.

---

[374] Rev 3:5
[375] Rev 3:21
[376] "Time" should not be considered as a moment in this case. It is translated from the Greek "kairos" which means "an occasion, i.e. Set or proper time: X always, opportunity, (convenient, due) season, (due, short, while) time, a while." – from Strong's Greek Dictionary #2540
[377] "Judging" is translated from the Greek 'krino' which means "properly, to distinguish, i.e. decide (mentally or judicially); by implication, to try, condemn, punish: -avenge, conclude, condemn, damn, decree, determine, esteem, judge, go to (sue at the) law, ordain, call in question, sentence to, think." – Strong's Greek Dictionary #2919
[378] Rev 11:17

and the purification and identification or selection of those permitted into his eternal kingdom.

The millennial years have a purpose and during that time Christ will rule with a scepter of righteousness. A determination will be made concerning the final disposition of all life on earth, including the lives of those who had made a claim of Christ's lordship and who had walked in darkness or who had loved to live a lie …those he did not "know."[379] As Malachi prophesied there will be a separation of the righteous and the wicked and those who serve the Lord and those who don't.[380]

> There will be a separation of the righteous and the wicked and those who serve the Lord and those who don't.

There is no basis for questioning the justness and integrity of God. All men will have been given generous opportunity to acknowledge who the Lord is and to respond appropriately according to the knowledge that has been provided them. Peter has recorded, "For Christ died for sins once for all, the righteous for the unrighteous, to bring you to God. He was put to death in the body but made alive by the Spirit through whom he also went and preached to the spirits in prison who disobeyed long ago when God waited patiently in the days of Noah while the ark was being built." (1 Pet 3:18-20) According to Peter, before Christ ascended to heaven, he went and preached to the spirits who had been held in prison from long ago. Those who had not had the privilege of his life-saving ministry were given it before Christ left this earth. Provision has been made for all, even those spirits from distant age to have the same hope as those of this age. Paul taught, "God presented him as a sacrifice of atonement through faith in his blood. He did this to demonstrate his justice because in forbearance he had left the sins committed beforehand unpunished-he did this to demonstrate his justice at the present time, so as to be just and the one who justifies those who have faith in Jesus." (Rom 3:25-26) God is just and he had left sins committed long ago unpunished in order that his justice would be equal for all people.

Likewise, those who had declared that Christ would be their lord and had yet rebelled against their proclamation will find opportunity to humble

---

[379] Mt 7:23
[380] Mal 3:18: "And you will again see the distinction between the righteous and the wicked, between those who serve God and those who do not." (NIV)

themselves under his righteous rule. Although they may be forever separated from him, his mercy and grace will prevent those who have come to a place of contrition during his reign from being cast into the lake of burning sulphur.

> The issue of judgment should be taken seriously; every single person will have to face the righteous judgment of Christ for the things done while in the body.

The issue of judgment should be taken seriously; every single person will have to face the righteous judgment of Christ for the things done while in the body. Hidden sins will be revealed, and careless words accounted for. It was Paul's admonition for every believer to work out his or her own salvation with fear and trembling. Each person will be treated impartially whether he or she be pastor, teacher, or the person who has defied the Lord's provision. Peter has written: "Since you call on a Father who judges each man's work impartially, live your lives as strangers here in reverent fear." (1 Pet 1:17)

The person who has claimed that Christ is his Lord will not be able to find security in a proclamation that Christ is his or her righteousness; Christ was their righteousness and they should have honored the grace of God as they walked this earth so that Christ could have lived righteously through them and in that sense, would have been their means of righteousness.

Chapter 7

Challenging Thoughts

7.1 Where is the Heavenly Kingdom?

It is a common presentation and understanding that heaven will be somewhere in the sky or heavens. The Word of God does not teach that this is so. The final word that is recorded states that following the descent of the New Jerusalem *to Earth*, God will dwell among his people. John has recorded, "Then I saw a new heaven and a new earth, for the first heaven and the first earth had passed away, and there was no longer any sea. I saw the New Jerusalem, coming down out of heaven from God, prepared as a bride beautifully dressed for her husband." (Rev 21:1-2)

> Although the earth will be greatly altered, it is to be the location of the Kingdom of God.

Although the earth will be greatly altered, it is to be the location of the Kingdom of God. A great deal has been written about the old earth passing away and a new earth being created. Prior to the Millennium the earth will be prepared for Christ's rule and there will be many physical changes made at that time.

The New Jerusalem that descends will have great high[381] and thick walls. It will be in the shape of a cube about 2,200 km on each side and the walls will be 65 meters thick.[382] The walls will have twelve foundations made of twelve kinds of precious stones,[383] and the city will be made from pure gold.

From this time forth there will be no sun or moon because they will not be needed. "The glory of the God gives it light and the Lord is its

---

[381] Rev 21:12
[382] Rev 21:16-17
[383] Rev 21:19

lamp." (Rev 21:23) The Bible has referred to outside the walls of the City as being "outer darkness." (Rev 21:18) "Darkness" probably refers to the absence of the presence of the glory of the Lord. John has recorded that the city has no need of the sun or moon to shine on it since the glory of God provides the light.

The glory of the Kingdom of Heaven -that was in heaven- will be revealed on earth and those who have prepared for it will dwell with God. "He will wipe every tear from their eyes. There will be no more death or mourning or crying or pain, for the old order of things has passed away." (Rev 21:4) The blessing of dwelling with God and in his Royal City will belong to those who "overcome." "He who overcomes will inherit all of this, and I will be his God and he will be my son." (Rev 21:7)

7.2 A Place for the Disobedient

The writer of Hebrews has written that "he [Christ] became the source of eternal salvation for all who obey him." (Heb 5:9) Although some accept that all the redeemed are obedient by compulsion the Word of God does not support this thought, neither could a person's life experience reveal it as truth. There will be some disobedient believers who have resisted the leading of the Spirit and who have allowed their walk to be in the sinful nature. These are the redeemed who "walk in darkness." [384]

John told his readers, "If we claim to have fellowship with him yet walk in darkness, we lie and do not live the truth." (1 Jn 1:6) His teaching references the way a person walks or lives out his life. It refers to a person's testimony of *faithfulness* to his Lord and to his brothers and neighbors.

In light of this, careful consideration needs to be given to the revelation of Jesus Christ, "Blessed are those who wash their robes ["do his commandments", KJV] that they may have the right to the tree of life and may go through the gates into the city. Outside are the dogs, those who practice magic arts, the sexually immoral, the murderers, the idolaters and *everyone who loves and practices falsehood.*" (Rev 22:14-15) Those who walk in darkness are those who love and practice falsehood. According to the Lord they will be found "outside" of his holy city separated from him.

---

[384] Mt 8:12, 22:13, 25:30, KJV

The "outside" is *not* the "lake of burning sulfur," but it is separation from the presence of Christ.[385] The Lord also revealed that "the kings of the earth" will bring their "splendor" into the city from the outside.[386] No splendor will be found in the lake of burning sulphur so the "outside" cannot be hell such as many would accept.

> The "outside" is *not* the "lake of burning sulfur," but it is a separation from the presence of Christ.

The prophet Daniel spoke of multitudes that will be raised to life following the Great Tribulation some of whom will awake to "everlasting life" and others to "shame and everlasting contempt." (Dan 12:2) His prophecy refers to those taking part in the first resurrection, that which precedes the Great Tribulation. Contempt does not come from a like-minded peer; it comes from another of a very different mindset. Those on the outside will suffer contempt from those inside, those who have given their lives for their Lord.

The believer should be prepared to exercise his faith through obedience. Those who have confessed that Christ is and will be their Lord and do not engage a righteous walk will be doomed to great disappointment when they find themselves forever separated from him. "The Son of Man will send out his angels, and they will weed out of his kingdom everything that causes sin and all who do evil." (Mt 13:41)

The city does not need the sun or the moon to shine on it, for the glory of God gives it light, and the Lamb of God is its lamp. (Rev 21:23)

The only light comes from inside the city. Outside is darkness-"outer darkness."

---

[385] Some would suggest that "outside" is the lake of burning sulphur; however, the lake of burning sulphur is for unbelievers (Rev 21:8) and for Satan. (Rev 20:10) The Word has several other references to the fact that outside are unfaithful servants. (Mt 22: 1-14, 24:42; 25:1-13, 30)

[386] Rev 21:24

7.3 Life in the Spirit and Religion

If given a chance people will change devotion to Christ into devotion to their church and its practices or into religion. Relationship is difficult as anyone who deals with people can attest. A mutually healthy relationship requires give and take, consideration, accommodation, sensitivity and respect. Commitment to church as an institution can exist according to a person's own terms and since the church is inanimate, affiliation is easier.

Religion without the Spirit does not please God and it will not bring anyone to eternal salvation or into his heavenly kingdom. Religion does not require a relationship with the Lord but is based on observance of prescribed practices, rituals, and observances. A person's need and God's desire is for his created people to have a holy relationship with him-to talk to him, to honor him, to love him. The issue of eternal salvation is one of the heart and of an intimate relationship, not of dogma, decree, or formality.

> Those who have confessed that Christ is and will be their Lord/lord and do not engage a righteous walk wil be doomed to great disappointment when they find themselves forever separated from him.

"You must love the Lord your God with all your heart, all your soul, and all your mind." (Mt 22:37, 38) It is this love expressed through obedience that results in the believer's transformation into a sacrifice acceptable to God.

Religion results when a person's "spiritual" focus is put on his or her church including his or her attendance, service, and fellowship rather than on the Lord. It is easy for a person to transition into this focus since the church -not the church of Christ- is visible and needy and has an element of spirituality in it.

Paul prophesied to Timothy that in the last days people will "have a form of godliness but denying its power. Have nothing to do with them." (2 Tim 3:5) There is nothing flattering in Paul's depiction to Timothy of those who have allowed themselves to be drawn into a form of godliness that lacks the Spirit.[387] Without his power the believer cannot become the sacrifice that God requires and his or her evil nature will continue to exercise itself.

---

[387] See 2 Tim 3:2-4; These people will be selfish, greedy with an interest in money and possessions, boastful, proud, abusive, disobedient to their parents, unholy, ungrateful, etc.

The church cannot bring anyone to eternal salvation which comes through the ministries of Christ as sacrifice, Holy Spirit, and High Priest and through the believer's personal commitment. The redeemed person is to use his or her gifting for the building of God's kingdom and God gives gifts so that everyone who has the Spirit can fulfill a particular service within the church.[388] There will be eternal consequences for those who neglect their gifting for service.[389] However, the believer's first obligation is to allow the Spirit of God to manifest his transforming power in his or her life. A person's focus should always remain on the Lord. The believer must cling to him and love him with all his or her mind, soul, body, and strength.

Paul addressed the requirements of a workman approved by God. "In a large house there are articles not only of gold and silver, but also of wood and clay; some for noble purposes and some for ignoble. If a man cleanses himself from the latter, he will be an instrument for noble purposes made holy, useful to the master and prepared to do any good work." (2 Tim 2:20-21) Only those who honor the Lord through their testimony or life example will be used for noble purposes.

> Relationship cannot exist without commitment and affection of the heart. This commitment is a measure of a person's *faithfulness*.

Relationship cannot exist without commitment and affection of the heart. This commitment is a measure of a person's *faithfulness*. Those who would resign it to formalities and ritual, to the mind and to knowledge, will never find a relationship with God or presence in his kingdom. Those who do not seek the heart of a loving God and creator and who cannot understand and respond to his heart cry must walk the path of frustration and emptiness, and eventually, eternal separation from him.

Eternal salvation is rested in the ministry of the Lord and Savior Jesus Christ as he mediates to bring a sinful and rebellious people in like mind with his or her holy God. It requires clinging with all of a person's heart, mind, and soul to the one who has promised to lead him or her to a heavenly dwelling. The mediation of the Lord is not only related to persuading the Father concerning the righteousness of a person, it also refers to his work within the redeemed as Holy Spirit. A person's sanctification is a component of Christ's mediation.

---

[388] Eph 2:10; Rom 12:6-8; 1 Cor 12:4-11, 28, 14:12
[389] 1 Cor 3: 12-15; Mt 25:14-30; Lk 1912-27

A loving relationship with God cannot be developed by obeying rules and procedures any more than it can with any other person. It comes through forging understanding based on knowledge and commitment to honoring the heart of the other. To put a person's eternal hope in obedience to the rules made by an institution, even a religious institution, is to place him or her again under a form of law.

Neither can the joy of pleasant and warm fellowship with other believer's and the practices that would enjoin close communion around the theme of God, as church gatherings often present, bring salvation. The Lord himself must be central in all things and honored with humility of heart. He offers a loving, caring, eternal relationship for those who would have it. Comfort and simplicity provided by formality of religion will not establish the relationship of heart that God desires, and neither do empty confessions, pledges, or promises to honor his sovereignty.

Christian faith is a person's obedient response to the persuasions of Christ. It is not just a possession but is a practice that compels its possessor to respond in compliance to that faith. Faith in practice is *obedience* and when it comes to obedience it is regarding the Spirit's leadership.[390] There is no other way to gain eternal salvation.

The Lord told Isaiah: "These people come near to me with their mouth and honor me with their lips, but their hearts are far from me. Their worship of me is made up only of rules taught by men." (Isa 29:13) The person who would find his or her eternal dwelling with the Lord must not allow religion to displace his or her faith in, and love for, Christ and his gospel.

7.4 Common Misrepresentations/Confusions Concerning Salvation

1. It is often presented that for the believer eternal salvation was accomplished at the cross by the sacrifice of Christ. Although the Word clearly teaches that his sacrifice "redeemed" the repentant sinner, it does not teach that this necessary and gracious act of our Savior meets the requirements for a person's eternal salvation. A person's redemption brings him

> A person's redemption brings him or her back to the place of fellowship with God and identifies him or her as a "servant" of Christ.

---

[390] Rom 8:4, 14; Gal 5:18

or her back to the place of fellowship with God and identifies them as a "servant" of Christ.[391] It also frees them from the jurisdiction of the Old Covenant.

The writer of Hebrews has recorded that eternal salvation requires a person's "obedience." (Heb 5:9) Paul recorded that it came *through the sanctifying work of the Spirit*. "From the beginning God chose you to be saved *through the sanctifying work of the Spirit* and through belief in the truth." (2 Thess 2:13). To Titus he wrote: "He saved us *through the washing of rebirth and renewal by the Holy Spirit*, whom he poured out on us generously through Jesus Christ our Savior." (Titus 3: 5-6)

To the Romans Paul taught, "Since we have now been justified by his blood, *how much more* shall we be saved from God's wrath through him!" (Rom 5:9-10) He distinguished the issue of "justification" from "being saved from God's wrath." That is, even though a person might have been justified at one time, he or she is not exempt from the wrath of God.

A person's justification is completed through the Lord's resurrected life[392] as he ministers as the Holy Spirit. Also, James has recorded, "You see that a person is justified by what he does and not by faith alone." (Jas 2:24) That is, the active ministry of the Spirit as permitted by the will of the redeemed person is necessary for his or her justification and their eternal salvation.

Through the sacrifice of Christ everything was made available for people to avoid God's wrath; however, his anger can only be avoided through a person's honoring of the provisions that Christ has made available. Since everything we need for life and godliness has been provided, and since righteous practices or godliness is expected, a person cannot continue to sin without suffering God's anger.

God's wrath does not necessarily mean that the sinner will be condemned to the lake of fire, since Paul taught that those who do not obey the gospel will be "punished with everlasting destruction and shut out from the presence of the Lord and from the majesty of his power on the day he comes to be glorified in his holy people." (2 Thess 1:8-9) Some will be condemned to the lake of burning sulphur[393] while others will be shut out from the presence of the Lord-outside the walls of the

---

[391] 1 Cor 7:22; 2 Co 1:22; Mt 25:21; Lk 12:47; Jn 15:20; Col 4:7; 2 Tim 2:24
[392] Rom 4:25
[393] Rev 21:8

Eternal Salvation

New Jerusalem. The writer of Hebrews has stated that those who are not holy will not see or lay eyes upon him.[394]

As well as suffering eternal separation and having to live in shame and everlasting contempt,[395] the wrath of God may be brought down on the disobedient as they walk this earth. The Lord punishes and disciplines those he loves. In Hebrews it is recorded, "My son, do not make light of the Lord's discipline, and do not lose heart when he rebukes you, because the Lord disciplines those he loves, and he punishes everyone he accepts as a son. God disciplines us for our good that we may share in his holiness. No discipline seems pleasant at the time, but painful. Later, however, it produces a harvest of righteousness and peace for those who have been trained in it." (Heb 12:5-6, 10-11) This discipline and punishment is to occur during a person's earthly experience while he is being fitted for eternity. Discipline is intended to correct inappropriate behaviour.

However, God's wrath is more eternal also. The Lord told his disciples: "Not everyone who says to me, 'Lord, Lord,' will enter the kingdom of heaven, but only he who does the will of my Father who is in heaven… Therefore, whoever hears these words of mine and puts them into practice is like a wise man who built his house on the rock." (Mt 7: 21…24) That is, although a person had been justified at the point of confession, only those who *do* God's will can gain entrance to the kingdom of heaven.

Eternal salvation is not achieved at confession of faith, but through obedience to Christ, the Holy Spirit, following confession and through a person's transformation of heart and mind-through the life of Christ lived out in him or her.

2. A person's understanding of "saved" and "salvation" must be clear. Because a person has been "saved" does not necessarily mean that he has been "saved" eternally; although, this is an accepted perception. In common usage a person can be saved from a multitude of dangers such as fire, drowning, and avalanches; all of them could have resulted in harm or death. "Saved" is used in a similar manner in the Word of

> "Saved" does not necessarily mean that a person has been "saved" eternally.

---

[394] Heb 12:14
[395] Dan 12:2

God. When the writers wanted to suggest that a person was delivered from an imminent danger, they indicated that he or she was "saved." Accordingly, the Scriptures state that the believer has been saved from his or her sins committed under the first covenant and from the dominion of the law, but they also talk about "eternal salvation." It should not be accepted that all usage of "saved" or "salvation" refers to a person's *eternal* salvation. Eternal salvation is only presented as coming through obedience.

3. It is often taken that because of humankind's inability to do anything good, their eternal salvation is provided directly by grace and as a gift. Of course, fallen people *cannot* do anything good, but the Spirit of Christ in him or her can and he is the source of a person's eternal salvation. It is the *means* of salvation that has been provided by grace, not eternal salvation itself. The blessings of God's grace have been explained earlier and as has been revealed, eternal salvation comes through obedience.

Paul has revealed that you have been saved by faith through grace because or since the believer is God's workmanship.[396] That is, the being that we become is the workmanship or product of the Spirit's ministry. Through a person's persuasion to obey him by practicing faith the person who is being saved is becoming an acceptable offering. Due to his or her having been persuaded they are being obedient to the Spirit's leading.

Because of the reality of the need for obedience some would teach that God compels the redeemed to be obedient. Such teaching would take away the God-given right of a person to exercise free-will and would even in the heavenly kingdom require that God continue to make people obey. His work would never end. Even through a person's own life experience following his or her redemption the believer can attest to the truth that he or she has not always been obedient. The believer is to love the Lord with all of his or her heart, soul, and mind. Love is not forced; it is chosen.

The Word of God also affirms the need of the believer to "sow to please the Spirit" if he or she wants to avoid destruction and find eternal life.[397] This warning is given to encourage a person in the pursuit of righteousness.

---

[396] Eph 2: 8-10
[397] Gal 6:7-8

Eternal Salvation

The issue of doing good is often not fully considered. Certainly, a person cannot maintain goodness in his or her walk without God's grace; however, following the gifting of the Spirit, he or she has been provided all that is necessary for life and godliness. They can walk in a godly manner, however doing so is a matter of their choices.

4. Eternal salvation is often presented as being through "belief," and it is; however, the word "belief or believe" is often left open to each person's interpretation. When it comes to "belief" as the means of bringing a person to salvation, a complete Biblical understanding needs to be appreciated. Belief should not merely be accepted as the mental assent to an idea; unless it refers to the belief that is required for a person's initial justification; it must be confirmed by the believer's practices.

The Word of God states that a person can be saved by 'believing on his name.'[398] The name was significant in the Lord's day. It signified the character and nature of a person. Sinners are given a new name[399] when they overcome the world. Their character and nature have changed. Belief in the sense used here indicates confidence based on the knowledge of who the Lord is. In some places Jesus told the lost that they were to "believe on him."[400] Often belief was to be rested in the gospel[401], the truth of Christ's words[402], "that he is, and that he is a rewarder of them that diligently seek him," (Heb 11:6) that "if you confess with your mouth, 'Jesus is Lord,' and believe with your heart that God has raised Christ from the dead, you will be saved." (Rom 10:9) [403] Belief is based on knowledge[404] and it is placed in Christ. Belief in the context of salvation goes beyond understanding that something is true; it means that a person has enough faith in Christ or is sufficiently persuaded concerning the being and mission of Christ that he or she is willing to entrust or commit their well-being to their

---

[398] Jn 1:12, 20:31; 1Jn 5:13
[399] Rev 2:17
[400] Jn 7:39, 6:29, KJV
[401] Mk 1:15; See also Acts 16:31
[402] Jn 5:47, NLT
[403] Although being "saved" as presented in this verse comes by belief, the meaning of "saved" being addressed is a person's deliverance from the Old Covenant and the gifting of the Spirit. See Heb 9:15.
[404] Lk 8:12

Savior's care and to accept his teachings. A person's understanding of "belief" should not be limited to mental assent but acknowledgment to the point that he or she is prepared to obediently cling to or cleave to the Lord. It means accepting as truth, his earthly ministry and his teachings about the gospel with the commitment to honoring them with his or her total being, all their mind, soul, and heart.[405]

> "To believe" means to obediently practice that which a person holds as his or her belief or persuasion.

"To believe" means to *obediently practice* that which a person holds as his or her belief or persuasion. A person's practices are a better testimony of his or her beliefs than are their proclamations.

In Jesus' day "to believe" was synonymous with obedience. "And to whom did God swear that they would never enter his rest if not to those who *disobeyed*? So, we see that they were not able to enter, because of their *unbelief*." (Heb 3: 18, 19) A person is expected to act according to what he or she believes. A person cannot truly believe something and act contrary to that belief. When "believe" is mentioned a person should accept that his or her actions must illustrate what they claim to believe. Belief will only result in a person's salvation if his or her actions are congruent with their beliefs and their beliefs are in accordance with the Word of God.

Today the most commonly presented view of the means of salvation seems to be by *assent* or acknowledgement that Christ will deliver the confessor into his eternal presence if he or she acknowledges that Christ is God, acknowledges that he or she is a sinner, and voices repentance concerning their sin. Many would also insist that a person's belief must be assent that exists in his or her "heart" or that their belief must be sincere. To accept the position that salvation comes through assent without requiring obedience, however, is contrary to much of the teaching of the New Testament. Belief "in the heart" means that a person accepts something as true in his or her core or with all their might; if so, their behaviours will be in accordance with their beliefs.

Whatever a person claims "belief" to mean, it must incorporate the necessity for obedience to Christ. He is to be lord and He is to be honored as Lord. Paul stated that salvation comes from confession or

---

[405] Mt 22:37, Mk 12:30, Lk 10:27

through a person's pledge or promise that Christ is his or her lord,[406] and their "belief" must recognize his lordship. It is through this belief that a person abandons personal lordship of his or her life and allows Christ to direct them in order that their heart might be transformed into that of the likeness of Christ.[407]

"Belief" does not save anyone since every person believes in something. That which results in a person's salvation is that which he believes and the way he proves that belief by his actions. Belief produces faith and faith unless it produces works, is meaningless.[408]

In order that no one should be left confused the Lord revealed to John, "Blessed are those who wash their robes or do his commandments, that they may have the right to the tree of life and may go through the gates into the city." (Rev 22:14) Only those with white robes, clothed in righteousness by *doing* his commandments, will be allowed entry into the New Jerusalem. That righteousness comes through belief in the truth of God's Word and through the Spirit's sanctifying work which the believer must allow and embrace.

> Enough belief for salvation is belief that presses the believer to follow the leadership of Christ as he ministers in a person's life through his Spirit.

Enough belief for salvation is belief that presses the believer to follow the leadership of Christ[409] as he ministers in a person's life through his Spirit. This belief needs to demonstrate faithfulness and must allow the believer to be led to develop holiness through the obedience of a righteous walk.

5. It is the teaching of some that upon confession of faith all sin has been forgiven-past, present, and future- consequently, a person's eternal salvation has been secured. However, having been forgiven or pardoned for sin at the time of confession is not the fullness of the believer's need. God's Word requires repentance and

> A person's having been forgiven or pardoned for sin is not the fullness of the believer's need.

---

[406] Rom 10:9, 10
[407] Rom 8:29
[408] Jas 2:17
[409] Heb 2:10

confession of known sin following his profession of faith in order that it might be forgiven.[410] The real necessity for eternal salvation is transformation of the heart and mind into a state of holiness from which freedom from sin through pardon and righteous practices are necessary components.

God's Word reveals that the propitiation offered by the blood of Christ was for past sins. "Being justified freely by his grace through the redemption that is in Christ Jesus: Whom God hath set forth to be a propitiation through faith in his blood, to declare his righteousness for the remission of sins that are past, through the forbearance of God." (Rom 3:24-25) The writer of Hebrews also presents that Christ died "as a ransom to set people free from the sins committed under the first covenant." (Heb 9:15) That is, the sacrifice of Christ was to cover the sentence of death that was the just penalty imposed by God for all sins committed under the first covenant so that a person might be free of the covenant of the law.[411] The law, established by God, had to be honored in order that he remain just in his judgments and government. The teaching of these verses does not support the idea that the sacrificial offering of Christ paid the penalty for all sin but that he was the atoning victim for the "sins that are past," for those that needed to be dealt with in order to complete the Old Covenant so that the New could be availed and for those *confessed* following a person's profession of faith.

The death of Christ released the believer from the death required by the law through Christ's having completed the righteous requirements of the Old Covenant for him or her. His death did not release the believer from their sinning ways or from their evil hearts since they are still in possession of their natural spirit, but through the Spirit of Christ, given following his resurrection, Christ provided a *means* of freedom

---

[410] 1 Jn 1:9

[411] Although Gentiles do not have the privilege of a covenant relationship with God, they are subject to fulfilling the law of the covenant for righteousness' sake. "For it is not those who hear the law who are righteous in God's sight, but those who obey the law who will be declared righteous. (Indeed, when Gentiles, who do not have the law, do by nature the things required by the law, they are a law for themselves, even though they do not have the law, since they show the requirements of the law are written on their hearts, their consciences also bearing witness, and their thoughts now accusing, now even defending them. (Rom 2:13-15, NIV)

from sinning and an *opportunity* for a transformed heart. A person's walk of righteousness and transformation is accomplished through obedience to the Spirit[412], "Christ in you; the hope of glory." (Col 1:27)

Once made friends with God through the atoning sacrifice of Christ, it is incumbent upon the believer to walk worthily in God's grace in order that righteousness and relationship might be maintained. John has made this clear: *"But if we walk in the light, as he is in the light, we have fellowship with one another, and the blood of Jesus, his Son, purifies us from all sin."* (1 Jn 1:7) In this passage John has put a *condition* upon the provision of the availability of the blood of Christ for a person's purification and that is, he or she must *"walk* in the light." No other provision except for an obedient walk along with repentance and confession for sin is made for a person to access Christ's blood for remission of sins following his or her redemption from the law.

A person's justification concerning the law is only permanent if he or she walks under the lordship of Christ and according to his leading. It should not and cannot be accepted that the person who was justified can go about living as he or she once did. The development of holiness[413] is essential for a person's salvation. God is holy and all who will dwell with him must be holy. Having been justified concerning the law may render a person innocent concerning that law *but it will not make him or her holy* in practice. They must be transformed. A person cannot rest his or her understanding in the thought that having been justified at one point, even if all sin and sinning *had been forgiven*, he or she will be made holy in thought and practice and will be made an "acceptable sacrifice" to the Lord. It will not fit them for the Royal Kingdom. Forgiveness only cleanses a person from the consequences of his sin. The preparation of a holy people for God is the very reason that Christ came to this earth.

The believer is justified concerning his or her past sins by the blood of Christ. However, this is *not* the end of justification. They are justified following this through the resurrection of Jesus. "He was delivered over to death for our sins and was raised to life for our

---

[412] Heb 5:9

[413] A person is made holy through the sacrifice of Christ, but that state may change as he or she lives out their life. The state of holiness that is necessary for eternal salvation comes through the Spirit's work in the believer's life. (See Gal 5:5)

justification." (Rom 4:24) Being justified following a person's release from the law of righteousness under the Old Covenant requires that Christ live his resurrected life through his Spirit *in the believer*. This life *must* be lived. James confirmed this thought. "You see that a person is justified by what he does and not by faith alone." (Jas 2:24) What a person does, or allowing Christ to live through him or her, is the means of eternal justification[414] and is the evidence of his faith. That is, it is the life of Christ in a person that allows him or her to defeat sin and be transformed into the likeness of God's Son.[415]

> What a person does, or allowing Christ to live through him or her, is the means of eternal justification.

The righteous practices and attitudes that he produces result in holiness[416] and allow a person to enjoy the eternal presence of God. Forgiveness is available for the redeemed who sin, if they are walking in the light or are striving to be led by the Spirit[417], provided they repent and confess the transgressions that the Spirit has revealed. "If we confess our sins, he is faithful and just and will forgive us our sins and purify us from all unrighteousness." (1 Jn 1:9) Since a condition for forgiveness is presented, it cannot be said that all sin has been forgiven.

There are specific passages that support the requirement of righteous living as well. Paul has recorded that a person cannot "mock" God by seeking "pleasure" in his or her sinful nature. "Do not be deceived: God cannot be mocked. A man reaps what he sows. The one who sows to please his sinful nature, from that nature will reap destruction; the one who sows to please the Spirit, from the Spirit will reap eternal life." (Gal 6:7-8) *[418]* Eternal life or destruction are determined by a person's walk in the Spirit.

---

[414] Heb 5:9
[415] Rom 8:29
[416] Rom 6:19, 22
[417] Rom 8:1...4, "Therefore, there is now no condemnation for those who are in Christ Jesus because through Christ Jesus the law of the Spirit of life set me free from the law of sin and death.... he [God] condemned sin in sinful man, in order that the righteous requirements of the law might be fully met in us who do not live according to the sinful nature but according to the Spirit." (NIV)
[418] Paul taught that, "if you live according to the sinful nature you will die." (Rom 8:13, NIV)

Peter has commented directly on the state of those who continue to sin after having escaped the corruption of the world through redemption. "If they have escaped the corruption of the world by knowing our Lord and Savior Jesus Christ and are again entangled in it and overcome, they are worse off at the end than they were at the beginning. It would have been better for them not to have known the way of righteousness than to have known it and then to turn their backs on the sacred command[419] that was passed on to them." (2 Peter 2:20-21) The writer of Hebrews also confirms that a person cannot deliberately continue to sin and enjoy forgiveness for its practice; the person who does so will lose his or her hope. "If we deliberately keep on sinning after we have received the knowledge of the truth, no sacrifice for sins is left, but only a fearful expectation of judgment and of raging fire that will consume the enemies of God." (Heb 10:26-27)

> A person cannot deliberately continue to sin and enjoy forgiveness for its practice.

Not only is future sin not forgiven, those in the Lord have a *responsibility* to pray for a brother who he or she sees sinning so that they can intervene with the Lord concerning that person in order he may be given life. "If anyone sees his brother commit a sin that does not lead to death, he should pray and God will give him life." (1 Jn 5:16) [420] This might be an aspect of the washing a brother's feet that had been commanded by Jesus. If sin can lead to death, a person cannot assert that all sin has been forgiven.

---

[419] The "sacred command" presents that if a righteous man turns from his righteousness and does detestable things that his righteousness will no longer be remembered with the result that he will die. See Ezek 18:24. Some suggest that the sacred command is to love the Lord with all one's heart, soul, body and strength. This kind of love does not allow for continued sinning and automatic forgiveness for rebellion.

[420] Some commentators accept that John is referring to the giving of physical life, or avoiding physical death, instead of the sinner being washed by forgiveness for his sin and escaping a death sentence for it. However, in no other place in John's book does he refer to physical death. His presentation concerns the Spirit and the defeat of sin. In the preceding verses his conversation has dealt with conditions that bring confidence of eternal life and God's provision for the believer. Even if a person understands this to be physical life that is given to the sinner, it would indicate that the sin had not been forgiven because its consequence was to be death. A consequence does not follow a pardon.

When addressing believers James has also recorded, "When tempted, no one should say, 'God is tempting me.' For God cannot be tempted by evil, nor does he tempt anyone; but each one is tempted when, by his own evil desire, he is dragged away and enticed. Then, after desire has conceived, it gives birth to sin; and sin, when it is full-grown, gives birth to death." (Jas 1:13-15) Clearly his understanding is that the believer must be careful not to let sin overtake him or her. All sin must not have been forgiven since giving in may lead to a person's death.

At the time of a person's initial confession only past sin, not sin that may be practiced in the future, was forgiven. The justification provided at the cross was made available to rid a person of the death that the law had brought. Through the cross and by his Spirit, the life of Christ will empower and direct the believer in the righteous practices needed to transform his or her mind and develop a state of holiness that is permanent. Christ as High Priest mediates with God regarding forgiveness of unknown sins, and known sins as they are confessed, following receipt of the Spirit.

Christ encouraged that his burden was not heavy.[421] It also needs to be clearly understood that the development of a state of holiness, as evidenced in a righteous heart and righteous mind, is the greatest need of humankind. It is enabled through God's willingness upon confession to forgive sin as the believer is being transformed by the Spirit. This cleansing and forgiveness is an expression of God's mercy, grace and love to a frail people. A transformation to the state of holiness is needed for entrance into the eternal Kingdom and this is being waited for as the Spirit performs his ministry in those who are willing to be led. "But by faith we eagerly await through the Spirit the righteousness for which we hope." (Gal 5:5)[422]

6. There is confusion between "redemption"[423] and "eternal salvation." While "redemption" refers to recovering something through purchase

---

[421] Mt 11:30

[422] A person should be careful not to dismiss "faith" as being a function of the mind. Faith must be put into practice. Faith really means "persuasion" and a person's persuasions direct his or her actions. Neither does the Spirit work without the believer's permission. He can be quenched, and the need of his ministry can be denied.

[423] "Redemption" is translated from the Greek *apolutrosis* which means; "(the act)

or by paying a ransom, salvation refers to delivering something from imminent danger and does not specifically refer to the means of that deliverance.

Generally, redemption means "deliverance" from an undesirable situation through purchase as might be understood from a person going to the market to purchase something that he or she desires by meeting the conditions necessary for transfer of ownership. Incumbent upon this understanding is that which has been redeemed has become the "property" of the person to whom ownership has been passed.

> The redemption that comes through the blood of Christ presents the Lord as purchasing the believer from the jurisdiction of the Old Covenant requirements.

The redemption that comes through the blood of Christ presents the Lord as purchasing the believer from the debt owed for his sin while under the jurisdiction of the Old Covenant requirements allowing him or her the enjoyment of the New Covenant.

The writer of Hebrews has recorded: "For this reason (to cleanse our consciences or moral consciousness) from acts that lead to death) Christ is the mediator of a new covenant, that those who are called, may receive the promised eternal inheritance-now that he has died as a ransom to set them free from the sins committed under the first covenant." (Heb 9:15) Paul has made the nature and purpose of this redemption clear. "Christ redeemed us from the curse of the law by becoming a curse for us, for it is written: 'Cursed is everyone who is hung on a tree.' He redeemed us in order that the blessing given to Abraham might come to the Gentiles through Christ Jesus, *so that by faith we might receive the promise of the Spirit.*" (Gal 3:13-14) According to the writer of Hebrews the purpose of our redemption is to free us from the consequence of sins committed under the first covenant and to bring to completion that Covenant for the person who is willingly led by the Spirit. According to Paul our redemption is so that we might receive the Spirit.

Many accept that once a person has been redeemed, he or she has become a member of the family of God and will find "eternal"

---

ransom in full, i.e. (figuratively) riddance, or (specially) Christian salvation: — deliverance, redemption." –from Strong's Greek Dictionary #629 salvation. Redemption has no application beyond the condition that Christ has purchased and taken ownership of the believer so that he or she might be freed from their "past sins" and might receive the Holy Spirit. That is, it does not mean to suggest anything more than that the redeemed person has become the property of Christ- in the case of a servant-so that he might receive a better hope. There are faithful and unfaithful, committed and uncommitted servants. What transpires in the final state of the redeemed will be determined by the Lord as the believer faces the judgment seat of Christ. It does not mean that he or she has been eternally saved as is often presented.

There are expectations put on the servant of Christ. The believer may dwell in the household of the family of God and may even be considered a member of the family, but his or her redemption and their *adoption* into the family of God has not been completed. Adoption only occurs at the "redemption of the body"[424] and is being waited for by the believer following the gifting of the Spirit. "But we ourselves who have the firstfruits of the Spirit, groan inwardly as we wait eagerly for our adoption as sons, the redemption of our bodies." (Rom 8:23)[425] Accordingly, the "redemption of the body" to which Paul is referring is not the redemption that came through the sacrificial offering of Christ's blood, but the redemption that takes place through the Spirit's sanctifying work and rids him or her of slavery to the body. The Lord told some Jewish believers, "I tell you the truth, everyone who sins is a slave to sin. Now a slave has *no permanent place in the family*, but a son belongs to it forever." (Jn 8:34-35) Paul has taught that a son is a person who is led by the Spirit.[426]

A person's eternal salvation was not accomplished by ransom from the first covenant but requires redemption and the sanctification that the Spirit completes in a person's life in conjunction with the believer's willingness to be led through righteous practices which result in a state of holiness. A person's redemption through the blood only brings the

---

[424] The body must be redeemed from its sinful desires and state…as Paul presents, it is "*the body of death.*"
[425] This "redemption" is the purchasing of the believer's body through the Spirit of Christ or Holy Spirit ridding the body of its unrighteous practices. Paul referred to this "justification" as coming through the resurrection of Christ." (Rom 4:25) See also Jas 2:24.
[426] Rom 8:14

believer back to relationship with his creator making Christ his lord and master.

7. The promises given to committed saints and to the apostles are often presented as applying to all of those who have claimed belief. This is error and care must be taken when a person applies the promises of those walking in a godly manner to all who have made a profession of faith. There are promises given to those in the seven churches of Revelation that apply to those who "overcome" and not to all. There are promises that are made to the Lord's disciples and yet not all who claim belief are disciples. When Christ made promises to his disciples, he often used the pronoun "you"; however, those promises did not apply to Judas or necessarily to those who have confessed belief. Those who love their family and even their own lives more than they love Christ cannot be his disciples.[427] Whoever does not bear his or her cross cannot be the Lord's disciple,[428] nor can anyone who is not prepared to give up everything he or she has.[429]

   When Paul wrote that "we will judge angels" (1 Cor 6:3) he did not mean to present that all of the redeemed would be the judges of angels but that some would be elevated to that position because of the nature of the lives that they had lived.

   Promises are given throughout the Scriptures that apply to specific people and not to all believers.

8. The truths of The Word of God are becoming increasingly more difficult to discern. This is not because those who study the Word are any less capable than those of other eras; it is because translations are becoming more 'interpretations' than translations. That is, "translators" are presenting their "translation" or interpretation to reflect their own bias. For instance, Romans 8:15 in the 1986 version (NIV) reads "*For you did not receive a spirit which makes you a slave again to fear, but you received the Spirit of sonship.*" The 2011 version reads, "*The Spirit you received does not make you slaves, so that you live in fear again; rather, the Spirit you have received brought about your adoption to sonship.*" While

---

[427] Lk 14:26
[428] Lk 14:27
[429] Lk 14:33

the first translation does not mention "adoption," the second says that it has been completed. This thought must be contrasted with verse 23 of the same chapter which in both translations says that *"we wait eagerly for our adoption as sons, the redemption of our bodies."* You can't both have it and be waiting for it. However, having received it fits more comfortably with current theology that teaches sonship to have been achieved at the time of confession of faith.

Revelation 22: 14 (NIV) states that *"Blessed are those who wash their robes, that they might have the right to the tree of life."* The KJV reads, *"Blessed are they that do his commandments, that they may have right to the tree of life."* In spite of the many references to the need for "obedience," (Mt 7:21, Heb 5:9 etc.) its need is being removed because obedience has been considered to be "works" which is seen to conflict with "grace."

The older KJV of Hebrews 10:10 has added in italics "for all" at the end to show that it was not in the original Greek. The KJV2000 has removed the italics implying its inclusion in the original text.

There are other instances where words once indicated as having been added are now being presented as a translation when they are, in fact, someone's interpretation. (Hebrews 9:12, "for us") It seems that "translation" is becoming more "interpretation" with an intrusion of bias. The effect is that God's "Word" is becoming corrupted and less reliable with the result that greater care must be taken to gain truth. The full gospel needs to be understood by theme as well as by verse.

Chapter 8

Conclusion

Considering the variety of denominational perspectives, many ways have been accepted by which a person might be eternally saved. The Lord himself said that since the time of John the Baptist people have been trying to "force" their way into the kingdom of God. Unfortunately, the "forcing" is still being attempted. Having made this comment, the Lord added that it was "easier for heaven and earth to disappear than for the smallest point of God's law to be overturned." (Lk 16:16, NLT) The law cannot be ignored. Christ said that he had come to complete it and Paul has taught that the righteous requirements of the law are fully met in those who live according to the Spirit. Trying to enter the kingdom of God in any other manner is an attempt to force a way in.

It is tempting to accept teachings that support the realization of a person's hope merely by their having been baptized or through having confessed faith at a singular event. The Word is replete with the need for commitment, obedience, and the expression of love to Christ and to others. It reveals the judgment that awaits all of humankind for the things done in the body, starting with the household of God. A person's commitment is to be complete. That is, the believer is to love the Lord their God with all their heart, their soul, and their mind. Less devotion will not please the Lord and will not enable righteousness. The Word speaks of the need to die to self-interest and for the believer to carry his cross so that he might crucify his or her body when it starts to take on life again, when personal interests start to emerge, and temptations become more real.

Eternal hope is not gained through a passive walk. Entrance to the Kingdom requires effort and a clinging to Christ. The Lord requires belief, but that belief must be to the extent that it is lived. It requires faith, but that faith must be demonstrated through the believer's obedient practices. The will of God must be done.

The doctrine of God's "sovereign grace" has permeated much of modern theology. Certainly, God is sovereign and all that he does and that he requires must be honoured. God's grace, however, has been allowed the understanding that nothing is required of the believer and that eternal salvation has been gifted or handed to him. God's grace is the manifestation of the life of Christ in and for the believer. His grace is the sacrificial offering of Christ on the cross, the gifting of the Spirit, and the constancy of God's working for good in the lives of those who have heard the call to live according to his purposes. A person is truly saved by God's grace, but It is not the "cheap" grace that is commonly presented.

All that is needed for life and godliness has been provided by God and those who dismiss their participation by ignoring the requirement to obediently follow Christ will one day suffer judgment for their disregard and they will be separated from their lord forever.

The need of humankind is not just to be pardoned for any sin they carry; it is to allow the Spirit to transform their hearts. It is to have them made a sacrifice acceptable to God, sanctified by the on-going ministry of the Spirit. It has been clearly revealed that the constant evil inclinations of the natural person pains God's heart. The evil heart was not the reality when God declared his creation to be very good and it will not be when his eternal kingdom is finally established. All of those who will find enjoyment with him will have been transformed into the likeness of his Son. God will be pleased and will once more walk and talk and even minister to his children. All sin will have been removed along with all who cause sin. What glory awaits those who are prepared to honour their Lord.

When considering a person's eternal salvation, it needs to be remembered that the plan was created by God and it will accomplish his purposes. Although humankind may have a special place in his creation, he loves all that he has created. People must honour his teaching and the role that he has ordained for them and even the state that he requires. God created for his good pleasure not for that of people.

There are many false and deceptive teachings in the Christian community and the Lord taught that many would be deceived and that only a few would walk the narrow road that leads to life. God's love and forgiveness should not be allowed to blind the believer to other teachings such as obedience, confession, repentance, and judgment- the gospel teachings that reveal the ongoing work of the cross. Each person needs to entrust his or her understanding of truth to themselves and to gain truth from the Holy Spirit and from their own studies. Paul wrote to Timothy, "For the time will come when men will not put up with sound doctrine. Instead, to suit their own desires, they will gather around them a great number of teachers to say what their itching ears want to hear. They will turn their ears away from the truth and turn aside to myths." (2 Tim 4:3-4) The person desiring entrance into the kingdom of God must not allow his hope to rest in a myth or in those who teach myths.

Chapter 9

Questions Answered

1. When does salvation take place?

Salvation means rescue from impending danger; accordingly, a person may be rescued or saved many times. The believer may rightly claim that he has been saved at the time of repentance and confession of faith. This "salvation" however, is deliverance from his past sins and from the legal jurisdiction of the Old Covenant. It is not "eternal salvation." Paul taught that a person could place himself or herself under the law again by rebelling against the Spirit of Christ who was given to provide victory over sin's temptation. In this sense, a person can lose that salvation. If he or she was saved from the law and from their past sins but continues to rebel against the leadership of Christ, they must work out their salvation totally by themselves; their initial deliverance will have had no lasting merit.

Of course, a person can be delivered from the temptations that he or she faces through the power of the Spirit and in this sense, they have been saved from the trials and judgment that would otherwise befall them.

"Eternal salvation" is the result of the believer's obedience to the Spirit's leading. It comes from striving for righteous practices as he or she is led and results when the body has been redeemed or when the believer has been transformed into the likeness of Christ and has been adopted as a son of Gd. For the faithful this salvation will happen at physical death.

2. Has all sin been forgiven?

The Word of God is very clear that upon confession of faith and through the pledge of Christ's lordship, a person's "past sins" have been washed away. It is equally clear that sins committed following the gifting of the Spirit are to be repented of and confessed if they are known, in order that they might be forgiven. "Unknown" sin will be mediated by Christ as high priest and will be forgiven and washed away through his advocacy

Eternal Salvation

and by the application of the blood of his sacrificial offering, provided he is walking in the light given him or her.

Sin can only be forgiven by the application of the blood of Christ, however the manner of gaining forgiveness is different following the gifting of the Spirit than it had been prior to that point.

3. *Can the believer have assurance of eternal salvation?*

The believer can have assurance of his or her eternal state, but that assurance may not come as some would present. The person who would "cling" to his or her Savior and who would love him with all of their soul, mind, body, and heart can have assurance that they *are being* delivered. The assurance cannot be based on a single act of faith, however. It can only rest in those who are being made holy-who are walking in the light- and who by practice are being obedient to the Spirit. "By that one sacrifice he has made perfect forever those who are being made holy." (Heb 10:14) Perfection *only* applies to those who "*are being made holy.*" This is not a past event but one that is ongoing and progressive.

Several passages speak of a person's need to persist in righteousness "to the end," [430] and to be faithful in service.

Paul's epistle to the Ephesians (1:13-14, NIV)[431] would seem to present a "guarantee" of a person's inheritance, however "guarantee" is an inaccurate translation of the Greek. On this occasion "guarantee" should be understood to be that the Spirit is a "deposit" representing God's *intense and serious state of mind* that those who have believed should inherit his kingdom. A deposit is not a guarantee and should not be taken as a surety. The Lord's own words state that one's place in his family might not be permanent. "I tell you the truth, everyone who sins is a slave to sin. Now a slave has *no permanent place in the family,* but a son belongs to it forever." (Jn 8:35) [432]

As presented on page 109, there are evidences in a person's life that can provide assurance of his hope.

---

[430] Mt 10:22; 2 Pet 2:21; Jn 8:34; Gal 6:8; Rev 21:7

[431] "Having believed, you were marked in him with a seal, the promised Holy Spirit, who is a deposit guaranteeing our inheritance until the day of redemption of those who are God's possession-to the praise of his glory."

[432] Christ considers the person who sins to be a slave to sin because he has provided all that is needed for life and godliness through his Spirit (2 Pet 1:3) so for a person to continue sinning indicates his slavery to it. The person who obeys the Spirit is a "son." (Rom 8:14)

4. Can the believer lose his "salvation?"

This question is often posed and deserves some consideration. There are many who argue adamantly for the position that a person has been eternally secured in his heavenly hope at the time of his or her confession of faith, and those who respond just as vehemently for the position that confession does not produce eternal assurance.

The query about whether a person can lose his salvation may be one that God would not have his children ask. What are the motives of the person engaged in such a query? Those asking the question have probably made a "confession of faith" and want assurance that they will be saved even if they fail to live that confession. Or, the question might be asked when hope and assurance are being sought regarding a loved one's outcome even though that person's life did not reflect a godly walk after having made a confession of faith. In either situation, the question is connected to spiritual failure.

Some have ventured that the assurance of eternal salvation is needful to motivate a person who has sinned to persevere in his or her spiritual walk. However, good teaching will inform all believers of the need to wash their robes or to repent and seek forgiveness when they have sinned. God is patient[433] and will strive with the wayward person. "Or do you show contempt for the riches of his kindness, tolerance and patience, not realizing that God's kindness leads you toward repentance." (Rom 2:4) God's Word has made it clear that a damaged relationship can be mended. The one ready to live in faith will respond in obedience to God's Word and to the Spirit's prompting. To fail to obey his Word is an act of disobedience, and failure to put confidence in the Word of God demonstrates a lack of faith-a lack of having been persuaded. Such a person needs to know how to be obedient, not assurance that despite such sinful activity his or her eternal hope has been left intact. God is loving and patient, but he is also holy, and without holiness no one will see him.[434]

God's Word resounds with the need for a person to be victorious, to overcome, and to persevere in order to inherit His blessings.[435] Believers are told to always be ready for his return-oil in their lamps[436]- and to be clothed in

---

[433] 2 Pet 3:9
[434] Heb 12 14
[435] Mt 10:22; Jn 8:34; Rom 11:22; 1 Cor 15:1-2; Gal 6:7-8; Phil 3:18-19; Col 1:21-23; 1 Tim 4:16; 2 Tim 2:12; Heb 6:4-6, 10:26-31, 36-39; 2 Pet 2:20-21; Rev 21:7
[436] Mt 25: 1-13

Eternal Salvation

righteousness. A person's final state is dependent on his faithfulness throughout the duration of his earthly life.[437] Falling from grace is not victorious living.

There are several passages that are often used to instill confidence in the concept of eternal security. They revolve around the proclamation in Scripture of a person's sonship, of God's guarantee, and of his sealing of the believer. These need to be examined.

a. *The Believer's Adoption*

The identification of the believer as a son of God[438] has often been credited as assurance of eternal security. The implication is that once a son, a person can never be *not a son*.

The designation as "sons of God" is given only to those who "believe" (Jn 1:12), who have "received him" (Jn 1:12), and who are "led by the Spirit of God." (Rom 8:14) Caution must be exercised when a person proclaims himself, herself, or another as a son of God.

Many assume their sonship based on a prayer once made or on the proclamation of another. However, the heart is deceptive, and the proclamation may be false. Faith and belief will prove themselves in a person's walk as his confession of Christ's lordship is lived out or has failed to be lived out. Paul told his readers to test their faith to see that it is sincere. "Examine yourselves to see whether you are in the faith; test yourselves. Do you not realize that Christ Jesus is in you--unless, of course, you fail the test?" (2 Cor 13:5) For this reason the believer should find his confidence in the evidences of the Spirit's work in his or her life rather than in a *moment* of commitment.

The person who is a son of God has Christ's Spirit and has allowed himself or herself to be led by his Spirit. He or she is "in Christ." There are many, however, who suppose that they are "in" Him but who do not permit Christ's leadership or lordship in their lives. Their claim is false, and their hope will be dashed. A son has many qualities that identify him as the father's son. For the believer who is following the Holy Spirit, the characteristics are those that reflect the Father, the qualities of his image. The person who would be God's son must put to death the misdeeds of the flesh and be transformed into his creator's image. This person does not

---

[437] Mt 10:22; Rom 11:22; 1 Cor 15: 1-2;1 Tim 4:16; 2 Tim 2:12; Heb 6: 4-6, 10:26-31, 36-39; 2 Pet 2:20-21; Rev 21:7
[438] Jn 1:12; Rom 8: 14; 19; Phil 2:15; 1 Jn 3:1, 2

wonder about his or her state, nor does he or she fear losing it. Their heart is set on loving their Father and through that love, practicing obedience.

"For if you live by the sinful nature you will die; but if by the Spirit you put to death the misdeeds of the body you will live, *because those who are led by the Spirit of God are sons of God.*" (Rom 8:14) The determination of 'life' and 'death' rests in a person's obedience to the Spirit. Only those who are "led" by the Spirit of God are sons of God.

The Lord addressed the matter of sonship when speaking to some Jewish believers. "Everyone who sins is a slave to sin. Now a slave has no permanent place in the family, but a son belongs to it forever." (Jn 8:34) Those whom He calls "slaves to sin" were once part of the family but their position was not *permanent.*

The "adoption" as a son of God will take place when our Savior returns, and not before that time. "Not only so, but we ourselves, who have the firstfruits of the Spirit, groan inwardly as *we wait eagerly for our adoption as sons, the redemption of our bodies.*" (Rom 8:23)

b. *God's "guarantee"*

Confidence in a person's eternal security is often placed in the "guarantee" provided by the gift of the Holy Spirit. "Having believed, you were marked in him with a seal, the promised Holy Spirit, who is a deposit guaranteeing our inheritance until the redemption of those who are God's possession--to the praise of his glory." (Eph 1: 13b-14) The word "guarantee" does not fairly represent the meaning intended by Paul as recorded in the Greek language. [439] It was God's intense and serious state of mind for those who "believe" to be given their inheritance. A person can gain assurance of his or her inheritance as they realize the Spirit's work in their life. He or she produces much fruit as they live in obedience, being led by him.[440] The believer must also be prepared to suffer trials, persecution, and even death[441] in defense of his or her faith.

---

[439] The word "guarantee" in this verse may not be the best English word to represent the intent of the Greek arrabwn'. To "guarantee" something implies a surety. When 'surety' is intended, the Greek word 'egguos' is used, as in Hebrews 7:22. The Old English word used by the KJV to represent the thought given by the Greek 'arrabwn' is "earnest." "Earnest" means "intense and serious state of mind."- from Merriam Webster's Deluxe Dictionary, Tenth Collegiate Edition "Earnest" does not imply "guarantee" but *intent* as in "intense and serious state of mind."

[440] See Rom 8:4

[441] Rev 12:11

The verse might be translated as, 'The Spirit is a *deposit* given as a result of God's intense and serious state of mind to provide for our inheritance until the redemption of those who are God's possession.'

The Spirit is God's "earnest" to give a person the inheritance, which is righteousness. "By his divine power, God has given us everything we need for living a godly life." (2 Pet 1:3) Our Father has provided *everything* in order that we might inherit the promise of righteousness; this provision is in accordance with His 'intense and serious state of mind." The provision comes short of a "guarantee," however. God's provision is not unilaterally applied. The "guarantee" of salvation is provided on the condition that he and his resources are honored. The thoroughness of his provision assures that the obedient might realize the inheritance he has promised. "But by faith we eagerly await through the Spirit the righteousness for which we hope." (Gal 5:5) God cannot and does not guarantee righteous practices in his created people. Humans were given free choice. If a person's choice is to respond in obedience and through God's provision to love his or her God, they will inherit righteousness; if they choose to live according to the sinful nature they will die.[442] The believer must partner with the Spirit in this process. "Dear children, do not let anyone lead you astray. He who *does* what is right is righteous, just as Christ is righteous." (1 Jn 3:7; 1 Pet 3:14)

The Spirit might be interpreted as God's "guarantee" if he can exercise his ministry as intended. It is not the mere presence of his Spirit that guarantees salvation, but the appropriation of his ministry. The Spirit might be quenched. Quenching the Spirit is a choice that the "believer" makes as he or she claims sovereignty over their life and denies Christ's God-given lordship and transforming work. The leading of the Spirit will be drowned out by the desires of the wicked heart.

The Spirit is the Spirit of Christ and he works in conjunction with his position of High Priest to effect righteousness and salvation. "Therefore, he is able to save completely those who come to God through him because he always lives to intercede for them." (Heb 7:25)

The "guarantee" is really a down payment for the souls that he will make righteous so that they might inherit his kingdom.[443] They have been purchased by his blood so that they might be given His Spirit. The gift of the Spirit is not a total payment but is a partial payment for righteousness

---

[442] Rom 8:13
[443] Eph 1:14

or for the inheritance which is his intention to provide. The possession of the Spirit cannot be the full price because the practice of righteousness is the full price. Through faith and belief, the believer must exercise his gifting that a transformed mind and righteousness might result. However, the Spirit can be quenched and with this act the source of life.[444] The believer must practice perseverance to the point of victory.[445]

Belief leads to a commitment to "fear the lord God, to walk in all his ways, to love him, to serve the lord God with all a person's heart and with all their soul, and to observe the lord's commands and decrees." (Deut 10:12)[446] The "guarantee" or "earnest" is the gift and possession of the Holy Spirit, who must, with the believer's consent, accomplish belief, love, service, and obedience.

c. Being "sealed"

Much emphasis is put on the words "seal" or "sealed". "He anointed us, set his seal of ownership on us, and put his Spirit in our hearts as a deposit guaranteeing what is to come." (1 Co 1:21b-22)

The "seal of ownership" is placed upon a person following his or her pledge that "Christ is Lord" (Rom 10, 9, 10) and upon his or her confession to willingly live as their master's servant. This being the case, they are given the Holy Spirit that seals the relationship or becomes the identifying *mark* that a relationship has been formed and that the believer has declared Christ to have sovereignty over his life.

An obedient servant does the will of his or her master and forgoes their own interests and desires. It must be recognized that a servant can refuse to relent to their master's leadership. Christ has said that the "unprofitable" servant will be cast into "outer darkness." (Mt 25:30)

The confession of the repentant person is his or her pledge, and on that promise Christ responds with the gift of his Spirit. This confession is only valid or true if it is honored; otherwise, it is a lie. Christ has revealed that "all who love to live a lie" will be found *outside* the walls of the New Jerusalem.[447] They will not see Christ who dwells inside.

---

[444] Rom 8:2
[445] Rev 21:7
[446] See also Mt 22:37, 38
[447] Rev 22:15, NLT

d. The believer has been "made perfect forever"

"Since that time, he waits for his enemies to be made his footstool, because by that one sacrifice he made perfect forever those who are being made holy." (Heb 10:14)

The true believer is told that he or she has been made perfect *forever*. That is, their perfection will never be tarnished and that they will always remain in fellowship with their God if they are "being made holy." The assurance of perfection rests in a person's attitude toward Christ and his Spirit, which is revealed through a person's readiness to practice righteousness leading to holiness. Christ, as High Priest, mediates for those who have sinned but whose hearts are set on being led by his Spirit. They are "walking in the light." (1 Jn 1:7) His blood cleanses them[448] and no condemnation rests on them if they are being led by him.[449] This verse might be more meaningful if read as, '*Those who are being made holy, he made perfect forever*.' The believer should understand that he *is being made* holy, not that he is holy in his practices. Holiness is developed through righteous living. Paul told the Romans to offer their body parts "in slavery to righteousness leading to holiness." (Rom 6:19, 22)

e. Sins no longer remembered.

The repentant sinner is forgiven, and God says, "I will never again remember their sins and lawless deeds." (Heb 10:17, NLT)

This promise was recorded in the book of Hebrews and as such has direct application to Israel and to her final generation; however, it also has application to all nations. When sin has been forgiven, it will no longer be remembered. Pardon from sin is given only upon repentance. This happens when a person is redeemed from his or her past sins through the sacrifice of Christ following which he or she is given the Holy Spirit, and for those sins committed after that point that have been confessed and for which forgiveness is sought. It does not mean that all sins ever to be committed by the willfully disobedient will be forgotten. "If we deliberately keep on sinning after we have received the knowledge of the truth, no sacrifice for sin is left, but only the fearful expectation of judgment and of fire that will consume the enemies of God." (Heb 10:26-27)

---

[448] 1 Jn 1:7
[449] Rom 8:1

Judgment awaits all of humankind for the things done in the body, both the redeemed[450] and the lost. "For we must all stand before the judgment seat of Christ, that each one may receive what is due him for the things done while in the body, whether good or bad." (1 Cor 5:10) Since judgment awaits all, their sins must not have been forgotten.

It is sin that separates humankind from his creator and if sin is remembered no longer, communion with God will remain complete, forever. The promise of sins being no longer remembered is given to those who have recognized their offence against God and have determined to live a life pleasing to him and who "are being made holy." God will never remember the sins of those "walking in the light".[451] When sin is forgiven it is forgotten.

f. God's keeping power

The writer of Hebrews states, "So God has given both his promise and his oath. These two things are unchangeable because it is impossible for God to lie. Therefore, we who have fled to him for refuge can have great confidence as we hold to the hope that lies before us. This hope is a strong and trustworthy anchor for our souls. It leads us through the curtain into God's inner sanctuary." (Heb 6: 18-19, NLT)

The writer of Hebrews has presented the *character* of God and according to his character he is not able to lie. Therefore, the person who flees to him for refuge can have great confidence in his promises. Because of this, a person should be confident in his or her hope and not lose it as far as it is consistent with the Word of God. It is a person's hope that leads him or her into relating to God through the curtain and into the inner sanctuary.

The inner sanctuary is the place of confession and doing business with God through Christ. The inner sanctuary is a place of holiness and is to be recognized as such. The high priest of the Jews entered fearfully and only once a year. The writer of Hebrews is presenting that the redeemed can enter confidently to do business with God.

Because a person can enter the inner sanctuary through Christ does not mean that he or she can have confidence in their eternal salvation, but that they can confidently approach the throne of grace to conduct whatever business is needful. This is a provision that has been made by Christ. God will not condemn or chastise the repentant heart. With this understanding

---

[450] 1 Pet 4:17
[451] 1 Jn 1:7

Eternal Salvation

a person can boldly approach and relate to his or her creator God. Because a person can confidently approach God, should he do so, God's keeping power will prevail; but, he or she must do so.

There are several passages that remind humankind that Christ "is able" to keep his own. "…for I know the one in whom I trust and am sure that he is able to guard what I have entrusted to him until the day of his return." (2 Tim 1:12, NLT) The writer of Hebrews states that, "he is able to save completely those who come to God through him, because he always lives to intercede for them." (Heb 7:25) Christ can keep unto salvation because of his authority and his priestly duties. These passages remind the reader of what he can do, not what he unilaterally does. The surety of salvation through Christ is based on his permanence, and in his ministry as high priest, and the reader is told that he can save completely because he always lives to intercede for him or her.

It is his intercessory ministry that enables Christ to save but this salvation is only for those who are walking in the light.[452]

Christ assures the believer, "My sheep listen to my voice; I know them, and they follow me. I give them eternal life, and they will never perish. No one can snatch them from the Father's hand." (Jn 10: 27-29)

This verse assures the faithful that they need not worry about what *others* can do to destroy their eternal hope because God is greater than all. It is intended only to affirm on the mind of each person who follows him that their salvation rests in a secure relationship between their Savior and themselves and cannot be affected by others.

In considering the question of eternal security, God's purpose for the creation of humankind and his eternal plan must be considered. It never was God's plan to dwell with sinners. God's nature could not tolerate that. He is holy and only those who are holy may dwell with him.[453] The question is, "How can holiness be achieved?" Some would say that the righteousness of Christ is "imputed" to the believer. The *imputation* of his righteousness applies only to the righteousness needed to establish a relationship with God so that his Spirit might be given for the pursuit of righteousness and the development of holiness. Prior to a person's redemption the sinner has no other means of gaining righteousness other than through the imputation of Christ's which is granted because of a person's confessed

---

[452] 1 Jn 1:7
[453] Heb 12:14

belief and willingness to make Christ his or her Lord. Those who have been gifted are expected to exercise faith and to respond in obedience to his leading. His word is clear when all is said and done the Lord will have created a "kingdom of priests, a holy nation." (Exo 19:6; 1 Pet 2:9)

Titus said, "He saved us not because of the righteous things we had done, but because of his mercy. He saved us through the washing of rebirth and renewal by the Holy Spirit, whom he poured out on us generously through Jesus Christ our Savior, so that, having been justified by his grace, we might become heirs having the hope of eternal life." (Titus 3:5) It is the Holy Spirit that accomplishes renewal and those who are not "in Christ" or walking in obedience to him, will not enjoy the salvation he has offered.[454] They will forfeit their hope of eternal life.

Can a person have assurance of salvation? Yes! John said that he had written his epistle so that "you may know that you have eternal life." (1 Jn 5:13) The evidences of salvation have been given.

Can a believer *lose* his salvation? When does salvation take place? Salvation cannot take place until the return of Christ, although a person might live in its promise. Paul said, "For all creation is waiting eagerly for that future day when God will reveal who his children *really* are." (Rom 8:19, NLT) It is God who knows a person's state of "belief."[455] For this reason it is not wise to depend on the occasion of professed faith as being true faith. Faith and belief must be practiced[456] and will be tested.[457] In his letter to the Corinthians, Paul cautioned his readers that those hopeful of salvation should test[458] their faith to make sure that it is genuine.

The assurance of salvation is there but it is for the faithful who persevere. It is for the obedient and for those who seek holiness. The prophet Ezekiel commented on the need to persevere in righteousness. "But if a righteous man turns from his righteousness and commits sin and does the same detestable things the wicked man does, will he live? None of the righteous things he has done will be remembered. Because of the unfaithfulness he is guilty of and because of the sins he has committed, he will die." (Ezek 18:24)

---

[454] 1 Jn 3:24; See also Heb 5:9
[455] "Belief", as intended by the Word of God does not merely mean a mental assent of something; it means absolute belief to the point where a person is compelled to act in accordance with his or her belief regardless of the circumstances.
[456] Jas 2:17, 20
[457] 1 Pet 1:7
[458] 2 Cor 13:5.

Eternal Salvation

John cautioned believers, "See that what you have heard from the beginning remains in you. If it does, you also will remain in the Son and in the Father. And this is what he promised us--even eternal life." (1 Jn 2:24-25) "If" is a word of condition. The condition of achieving eternal life is that of remaining faithful to the Word.

Peter also clarified when talking about false teachers: "If they have escaped the corruption of the world by knowing our Lord and Savior Jesus Christ and are again entangled in it and overcome, they are worse off at the end than they were at the beginning. It would have been better for them not to have known the way of righteousness than to have known it and then to turn their backs on the sacred command[459] that was passed on to them." (2 Pet 2:20-21) This passage also begins with the conditional "if". It is a statement of condition and was given for a purpose. Although some false teachers may have never known "the way of righteousness", undoubtedly some did; otherwise, the verse is without purpose.

The "sacred command" referenced above refers to the need to remain faithful. The writer of Hebrews also reminds of the need for faithfulness. "It is impossible for those who have been once enlightened, who have shared in the Holy Spirit, who have tasted the goodness of the word of God and the powers of the coming age, if they fall away, to be brought back to repentance, because to their loss they are crucifying the Son of God all over again and subjecting him to public disgrace." (Heb 6:4-6) The writer also adds that, "If we deliberately keep on sinning after we have received the knowledge of the truth, no sacrifice for sins is left, but only a fearful expectation of judgment and of raging fire that will consume the enemies of God." (Heb 10: 26-27)

Does the believer have eternal security? God's Word gives many warnings about falling away and says that in the last days some will abandon the faith[460] and that others would live a lie. He has also provided all that is necessary so that the believer might live a godly life. There are many references regarding the need to walk in the light. Paul told the Philippians to "continue to work out your salvation with fear and trembling, for it is God who works in you to will and to act according to his good purpose." (Phil 2:12-13) His purpose for the redeemed is that they bring glory to his

---

[459] The "sacred command" references Ezek 18:24, Heb 6: 4-6, 10:26, 27 at 2 Pet 21 in the NIV
[460] 1 Tim 4:1

name through righteous practices. There is a responsibility placed on the believer and that responsibility must be borne. John encouraged believers to pray for brothers who they have seen commit a sin so that brother might be restored to life. "If anyone sees his brother commit a sin that does not lead to death, he should pray and God will give him life." (1 Jn 5:16) If the *brother* had not died because of his sin, he would not have a need to be *restored* to life. Will some fall? Yes. However, the person with his or her sight set on heavenly things need not fear. There will be many warnings and much discipline before failure becomes complete. God's patience will come to an end for those not striving with him, however.

Complacency should be far from the believer's heart. For those who would rest in the confidence of being eternally secure in the Lord's presence, Paul has revealed his thoughts concerning his own eternal state. "I want to know Christ and the power of his resurrection and the fellowship of sharing in his sufferings, becoming like him in his death, and so, somehow, to attain the resurrection from the dead. Not that I have already obtained all this, or have already been made perfect, but I press on to take hold of that for which Christ Jesus took hold of me. Brothers, I do not consider myself yet to have taken hold of it. But one thing I do: Forgetting what is behind and straining toward what is ahead, I press on toward the goal to win the prize for which God has called me heavenward in Christ Jesus." (Phil 3: 10-14) Paul had great faith as proven through his life and yet he was not sufficiently confident to claim to have heaven's grasp within his hands. He felt it necessary to "press on toward the goal." If Paul did not accept that he had obtained the resurrection, neither should those less committed. The race must be run till the end and not rested in a prayer of confession at the beginning.

5. *Are the believer's sins forgotten?*

Sins committed prior to a person's confession of faith are forgotten. Sins that have been revealed and have been confessed following the believer's confession by those striving for righteousness are also forgiven and forgotten, as well as sins committed by the confessed believer about which he is unaware. Intentionally continuing to sin, known sin that has not been confessed, and sins committed as a result of denying the Spirit's ministry in a person's life are left for the "believer" to address before the judgment seat of the Lord.

6. *Can a person be eternally saved and not transformed?*

No! A person's evil imaginations arising from the heart bring God pain.[461] He will not dwell eternally with those who bring him pain. Paul has revealed that those who will find God's kingdom will be in the likeness of the Son of God.[462] They will be righteous in their practices and will be able to relate to him in the manner and for the purpose for which they had been created. "Neither circumcision nor uncircumcision mean anything; what counts is a new creation." (Gal 6:15)

7. *Why is "faith" necessary for a person's salvation?*

Faith means "persuasion" or "having been persuaded." God will not save those who have not been persuaded about him or about his sovereignty. It is his kingdom that he is establishing. People who maintain such pride as to defy him and his government would be a constant problem in his eternal kingdom, just as they are on this earth. If a person is persuaded of the awesomeness and authority of God, he will relent to the Lord's right to rule and will practice obedience.

Faith is displayed in a person's practices and is not merely a possession. If a person really believes or has faith in the Lord, or in anything for that matter, his or her practices will reflect that persuasion. Without faith it is impossible to please God. A person must be persuaded to the extent that he or she is prepared to abandon any right to self in favour of the Lord's right to him or her. James spoke of Abraham's faith. "You see that his faith and his actions were working together, and his faith was made complete by what he did." (Jas 2:22)

8. *How is the resurrection of Christ a significant aspect of salvation?*

The resurrection of Christ demonstrates God's sovereignty and power and provides evidence of the hope of life after death for those in whom Christ dwells. His resurrection also makes his Spirit available.

The death of Christ justifies the believer concerning his past sins[463] but the resurrected life of Christ allows his life to be lived in the believer[464], and his priestly ministry, justifies the repentant one concerning the sins that follow.

---

[461] Gen 6:6
[462] Rom 8:29
[463] Rom 5:9; Heb 9:15
[464] Rom 4:25; 1 Jn 1:7; Jas 2:24

Without his resurrected life the believer would have no eternal hope because he would not have the Holy Spirit to enable him or her.

Justification means 'acquittal.' That means that the resurrection of Jesus provides the way for a person's acquittal concerning judgment or his or her being discharged from any consequences of sin. This acquittal is accomplished as the Lord lives his life through one. First, sin is being eliminated through righteous practices. Secondly, the blood of Christ is applied to the sin of those who are walking in the light.[465] Thirdly, as high priest Jesus advocates with the Father pleading his blood offering for sins committed in ignorance.[466]

Although the Lord's resurrection gives confidence of the hope through example of a person's resurrected life, his resurrected life provides the means for it as well.

9. *Who are the victorious?*

The victorious are those who have overcome the world, the evil one, and their natural spirit. The Lord has promised that they will enjoy a dwelling in the New Jerusalem with him.[467] They will have walked in the light having practiced obedience to the Spirit. They are sons of God.[468]

Revelation 21:7 (NIV) specifically reveals that those who "overcome" will inherit a presence in the New Jerusalem. Earlier in Revelation the Lord addressed the seven churches and praised them for their merits and condemned them for their failures. To each church He identified an issue that needed to be "overcome." These issues apply to his people today.

Believers are expected to:

1. love Christ and others as much now as they did in the beginning.[469]
2. persevere in suffering.[470]
3. remain faithful in teaching so that sinning is not encouraged nor tolerated for benefit.[471]

---

[465] 1 Jn 1:7
[466] Heb 9:24 and 9:7
[467] Rev 21:7
[468] Rom 8:23
[469] Rev 2:4
[470] Rev 2:10
[471] Rev 2:14

4. be true in teaching so that those present do not fall into sin.[472]
5. meet the requirements of God by *living* the truths they know, not merely proclaiming truths. To practice holiness.[473]
6. persevere in weakness and trials or persecution.[474]
7. abandon indifference and to passionately seek holiness or "white garments."[475]

---

[472] Rev 2:20
[473] Rev 3:2, 3
[474] Rev 3: 10, 11
[475] Rev 3:18

Chapter 10

Study Guide

Introduction

    a. Can you clearly explain the means of a person's eternal salvation? If you can, find someone with whom you can share your understanding. Have that person share theirs with you. What are the similarities and the differences between you?

    b. If you were to witness to another could you show Biblical proof for your understanding? In Philippians 3: 10-14 Paul reveals his understanding of his own eternal hope. Since he is the recorder of many of the gospel teachings, how do his words in this passage impact you?

Understanding the Issue

    a. In your opinion, why is God redeeming a people for himself? What would his redeemed people be like?

    b. What does Genesis 6:5-6 reveal about God? What might this understanding have to do with the issue of eternal salvation? Would your understanding of eternal salvation satisfy the heart of God? Why or why not?

    c. John 3:16 is a well-known passage. According to this passage what is the focus of God's love?

    d. Why must God make a separation among created people so that some are rejected from his eternal presence while others are preserved?

    e. Briefly summarize the issue that has brought about the separation of God from mankind. What does this tell you about humankind's need?

About Humankind

  a. Why are humans especially culpable for their sin?
  b. How would you distinguish between the soul and the spirit? How many spirits can a person possess?
  c. Why is the Holy Spirit a significant gift?
  d. By what means does a person gain "knowledge" from the world?
  e. Why does a person's body create so many issues in relation to his spiritual life? How can a person's senses bring God's wrath upon them?
  f. According to Ecclesiastes 12:7 what happens to a person's spirit upon death?
  g. Why does Paul say to think about things that are lovely, admirable, excellent or praiseworthy? How well do you practice this teaching?
  h. According to Romans 15:16 what was the purpose of Paul's ministry?

God: Sovereign, Just, and Holy

  a. According to Hebrews 11:6, what are the two components of faith in God? According to your understanding would this measure of faith be enough for a person to gain eternal salvation? Discuss.
  b. Although God has many attributes, there are two that are particularly relevant to the believer in his hope to find everlasting salvation. What are they? Discuss the implications of these two as to how they affect a person's eternal hope. How does knowledge of God's possession of these attributes impact your heart?
  c. Some accept that God's "grace" has removed any requirements for the believer to change his behaviour in any way. What are your thoughts about having to participate in your eternal salvation?
  d. What is meant by the teaching that God has and must have an intimate relationship with those who will be eternally saved? How is this both unsettling and wonderful?
  e. Christ did not come to do away with the law but to fulfill it. How did He accomplish this? This concept is vital to understanding the means of a person's eternal salvation. Reflect on it as you go through the remainder of the study.
  f. According to Galatians 5:6-7, how can a person be deceived?

God Declared His Creation to be "Very Good!" so, What Happened?

a. Consider: Why did God designate the tree in the middle of the Garden of Eden to be the tree of the knowledge of good and evil? How would his creation be different if such a tree had not existed?
b. Notice that Eve's enticement came through her senses. Accordingly, how should a person consider his or her senses when it comes to temptation? Can you think of a time when temptation to sin was presented through your senses? What was the temptation?
c. What is the great hope for the soul? (2 Cor 4:16)
d. Why is it important to retain "knowledge of God?" Is this important today? What might be the consequence of *not* retaining that knowledge?
e. If the whole creation is struggling in the pains of childbirth, what implications might this have for the future?
f. Romans 15:16 reveals Paul's "priestly duty" (NIV). What did he consider to be his ministry to the Gentiles? How does this revelation affect your understanding of "eternal" salvation?
g. In Colossians 1:27 Paul has revealed the source of a person's hope of glory or hope for glory. Why do you think that this truly is a person's hope of glory? How does this affect your understanding of the path to eternal salvation?

Sin and Mankind

a. Why is the heart deceitful?
b. Genesis 6:5-6 presents God's view of mankind. What does this tell you about sin? about God? about you? Does the Lord's revealed heart-state suggest any implications for a salvation plan?
c. According to Galatians 6:15, what is revealed as being very important?
d. God's Word reveals that "all have sinned" (Rom 3:23). According to Isaiah 59:2, what is the consequence of sin? How was this resolved?
e. Hebrews 10:14 (NIV) stipulates exactly who "has been made perfect forever." What is the requirement that is presented? What is your understanding of this requirement? How do Romans 6:18, 22 affect your understanding?
f. God has given humankind "free-will." What does this mean? What are its implications? It was with humans having this right

that the Lord declared his creation to be "very good." Why do you think he has preserved this privilege that he had given people? Why do you think that it was given?

g. The Lord stated that the believer must "stand firm to the end." How does this teaching affect your understanding of eternal salvation? What are its implications?

h. Hebrews 5:9 is the only verse in the whole of God's Word that contains the term *'eternal salvation."* What is presented as its means? How does John 10:27 support the teaching?

i. How is one to avoid "condemnation" in the end? (Rom 8:1-4) How does this enlighten the Lord's teaching in Matthew 5:17?

j. What are the two covenants that impact one's eternal salvation? (Heb 9:15)

Becoming an Offering Acceptable to God

a. Paul has stated that the kingdom of God is a matter of "righteousness, peace, and joy in the Holy Spirit." (Rom 14:17-18) Consider each of these qualifiers as to how they are achieved in a person's life apart from the Spirit. How does the Spirit aid in their development? Why would the Lord desire that his people possess these attributes?

b. Becoming "an offering acceptable to God" is through the "sanctifying ministry" of the Holy Spirit. "Sanctified" in this case means, "to make holy, i.e. (ceremonially) purify or consecrate; (mentally) to venerate: —hallow, be holy, sanctify."[476] What does this mean to you?

c. 2 Thessalonians 2:13 uses "sanctification" to mean **"purification, i.e. (the state) purity; concretely (by Hebraism) a purifier: — holiness, sanctification"**[477] Titus teaches that a person is saved through "the washing of rebirth and renewal by the Holy Spirit." (Titus 3:5-6) What do "rebirth" and "renewal" mean? How would you distinguish them? How does the Holy Spirit accomplish these needs? What do "washing" and "renewal" have to do with making the believer "an offering acceptable to God?" When is the believer's "renewal" completed?

---

[476] Translated from the Greek *hagiazo* according to Strong's Greek Dictionary **#37**
[477] Strong's Greek Dictionary #38

d. Jesus told Peter, "*Unless I wash you, you have no part with me…A person who has had a bath needs only to wash his feet; his whole body is clean.*" (Jn 13: 8…10) Why did Jesus tell Peter that without having his feet washed, the Lord could have no part with him? How can you "wash the feet" of a brother in the Lord?
e. The issue of "deception" is vitally important since those who have been deceived will not dwell with the Lord? Paul implies that deception is "mocking" the Lord. According to Galatians 6:7-8, what practices reveal that a person has been deceived? What does Paul present as the consequence?
f. Some present that a person's needed righteousness following confession of faith is "imputed." What word in Galatians 5:5 reveals that this is not so? Why?
g. According to Romans 8:29 what must be the state of those who are to dwell with the Lord? Would "imputed righteousness" achieve God's goal?
h. Ephesians 2:8-10 states that through God's "grace" and our "faith" we are being made into a 'product' acceptable to God since we are his "workmanship" (NIV) or "masterpiece" (NLT). If his "grace" applies to the creation of this acceptable product or sacrifice, how does is your understanding of "grace" affected?

The Gospel of Christ

a. "Gospel" stands for 'good news." What is the mystery that was hidden and is now good news for humankind?
b. Why is the New Covenant more desirable than the Old Covenant?
c. How do you know that being justified by the blood of Christ is not enough to avoid the wrath of God?
d. How can a person know if he or she is "in Christ?"
e. How do you know that Christ is able to accomplish a life of sinless living in you?
f. Christ said that he came to "fulfil" the law, not to abolish it. How does he accomplish this?
g. What is a requirement for being a "son of God?"
h. What assurance does a believer have that he or she has all that is required for life and godliness?
i. What happens to those who do not "obey" the gospel of Christ?

j. How was Christ like you? How was he different?
k. Did Christ suffer with temptations? How does his struggle help you?
l. What is meant by having your "moral consciousness" cleaned?
m. What stands in the believer's way to prevent him or her from walking righteously before God?
n. How does Genesis 6:5-6 reveal truth concerning eternal salvation?
o. Can the practice of sin be excused? Why?
p. Can you articulate the gospel of Christ?

A Synopsis of Eternal Salvation

a. Knowing that creation was for *God's* pleasure and that you are a part of it will give you cause to think about the nature of his eternal kingdom. What understanding does this give you?
b. What is rebellion against God? How and why does rebellion affect a person's eternal state?
c. How are a person's rebellious practices overcome?
d. What are the Lord's ministries in the accomplishment of a person's eternal salvation?
e. What profession, pledge, or promise must a person make if he or she is to gain salvation?
f. How will this affect the believer's practices?
g. What can happen if a person does not honor this profession, pledge, or promise?

Putting "Salvation," "Saved," and "Eternal Salvation" into Perspective

The terms 'save,' 'saved,' 'salvation,' and 'eternal salvation' are often misinterpreted. They are English words used to express an idea. They proclaim a 'rescuing' or 'deliverance but the nature of their rescuing depends upon the circumstances in which the words are used. Save, saved, and salvation do not necessarily mean 'eternal salvation' and they should not be always understood to mean it.

a. What are the situations from which a person must be delivered if he or she is to gain eternal salvation?
b. According to Hebrews 5:9 what is required for "eternal" salvation? How do Revelation 21:7, Matthew 7:21, Revelation 22:14 (KJV), John 10:27, Romans 8:14, and Galatians 5:18 support this idea?

    c. According to Hebrews 9:15, what salvation or deliverance did the ransom of Christ accomplish?
    d. Who are God's angels going to weed out of his kingdom?
    e. What do 1 Corinthians 15:2 and Matthew 24:10…13 teach about salvation?
    f. In John 8:34 and 15:1 the Lord reveals important realities about eternal salvation. What are those realities that should be of concern to the believer?
    g. What is the commitment that the Lord expects of the believer if his or her life is to be "saved"?
    h. How do these teachings about "salvation" and "eternal salvation" comply with God's purpose for saving or separating a "peculiar" people from the masses of humanity?

The Sacrifice of Christ on the Cross

    a. What are the three accomplishments of the sacrifice of Christ on the cross?
    b. According to Hebrews 9:15, from what sins did the Lord's sacrifice provide freedom?
    c. What is required for the blood of Christ to be applied to sins following the point of confession of faith?
    d. What does "walking in the light" mean?
    e. According to Galatians 3:13-14, what was the great gift that was given following a person's redemption? Why is that gift of grace so necessary for the believer's *eternal* salvation?
    f. Why is it the Spirit *of Christ* who saves? Why was the Lord's sacrifice necessary in order that the believer might gain the Spirit?

The New Covenant

    a. How is the nature of the New Covenant different from the Old?
    b. What did the Old Covenant require?
    c. According to 2 Corinthians 3:6, the New Covenant is a covenant of the _____.
    d. In accordance with the New Covenant, how is the Lord able to satisfy the righteous requirements of the law? Are they met through the crucifixion of Christ?

Eternal Salvation

    e. What is the relationship between the Holy Spirit and the Lord Jesus Christ? (2 Cor 3:18-19; Col 1:27)
    f. Can the believer justify saying that he or she was unable to meet God's condition of godliness? (2 Pet 1:3; 2 Cor 3:6)
    g. How was the believer's deliverance from the jurisdiction of the Old Covenant accomplished? What is the condition for his or her release from its jurisdiction? (Gal 5:18)
    h. What happens if the believer lives his or her life according to the leading of (sows to please) his or her sinful nature?
    i. Did the sacrifice of Christ on the cross provide the fullness of the righteousness for which we hope? (Gal 5:5)
    j. What is the requirement for a person to "see" (lay eyes upon) the Lord?
    k. Since the believer is competent to keep the New Covenant, what is the basis for the judgment of believers?

Being "in" Christ

    a. What is the advantage of being "in Christ?"
    b. What scriptural evidence is there that a person may not remain in Christ? What are the implications for the "believer" of not remaining in him?
    c. What is required in order to remain in Christ?
    d. How can a person know whether he or she is in Christ?
    e. Is it Christ's responsibility to keep the believer in him? Explain?

The Path to Eternal Salvation

    a. According to Paul what are the two requirements necessary for salvation?
    b. Why do these two requirements refer to deliverance from "past sins" and the law and not to "eternal" salvation?
    c. When is the Spirit given? For what purpose?
    d. Can a person have the Spirit and not acquire "eternal" salvation?
    e. How does the Holy Spirit enable a person to obtain "eternal" salvation?
    f. Why is perseverance necessary for the believer to gain the kingdom of God?
    g. In what manner does the Lord say that a person is to treat his own life?

    h. What happens if the believer does not follow the leading of the Spirit? What practices regarding the Spirit will bring about his or her destruction?
    i. Who is the Spirit and what is his purpose?
    j. Hebrews 5:9 is the *only* passage in the Bible that directly references "eternal salvation." According to this passage what is its requirement?
    k. Who will have "no permanent place" in the family?
    l. On what basis will the believer be judged?
    m. What aspect of humans allows them to be guided by the Spirit?
    n. There are two kinds of sins-those committed "in ignorance" and those that are "known" because they have been revealed. What is the difference in their treatment in order that a person might find forgiveness and be cleansed?
    o. What is the relationship between "free-will" and "true love?"
    p. Why is pardon for "past sins" not enough for a person to gain his or her eternal hope?

More about Gaining the Spirit

    a. According to Peter what is required for the Father to give the Holy Spirit?
    b. What is the significance of water baptism and the gaining of the Spirit?
    c. Peter calls water baptism a "pledge." What is the essence of this pledge? To whom is it addressed?
    d. What is required for the Father to entertain the gifting of the Holy Spirit?

The Life of Faith

Understanding "Faith"

    a. What does "faith" mean?
    b. Is faith a possession or a practice? Why? How do the different understandings impact a person's spiritual life?
    c. Are there different levels of faith? If so, how are differing levels of faith revealed in the lives of those who have claimed "faith?"
    d. How can interpreting "faith" as "trust" affect a person's understanding of the Scriptures?

e. How is true "faith" displayed in the believer's walk?
  f. What is the measure of faith required by God?
  g. Is "saving" faith different from the faith that results in "eternal salvation?"
  h. How does "faith," meaning "persuasion," impact the way Christ came to fulfil the law?
  i. Is the life of faith difficult? Why?
  j. How is salvation by "faith" different from salvation by "works?"
  k. How can the believer use all that has been provided by God to equip himself or herself for a life of faith?

Death to Self

  a. If your body has died with Christ, how are its interests affected? What parts of the believer do not die following death of the body?
  b. The believer has both his natural or evil spirit and the Holy Spirit within him or her? What problem does this create for them? How are they to deal with this problem? What is the outcome if the natural spirit can rule? Is the old nature still able to affect the believer after the Spirit has been received? Explain.
  c. How would you know if someone has truly been baptized into the death of Christ?
  d. What aspect of a person is the believer to guard? Why?
  e. If a person has been "saved" from the law of sin and death, can he or she return to the jurisdiction of that law or *lose that salvation or deliverance*? (Eph 2:17; Gal 5:18; Heb 10:26; Jn 15:1, 10)
  f. According to John 6:63, what is the source of life? What does Hebrews 5:9 give as the requirement for "eternal life?"
  g. Summarize your thoughts on "death to self."

Slavery and the Believer

  a. What kind of slavery is it that Paul teaches will lead to holiness and eternal life?
  b. The believer is a slave. According to Paul to whom can he be a slave? (2)
  c. According to the Lord, what is the consequence of unrighteous slavery?

4. Many think that all of the redeemed are "sons of God." Who does Paul present as being a son of God? (Rom 8:14) When does a person's adoption as a son take place? (Rom 8:23)

Eternal Salvation through Relationship

One's hope of eternal salvation is through Christ's presence in him or her and through his on-going ministry. This demands love for Christ, commitment to him, and a clinging so that the believer remains "in" him.

a. What does the Lord present as being love for him?
b. The Lord requires that you "fear" him. What does that mean? Can a person who hopes for eternal salvation live without regard for the Lord? Why?
c. What does the Lord require of his sheep? What does this have to do with belief? (Heb 3:18-19) What does this require of you?
d. Many people accept singing as their act of worship. What does Paul say is proper worship? (Rom 12:1)
e. What is the evidence that a person "knows" Christ?
f. Christ did not come to abolish the law but to fulfil it. How does he do this?
g. Can a person abort his relationship with Christ? (Mt 10:22; 1 Cor 15:2) What is required of the believer in order to "remain" in the Lord? What happens if a person leaves this relationship?
h. Christ revealed the nature of this relationship to his disciples. (Jn 14:20) What is your understanding of "being in" Christ? Of his "being in" you?

The Practice of Being Led by the Spirit

a. Paul has taught that the believer is saved through the "sanctifying work" of the Spirit. (2 Thess 2:13; Titus 3:5-6) What is meant by "sanctifying"? by the "sanctifying work" of the Spirit?
b. Refer to Genesis 6: 5-6. Why do those who are to dwell eternally with the Lord need to be transformed (sanctified)?
c. When Christ said that he was "the life," (Jn 14:6) what did he mean?

Eternal Salvation

    d. What are the three sources of evil influence upon the believer? Accordingly, why can a person not accomplish eternal salvation by his or her own "works?"

    e. Once a person has been gifted with the Holy Spirit (Spirit of/for Holiness) what aspect of a person does the Spirit use to guide the believer?

    f. God condemns "blasphemy" of the Spirit? Why?

    g. What happens to the person who is not led by the Spirit?

The Leading of the Spirit for Righteousness

    a. Why is "knowledge" of God and God's Word important to have if a person is to be led?

    b. What role does prayer have in a person's being led?

    c. Why are people brought into God's kingdom?

    d. Why is it false thinking to accept that the believer will be given a life of ease, peace, and comfort?

    e. Why does God allow trials? Romans 8:28 should provide comfort for those going through trials. Why? To whom is this promise directed?

6. Why do you think Christ said that only "a few" people would find the gate that leads to life? Who are the "few"? What other means does God have for leading by the Spirit? Why should a person be cautious in claiming that he or she is being led by the Spirit?

The Leading of the Spirit for Service

    a. The Lord gives a spiritual gift to all his children for the building of his kingdom. (1 Cor 12: 7-11) Is the believer accountable for his or her use of those gifts? To whom are the "noble" gifts given?

    b. How can you know your gifting? What is it?

Facing Trials

    a. What outlook should a believer have when trials come? What attitude should he or she avoid?

    b. Paul taught that the believer is to put to death the interests of the earthly nature and interest in the things of the world? Why? What does this mean to you?

    c. Think of a time when your parents disciplined you. How did you feel about it? What do you think might have been their reasoning? Why does God discipline the believer?
    d. Why does the believer need to persevere under trials? What happens if he or she doesn't?

The Fight for Victory

    a. Why must *the believer* fight for victory? What is there about him or her that requires a fight in the first place? Can the believer be passive and assume that God will win the victory for him or her? Why?
    b. Paul addressed the issue of how a person is to be fitted for the fight as putting on the "armour of God." What is the armour of God? How do you understand the elements of the armour as providing protection for you?
    c. Why is it important to win the victory?
    d. Can there be such a thing as a passive believer? Why?
    e. When a person sins is he or she "in Christ?" Why?
    f. Is there ever a valid excuse for giving in to temptation? Explain.

Gaining Victory

    a. Some think that victory is something that is given a person as opposed to being available for him or her. How is victory achieved?
    b. Why is it important to "overcome?" Besides giving access to God, why is it important that the veil that hid God from the believer was taken away?
    c. Why is it error in thinking that the new person is put on instantaneously at the time of confession of faith? (2 Cor 3:18)
    d. What does it mean to "walk in the light?" Why is it unacceptable for the "believer" to "walk in darkness?"
    e. According to Romans 1:28, what could happen to those who do not "obey" the gospel?
    f. What is required of the believer for the blood of Christ to cleanse him or her of all unrighteousness?
    g. What is the purpose of our redemption? (Gal 3:14; 1 Pet 3:18)

Repentance and Salvation

    a. What does "repentance" mean? What does a lack of repentance reveal?
    b. What does God require in order that his grace and mercy rest on one?
    c. Following confession of faith what does John teach as a requirement for the forgiveness of sins?
    d. For a person to dwell with God in his eternal kingdom, what is a person's state to be like?

The Issue of "Works" and "Grace"

    a. In Genesis it is recorded that people were created in the image of God. (Gen 1:27) What is your understanding of this? Comparing this thought to Romans 8:29, what does this reveal about the process of eternal salvation?
    b. Genesis 6:5-6 discloses God's heart on the condition of people. How does this revelation impact your thinking about whether a person's eternal salvation is dependent upon his or her transformation or their having been forgiven?
    c. What steps has God taken to separate a righteous people for himself?
    d. Why isn't salvation by the "works of the Law" effective in satisfying God's righteous requirements?
    e. When Paul writes that we are God's "workmanship," what does he mean?
    f. What is meant by the "works of the law?"
    g. According to Romans 8:4 how can a person accomplish the righteous requirements of the law?
    h. How does the believer meet the righteous requirements of God? Can he or she be indifferent in their walk?
    i. Why is salvation by grace?

The Law and Salvation

    a. Many think that the Old Covenant requirement for righteousness does not apply to the believer? What are your thoughts?
    b. What is it that a person can do concerning the law and is dangerous for him or her to do?

c. What is required for known sin to be forgiven under the New Covenant?
   d. Is the law important to God under the New Covenant? Explain.
   e. Many say that Christ has won the victory for them. In what ways is this true and in what ways is it false?

Conditions Applied to Eternal Salvation

Conditions that limit are often preceded by the word "if," meaning that provided something occurs a certain result will follow. Sometime the conditions are implied by the opposite of an assertion. Consider the conditions in this section.

   a. What is the importance of the three "if" statements?
   b. Examine the verses referenced in footnote 489.
   c. The need to persevere to the end is presented as a condition. Explain why perseverance to the end is a need?
   d. What might be "startling" about Paul's revelation concerning his own hope?

How Can You Know that You Enjoy the Hope of Eternal Salvation?

   a. Examine the fifteen (15) evidences of the Spirit-filled life. Which apply to you? What does your evaluation tell you?
   b. What do these evidences suggest about why a person cannot be saved by his or her own "works?"
   c. What is a requirement of God for each person who would enjoy his eternal presence?
   d. In his gospel concerning God John writes, "He cuts off every branch in me [Christ] that does not bear fruit, while every branch that does bear fruit, he prunes so that it will be even more fruitful." (Jn 15:2) How would you connect the evidences in Revelation with the teaching in John's gospel?

Judgment

   a. What are your thoughts about facing the judgment of Christ? Will you be confident, anxious, or fearful?

Eternal Salvation

b. How will a person's choices, or use of free-will, affect his or her judgment at Christ's return?
c. What must be the believer's attitude if he or she is to avoid the "wrath of God?"
d. The Lord has revealed that "few" would find the road that leads to life. What does "few" mean to you? Who will comprise the few?
e. What did Paul consider to be his ministry to the Gentiles?
f. Who will suffer God's "wrath?"
g. On what criteria will judgment be based?
h. Paul taught that a person is not to allow himself or herself to be deceived. What is the nature of the deception about which he is referring in Galatians 6:7-8? Will judgment apply to those who have been deceived? To those who deceive?
i. Is "negative" judgment a "fair" outcome considering God's provision? Explain.
j. When considering Christ's revelation that not all who call him, "Lord, Lord," would enter the kingdom of heaven, what thoughts and feelings are stirred within you?
k. What are your thoughts concerning the relevance of the law when considering the New Covenant?
l. According to God's revelation, why is he going to destroy the earth? What does this tell you about the value he places on his laws, his statutes, and his Covenant? What does this reveal about him?
m. Do you think that "cheap grace" is being taught in the church today? Has it affected your understanding and life?
n. Who will be "weeded out" of God's kingdom? The Lord promises rewards for the "overcomers." (Rev 21:7) These rewards are being offered for victory over specific issues as revealed to the seven churches. Consider which rewards apply to which victory.
o. God takes a person's lack of commitment very seriously. How is this revealed? What is to be the outcome for those whose service proves to be lacking?
p. Why do you think that the Father has allowed judgment to rest in Christ? The Millennium may not be adequately appreciated. What is your understanding of this era? How does it apply to judgment?
q. Who is to be judged? Will pastors and teachers be judged any differently than the meekest labourer? (See Jas 3:1)

Where is the heavenly kingdom?

Where does Christ's final revelation present God's heavenly kingdom as being? Does this challenge your current understanding?

A Place for the Disobedient

   a. What does God require of those who will find eternal salvation?
   b. Who are those who will be found outside the Royal City and separated from God's presence?
   c. Some suggest that the "outside" refers to hell; however, Revelation 21:21 would make this impossible. Why?
   d. Some of those who will be raised at the time of the first resurrection will suffer shame and everlasting contempt? From whom will they suffer contempt? Why?

Spiritual Life and Religion

   a. Many allow themselves to accept religion as "faith." What is the difference between the two? What must you do to assure that your faith does not become "religion?"
   b. What did Paul caution Timothy to resist? What does 'denying the power of God' mean?
   c. To whom or what is the believer to be personally committed?
   d. How is "faithfulness" measured? How does "obedience" relate to faith?

Common Misrepresentations Concerning Salvation

If you are going to come to a true understanding of Biblical salvation you need to grasp these points. Find at least another person with whom you can carefully consider the issues presented. Do not hesitate to form an objection; but make sure you explore your objections and concerns within the full body of the Scriptures.

1. The believer is redeemed through the sacrifice of Christ on the cross, but his redemption does not mean that he has "eternal salvation"

a. Why is "redemption" only a part of God's salvation plan? How is a person redeemed? What does "justified" mean? Is a person fully justified through the sacrifice of Christ? Why?
b. How is it possible to be "justified" and to still suffer God's wrath?
c. Why does the Lord say that *not* everyone who calls him "Lord" will enter the kingdom of heaven?
d. What does Paul teach about the means by which a person is "saved?"
e. Why is "eternal salvation" accomplished "through" the cross and not "at" the cross?

2. Review the section "*Putting 'Salvation,' "Saved" and "Eternal Salvation" into Perspective.*"

a. What does "saved" mean? The word "eternal" in "eternal salvation" is a limiter or definer. Its usage denotes a salvation that is "eternal" whereas "saved" can be applied to many different situations.
b. What verses differentiate between "salvation" and "eternal salvation"?

3. a. Is eternal salvation" a gift if it requires "obedience?" (Heb 5:9)
b. What is the meaning of God's "workmanship" or "masterpiece" (NLT)? What is God endeavouring to create in the believer? (Rom 8:29, 15:16) Why is this necessary? (Gen 6: 5-6)
c. What does "faith" have to do with the accomplishment of God's workmanship?
d. How would you explain God's grace in the accomplishment of that which he desires?

4. a. What is your definition of "belief?"
b. How does a person reveal his or her beliefs?
c. If someone believes in Christ what would you expect of him or her?
d. Belief is based on "knowledge." Why is knowledge necessary for a person to satisfy the heart of God? How is knowledge gained concerning the ministry and expectations of Christ?
e. From a Biblical perspective what does "believe" or "belief" mean?

5. a. Have all (past, present, and future) sins of believers been forgiven? What does Hebrews 9:15 teach?
What about 1 John 1:9 and Romans 3:24-25?

b. What is expected of the believer for him or her to be forgiven of all sin?
   c. What other evidences does God's Word give that reveal that a person must bear the penalty for continued, unconfessed sin?
   d. What responsibility does one believer have for a fellow believer?
   e. What does James say is the result of "full-grown sin"?
   f. How can the believer avoid sin, or live a victorious life?

6. a. Once redeemed what is the relationship of Christ to the redeemed?
   b. What does the parable of Christ teach about unfaithful servants? (Mt 25:14-30)
   c. From what is the believer redeemed? Why does Christ redeem?
   d. What is required for one to be adopted into the family of God? When does one's adoption take place?

7. a. Do you think that the promises made to the apostles should apply to all the redeemed?
   b. Should those who give their lives for the Lord and those who have confessed belief and have lived comfortably receive the same rewards?

Consider the objections and confusion that you might still have regarding the above issues. Record your thoughts and investigate further if necessary.

Chapter 11
Sharing Your Faith

Not knowing the Word of God to the point of personal comfort prevents many from sharing the gospel message. Identify any issues of confusion and seek clarification. (Take time to resolve your confusions.) Establish your truth on the Word of God and its evidences. Discomfort with your understanding will hinder boldness.

The sinner's understanding needs to begin in the book of Genesis. For a person to understand Christ's ministry as it relates to forgiveness is not enough. He or she needs to understand their need for a transformed heart. God's forgiveness will not allow the believer an honorable place in his heavenly kingdom.

1. No person can "save" another. The hope of salvation comes through Christ. It is the duty of the believer to help build the kingdom and to do so he or she must walk righteously before God and seek the direction and power of the Spirit. Any attempt to bring another to the Lord should be couched in prayer in order to seek the Lord's grace and mercy for the lost soul. Neither should the evangelist harbour disappointment for failure to see a lost soul one come to the kingdom-such deliverance is not his or her responsibility; however, he or she must be ready to honor God as he calls upon the believer for service is this matter.

2. The sinner needs to know that there is a sovereign God and creator and that he has the authority to allow or deny access to his Kingdom.
   The fact that God created all that is and that he is sovereign needs to be made clear *and must be accepted*. The issues of heaven and hell and of righteousness will not make sense apart from a person's faith (persuasion) in the reality of God. Hebrews 11: 6 states, "And without faith it is impossible to please God because anyone who comes to him must believe that he exists and that he rewards those who earnestly seek

him." If a person believes in God, he will have little difficult accepting God's sovereignty. According to Paul, the awesomeness of God's creation should provide enough evidence of his existence. Romans 1:20 states, "For since the creation of the world God's invisible qualities-his eternal power and divine nature- have been clearly seen, being understood from what has been made, so that men are without excuse."

In this day and age, a person must be prepared to battle the false teachings about macro evolution.[478] The evangelist should never try to excuse or deny science; after all, "science" is a human effort to make sense of God's creation; however, many ideas that are presented as truths of science are not, in fact, truths.

3. It must be accepted that people were created in the likeness of God (Gen 1:27[479])- morally pure or flawless (holy), virtuous in character- and that God was pleased with this state. (Gen 1:31[480])

4. The sinner needs to know of God's hurt and displeasure with the state of his or her heart and mind. "The Lord saw how man's wickedness on the earth had become, and that every inclination of the thoughts of his heart was only evil all the time. The LORD was grieved that he had made man on the earth, and his heart was filled with pain." (Gen 6:5-6, NIV) Have the seeker consider whether God would like to dwell eternally with those who would bring him "pain."

5. The cause of pain to the heart of God cannot be resolved without a changed heart and without this no one will "see" God. (Heb 12:14[481]). In fact, a person must be changed into the likeness of Christ as people had been originally created, if he is to be "saved" into the presence of God, his

---

[478] "Macro" evolution is the teaching that one *species* evolved or transitioned into another species. Micro evolution does occur, however. That is, several hundred years ago people were on average shorter than they are today. There are other examples such as domesticated animals and plants to illustrate its existence.
[479] "So God created man in his own image, in the image of God he created him." (NIV)
[480] "God saw all that he had made, and it was very good." (NIV)
[481] "Make every effort to live in peace with all men and to be holy; without holiness no one will see the Lord." (NIV)

creator. (Romans 8:29[482]) This truth reveals the nature of the ministry of Christ and should allow the sinner to recognize his or her need.

6. The sinner or rebellious person cannot change into the likeness of Christ by himself or herself. Their natural self will not let them do so. Love for the world and its comforts, the body's demand for pleasure, and a person's own self-interests are too powerful to be overcome. (Rom 7:23-25[483]) Many will not be prepared to make a commitment to Christ because the world and its comforts have too great a draw on them. Until the strength of their faith (persuasion) in God surpasses their love of the world they must remain hopelessly lost. This is the great obstacle that the evangelist must overcome. The sinner should not be encouraged to accept the thought that he or she will be eternally free from "God's wrath" by merely confessing faith. (Rom 5:9-10))

7. The problem to be faced is that *if a person needs Christ* to help him or her, they must address their need for the Savior to God. They must be humble before him (Isa 59:2[484]) and recognize their offence and his right to rule. Without a person's recognition that he or she has offended their God and creator by entertaining thoughts and behaviours that are rebellious to him, God will not commune with him or her or provide the help that they desperately need.

   The person who does not recognize that he has offended God needs to be taken through the Ten Commandments. (Ex 20:3-17; Deut 5:6-21) If he or she is still unable to recognize their state as a sinner refer to Romans 3:23. "For all have sinned and fall short of the glory of God" (NIV) or Romans 5:12.[485] The seeker needs to know that whether he thinks he is a sinner or not, God does and God is

---

[482] "For those who God foreknew he also predestined to be conformed to the likeness of his Son, so that he might be the firstborn among many brothers." (NIV)

[483] "But I see another law at work in the members of my body, waging war against the law of my mind and making me a prisoner of the law of sin at work within my members. What a wretched man I am! Who will rescue me from this body of death! Thanks be to God-through Jesus Christ our Lord! "(NIV)

[484] "But your iniquities have separated you from your God; your sins have hidden his face from you, so that he will not hear." (NIV)

[485] "Sin entered the world through one man, and death through sin, and in this way death came to all men, because all sinned. (NIV)

sovereign. The sinner brings pain to God's heart and so his or her destiny is death. The person who sins (rebels) against God will die. "For every living soul belongs to me, the father as well as the son-both alike belong to me. The soul who sins is the one who will die." (Ezek 18:4) Or, "For the wages of sin is death, but the gift of God is eternal life in Christ Jesus our Lord." (Rom 6:23)

8. Being made right with God is the sinner's first requirement. The psalmist has written, "The sacrifices of God are a broken spirit: a broken and a contrite heart, O God, thou wilt not despise." (Ps 51:17, KJV) [486] A person's pride must be broken, and truth must be faced. Contrition of heart needs to be voiced to God through prayer.

   God requires a repentant heart-one that recognizes the hurt and pain that has been caused through rebellion. "But unless you repent, you too will all perish." (Lk 13:3, 5) Repentance and contrition are not revealed through a mere verbal acknowledgment but through heart-felt sorrow. God's heart has been "pained" by the sinner and this needs to be appreciated.

9. The new believer needs to recognize the sacrificial offering that Christ has made for him or her through his atoning work. That is, they need to know that Christ has taken the penalty for their sin, which is death, and has cleansed them from those sins which separate. "Christ is the mediator of a new covenant, that those who are called may receive the promised eternal inheritance-now that he has died to set them free from the sins committed under the first covenant." (Heb 9:15) His or her "past sins" have been wiped away and he or she has been brought back to God.[487] Having been brought near, God's favour rests on him or her; they are redeemed from the curse of the law and are given the Holy Spirit[488] to enlightened, guide, and empower them for the needed transformation.

---

[486] See also Psalm 34:18: "The LORD is close to the broken-hearted and saves those who are crushed in spirit." (NIV)

[487] Eph 2:13…14, "But now in Christ Jesus you who once were far away have been brought near through the blood of Christ." (NIV)

[488] Gal 3:13, "Christ redeemed us from the curse of the law…so that by faith we might receive the promise of the Spirit." (NIV)

Christ, through his Spirit, will satisfy the righteous requirements of the law for those who are obediently led,[489] and they will escape the wrath of God. His grace in this regard is only available to those who are willing to walk in obedience to the Spirit, however. God requires faithfulness "to the end,"[490] and obedience is faith in practice.

10. All will face judgment for things done in the flesh,[491] starting with the household of God.[492] There will be consequences for those who continue to rebel. "He will punish those who do not know God and do not obey the gospel of our Lord Jesus Christ. They will be shut out from the presence of the Lord and from the majesty of his power when he comes to be glorified in his holy people and to be marveled at among all those who have believed." (2 Thess 1:8)

11. The Lord will never leave the believer, nor forsake him or her.[493] They have been given everything that is needed for life and godliness.[494] However, they are to work out their own salvation with fear and trembling.[495] The walk of the believer is not easy, however the rewards are great and the Lord expects those who will dwell with him forever to love him with all their minds, hearts, bodies, and souls…to obey him completely. The alternative…to disobey God and reject his provision is eternally severe. "But the cowardly, the unbelieving, the vile, the murderers, the sexually immoral, those who practice magic arts, the idolaters and all liars-their place will be in the fiery lake of burning sulphur." (Rev 21:8)

---

[489] Rom 8:3-4, "For what the law was powerless to do in that it was weakened by the sinful nature, God did by sending his own son in the likeness of sinful man to be a sin offering. And so he condemned sin in sinful man, in order that the righteous requirements of the law might be fully met in us, who do not live according to the sinful nature but according to the Spirit." (NIV) Also note: "He [Christ] became the source of eternal salvation for all who obey him." (Heb 5:9, NIV)

[490] Mt 10:22

[491] 2 Cor 5:10 "For we must all appear before the judgment seat of Christ, that each one may receive what is due him for the things done while in the body, whether good or bad." (NIV)

[492] 1 Pet 4:17

[493] Heb 13:5

[494] 2 Pet 1:3

[495] Phil 2:12

12. Those who "overcome" (Rev 21:7) will dwell with God forever. They will be his people and He will dwell with them. He will wipe every tear from their eyes. There will be no more death or mourning or crying or pain.[496]

The sinner who has become a believer is to count the cost of faithfulness and is to commit to loving the Lord with all his or her mind, body, and soul. A person should not be deceived into thinking that their sin will be overlooked. God is holy and those who are to dwell with him must be holy. "Do not be deceived: God cannot be mocked. A man reaps what he sows. The one who sows to please the sinful nature from that nature will reap destruction; the one who sows to please the Spirit from the Spirit will reap eternal life." (Gal 6:7-8)

Too often false promises are made to those who are willing to confess belief. The goal of the evangelist is to present sinners with the truth of the Word of God and to let the Spirit do his ministry. No ministry effort will be forgotten. The person who makes a commitment after having counted the cost must be prepared to honor it. He or she needs to be encouraged to seek further knowledge through the Bible and with the help of others and needs to commit his or her way through prayer and obedience to the leading of the Spirit.

The salvation plan was instigated for God's purposes, not with its focus on humankind. In the end his creation plan will have been completed and he will have a royal priesthood and a holy nation and it members will be committed to him through love, just as the Son has demonstrated.

---

[496] Rev 21:4

www.ingramcontent.com/pod-product-compliance
Lightning Source LLC
Chambersburg PA
CBHW052027070526
44584CB00016B/1932